THE USSR ARMS
THE THIRD WORLD:
Case Studies in Soviet Foreign Policy

THE USSR ARMS THE THIRD WORLD:
Case Studies in Soviet Foreign Policy

Uri Ra'anan

THE M.I.T. PRESS
Cambridge, Massachusetts, and London, England

*Sponsored by the Research Institute
on Communist Affairs,
Columbia University*

SBN   262 18033 2   (hardcover)

Library of Congress catalog card number: 75-87303

To Estelle, Gavy, Micha,
  and my parents

Preface

This study was written under the auspices and with the financial support of Columbia University's Research Institute on Communist Affairs. The author owes more than words can express to the Institute's Director, Professor Zbigniew K. Brzezinski, whose unfailing encouragement and assistance (as well as patience) made possible not only the birth of this work but also the author's return to academic life. Acknowledgment is also due to various colleagues and to the staff of the Institute, including Mrs. Christine Dodson, for their kind support.

In addition to the material available at Columbia, the author was able to utilize the facilities of Radio Liberty and Radio Free Europe and wishes to express appreciation to Mr. Bela Kardashinetz at RFE for the assistance extended. The staff at the library of the Council on Foreign Relations also proved most helpful, as did the staff at the library of Harvard's Russian Research Center. Special thanks are owed to Professor Philip E. Mosely for making available material from his own valuable research files and to Mrs. David Dallin for opening up some of the late Professor David Dallin's papers.

The author is deeply beholden to Professor William E. Griffith of M.I.T.'s Center for International Studies, without whose understanding and support the work could never have been completed and whose magnificent—indeed unique—collection of material on international communism proved invaluable. Gratitude is also due to many other colleagues at the Center and to the staff, especially Miss Mina E. Parks.

Finally, the author wishes to thank his own Fletcher School of Law and Diplomacy, where Dean Edmund A. Gullion has done his utmost to provide the faculty with an atmosphere congenial to productive work. In his present effort, the author received special help from Assistant Dean Charles Shane and from Miss Harriet Emery and Mrs. Helene Nelson. Appreciation is due also to Mrs. Elizabeth G. Smith, whose work on manuscripts is a joy to behold.

In this, as in all other matters, the author owes whatever he may be able to achieve to his wife and children, without whose love and patience creative work would be unthinkable.

URI RA'ANAN

Lexington, Massachusetts
April 1969

Contents

THE USSR ARMS
THE THIRD WORLD:
Case Studies in Soviet Foreign Policy

Introduction

During 1967–1969, dramatic developments in the Third World, including the Near East and East Asia, once again drew attention to the highly problematic aspects of Soviet policy toward that part of the globe. At the same time, new indications appeared that Moscow's performance in Afro-Asia had generated controversy domestically no less than internationally. Tantalizing signs that factional clashes in the Soviet capital were perhaps not entirely unrelated to this problem caused observers to speculate anew about the mechanics of the decision-making process in the USSR, with special emphasis on foreign policy.

In all probability, it is still too early to delve into current manifestations of this topic, since Western observers can as yet obtain very little by way of basic documentation. However, the time has surely come to start gathering at least such evidence, both direct and circumstantial, as may help to shed light upon the *origins* of present Soviet temptations—and dilemmas—in the Near East and other regions of the Third World.

With this task in mind, the author has prepared two case studies concerning a particularly poignant aspect of the initial Soviet thrust into the developing areas, namely, the troubled and complex relationship between the USSR, in its role as a military donor, and various Afro-Asian recipients of Russian weapons. In Part I of the present work, he offers a reappraisal of the genesis of Moscow's first offensive into the "nonaligned" regions, that is, the prehistory of the famous 1955 arms transaction with Egypt, while, in Part II, he attempts to deal with the tangled web of relations between a particular arms recipient, Indonesia, and several actual and potential donor powers.

Part I: Genesis of an Arms Deal—Egypt, 1955[1]

It is now well over a decade since the Soviet presence materialized upon the Afro-Asian scene with the startling news that a "Czech"-Egyptian arms deal had been concluded. Although by no means the first, it was by far the most unmistakable manifestation that a turning point had been reached in Moscow's policy toward the Third World.

Since then it has been unusual to encounter a book or major article about Soviet—or, for that matter, U.S.—foreign policy that has not at least touched upon this historic event. However, upon closer study, it transpires that the countless publications in question contain little more than brief mechanical repetitions of a few unverified, intellectually unsatisfactory (and mutually contradictory) versions concerning the antecedents, course, and implications of the famous Arms Deal. The accounts published so far do not stand up well to any kind of searching examination—either with regard to political plausibility or as far as the hard facts of chronology are concerned (that is, the logical sequence of cause and effect). Nevertheless, imposing structures of far-reaching (and unchallenged) conclusions have been erected upon such dubious foundations.

Thus U.S. foreign policy during the 1950s has been subjected to scornful criticism with hardly a dissenting voice, not least because

---

[1] With regard to the subject of Part I, it should be pointed out that the author originally did not intend to include a case study of this particular topic in his present work. However, in the course of his research, he came across new—or previously overlooked—material, which left little doubt that current historical interpretations concerning the genesis of the 1955 Arms Deal required serious revision. Since this massive transaction between a communist power and a nonaligned country has generally been regarded as one of the dramatic turning points of the mid-fifties, and since a reappraisal might, therefore, shed new light upon the whole history of the period, the author felt he could not very well ignore his own findings. In pursuing the matter further, he had to do violence to his own inclinations, being only too conscious of the fact that any subject even tangentially related to the Near East constitutes a veritable minefield for the unwary academician. Since, in this section of the book, the author must tread—lightly, he hopes—upon delicate ground (rather than skirt around it, as all his instincts urge him to do), he can only pray that he will be protected by that power which traditionally shields animals, children, and the feeble of mind.

the genesis of the Arms Deal allegedly illustrates Washington's insensitivity at that time toward the newly emerging Afro-Asian world. The State Department, it is claimed, missed repeated opportunities of preempting the Soviets during the many months that are said to have passed before Egypt's leaders finally turned toward the East. Consequently, Russian actions during this episode are viewed simply as opportunistic efforts to exploit openings provided by Western clumsiness. At the same time, extravagant praise has been heaped upon Khrushchev personally for being shrewd enough to make the most of Near Eastern opportunities supposedly ignored by Stalin and his spiritual heirs prior to the fall of 1955. Uncritical reliance upon the traditional versions of the genesis of the Arms Deal also led historians to underestimate the complexity both of the Near Eastern situation and of the circuitous course steered by the (then) youthful Egyptian leader, Colonel Nasser, during this "delicate" and carefully manipulated operation. Thus Nasser's part, too, has been relegated to the role of a participant who merely reacted to the blunders of others, a man allegedly guided by impulse rather than calculation.

A little reflection will show just how much this portrayal of events during 1955/56 still colors current appraisals of the U.S. and Soviet roles in the Third World—of the precepts that (so commentators claim) must guide all great powers in their relations with the proud and touchy leaders of Afro-Asia. A reexamination of this important turning point of history, therefore, is urgently required to shed some light upon the origin and nature of problems that continue to be very much with us. The solution to these questions still evades contemporary analysts; above all, observers of the Soviet scene continue to grope for an understanding of the forces at work in shaping Moscow's policies toward the Third World. Thus the complex problems raised by the new relationships between the great powers and the Afro-Asian countries would, most probably, be seen in better perspective as the result of a successful attempt to elucidate the genesis of the Arms Deal and to investigate the political struggle within the Soviet elite that made this episode possible.

Nevertheless, the analyst embarks upon this venturesome task with great trepidation. It is perfectly true that some additional evidence of a documentary nature has appeared in recent years, which either was overlooked or received relatively scant attention in the West. This new material alone would tend to throw grave doubt upon the authenticity of the accepted accounts concerning the Soviet thrust into the Near East. Unfortunately, the very nature of an arms deal—a particularly confidential and intimate transaction, especially when concluded between two "closed" societies—reduces the likelihood that such documentation might proliferate to the point at which an uncontroversial, definitive, and watertight history of this episode could be presented to the reader. Of necessity, therefore, the historian has to resort to such additional evidence of a more circumstantial and indirect nature as he can excavate, including a great deal of material that can best be uncovered by the method known as content analysis (or, pejoratively, as "Kremlinology"). While perhaps not as dependable and scientific a tool for the elucidation of the post-Stalin period as of the previous era, the repeatedly proclaimed demise of content analysis as a useful adjunct to Soviet and communist studies ought, nevertheless, to be considered highly premature. This holds true especially of an inquiry dealing with events a mere one or two years after Stalin's death; needless to say, the Sovietological approach must be used far more circumspectly when applied to the increasingly complex realities of the present day.

In observing a group as conscious of power relationships and their external symbols as is the communist elite, with its particular sensitivity to the precise "scientific" meaning of party jargon, the historian is ill-advised to shrug off the significance of esoteric but very meaningful forms of intracommunist communications. Indeed, during recent years, those Western scholars who persisted with their practice of content analysis, especially in relation to the Sino-Soviet conflict, have received unexpected accolades from communist historians in countries like Czechoslovakia (who have paid them the great compliment of open and avowed imitation).

The fact is that significant traces of the political interplay that produced the Arms Deal can be uncovered by a careful sifting of communist party literature and other Soviet, Near Eastern, and Western sources, as well as of various accounts, both contemporary and subsequent, of relevant political manipulations and "economic" transactions in the year 1955. The inferences derived from this material corroborate and lend perspective to the important new data contained in recently published, more direct, and explicit documentary references to the subject. Even so, this methodology cannot suffice to produce the type of straightforward, painstaking diplomatic history that scholars have been able to distill from the published archives of various foreign ministries, for instance, when analyzing Soviet-Western relations during World War II.

Such serious drawbacks notwithstanding, it appears to be well worth making an attempt to reevaluate the history of Russia's original leap into the Third World; the traditional views clearly need to be reexamined in the light both of new material and of circumstantial evidence (however laborious the process of excavation may seem). Admittedly, the nature of the available sources makes for a somewhat elaborate and circuitous approach, which does little to ease the task of writing. Such difficulties are compounded by the plethora of "actors" crowding the "stage" in this particular drama. Their conflicting and/or overlapping aspirations and motivations have to be carefully sifted and appraised so that the episode may be viewed in the full perspective of the factors involved.

Among the subjects to be analyzed in this fashion, one must include (a) the strategic and political East-West equation as it appeared in 1954/55; (b) the place of the Near East in the equation, as well as the local crosscurrents within that region; (c) the precise part played by factional conflicts in the Kremlin during the fateful opening days of 1955 when (as this study hopes to demonstrate) the initial moves toward the Arms Deal were actually made; and (d) significantly, Peking's repeated response to appeals for intervention on behalf of one Soviet faction or another, to the point where Chinese views came to be of importance at a fateful moment in Soviet-Egyptian relations.

Such an approach may seem to produce an unduly orchestrated view of political history, but it would be an oversimplification to treat the subject without taking into consideration the crowd of participants, both direct and indirect, and the specific part played by each in affecting the final outcome. If this makes for complexity, with repeated flashbacks, references to subsequent pages, and occasional repetitions, the author can but sympathize with the reader.

The organization of the present study was governed (1) by the necessity of demonstrating the implausibilities inherent in the currently accepted versions of the genesis of the Arms Deal, and (2) by the need to examine the implications of additional available evidence that point in an entirely different direction. Consequently, in Chapter 1 of this book, the author has attempted to analyze the situation prevailing in 1955 and the precise considerations guiding the various parties involved, so as to indicate the logical conclusions that can be deduced from these factors; in Chapter 2, he has summed up the several accounts that, until now, have been generally accepted as accurate portrayals, showing not only the implausibilities and basic contradictions contained in these versions but viewing them against the background of the 1955 situation and its logical requirements as outlined in Chapter 1; in Chapter 3, he has proceeded to advance the thesis that an entirely different chronology for the genesis of the Arms Deal must be postulated (and can, in fact, be clearly demonstrated from the documentation available)—thus the various developments attending this event have to be regarded in an altogether new light since they must be entered upon the logical chart of causality in a completely changed sequence.

Briefly, the present study indicates that initial Soviet-Egyptian contacts to foil the incipient Baghdad Pact followed immediately upon the earliest intimations that the cornerstone of this Western defense arrangement—in the form of a Turkish-Iraqi treaty—was being prepared, that is, during the first weeks of 1955. This development led rapidly, in mid-February 1955, to an Egyptian-Czech arrangement that contained the nucleus of the future Arms Deal; an authoritative Soviet publication has revealed the date of this transaction, and its accuracy is corroborated by various contemporary Western and Near Eastern sources that seem to have been completely overlooked at the time.

It can, moreover, be demonstrated that the decision to dispatch a Czech delegation to Cairo coincided, almost to the day, with the climax of a factional struggle within the Kremlin, during which Khrushchev and Molotov, after having joined hands to oust Malenkov, started to fall out over the division of the prospective spoils and the future policies to be adopted. (The Soviet line in the Near East appears to have been one object of contention.) In Chapters 4 and 5, the author has attempted to follow this conflict and its manifestations in microscopic detail, because he feels that content analysis can be used to advantage in tracing the ups and downs of the struggle almost moment by moment; consequently, it is possible to establish—at least tentatively—which group or personality in the Soviet leadership may be linked to a particular expression of views or action in the field of international affairs. In this fashion, one can hope to shed new light upon an unusually significant event in Soviet foreign policy as well as upon the Kremlin's decision-making process itself. The author has, in fact, found it necessary to analyze the effects of Moscow's internecine struggles not only upon Soviet Near Eastern policy but also upon the Soviet-Chinese and Soviet-Yugoslav relationships, since (as the present study indicates) these questions were, to some extent, linked.

The material demonstrates that in this, as in several other instances, Khrushchev and his supporters constituted the ebullient, adventuristic, "forward" faction, while the "Stalinists" (if, indeed, such nomenclature can fairly be applied to Molotov and his allies) were the moderate, conservative, cautious element in the Kremlin. Looking back and considering the serious dangers and grave embarrassment Moscow was to encounter during its Third World offensive—the Cuban missile crisis, the 1956, 1958, and 1967 Near Eastern outbreaks, the Southeast Asian conflagration, and the overthrow of radical associates in Algeria (1965) and Ghana (1966)— the policies of consolidation and restraint advocated by Molotov appear to have been wise, especially since Khrushchev's "leap southward" failed to achieve either enduring gains or solid "leverage" for the USSR. The Chinese leaders, correctly regarding Molotov's attitude as a state-centered, pragmatic (or selfish) view that would not permit Soviet resources to be dispersed or risks to be taken, whether on behalf of "fraternal" communist regimes or for the sake of dubious "revolutionary" offensives in Afro-Asia, instinctively backed Khrushchev in this dispute, however much cause they may have had later to regret this step.

In a sense, Molotov was fighting a lost battle, since Khrushchev, in typical conspiratorial fashion, with his state security (KGB) and military intelligence (GRU) allies had already begun to create a fait accompli in the form of an entente with members of the Cairo junta (an indispensable part of any Soviet offensive southward). This move was made at a very early date in 1955, at least three or four months before the West could or did become aware that there was even a serious possibility of such a development. In view of the secrecy enveloping these initial steps and the fact that Colonel Nasser's relations with the West did not begin to reflect the new development until preparatory arrangements for a "Czech" arms deal had already been completed (as the present study shows), it seems rather harsh to blame Secretary Dulles for having failed to prevent this untoward event. Moreover, considering the clear and binding provisions of congressional enactments concerning military aid, as well as U.S. international commitments

under the 1950 Tripartite Declaration, there is very little that the
Eisenhower administration would have been at liberty to do by
way of preventive measures, even if intelligence of Russia's Near
Eastern operations had reached Washington at an earlier date. The
only recourse open to the West was to stage a massive counteraction, namely, a politico-military operation à la Guatemala to
interdict the "Czech" transaction; such a possibility does appear to
have been considered for some time, but was finally rejected.

To the possible contention that some of his tentative findings
must, of necessity, appear speculative, the author can only plead
that this is unavoidable in the present case; the attempt nevertheless seems worthwhile, because new material makes a reevalua-
tion of the episode inescapable and because this is an excellent
subject on which to demonstrate both the possibilities inherent in
content analysis and its limitations. In other words, the present
study constitutes an attempt not only to elucidate a very dramatic
development in Soviet foreign policy but also to apply, in fairly
systematic fashion, a useful methodology to a period of Soviet
history for which it certainly has not lost its relevance (if, indeed,
it can be said to have done so even today).

*Part II: Relations Between Recipients and Donors—Indonesia,
1956–1960*

The first section of the present work, especially Chapter 6 (Epilogue), raises the question of how much leverage the USSR can
actually exert over the Afro-Asian recipients of Soviet hardware.
Part II investigates Indonesia's incipient military relationship
with the Soviet Union and her dealings with other actual and
potential donor states; this case study suggests that the leaders
of a recipient country can learn to maneuver adroitly between
Moscow, Peking, Washington, and other capitals, evading foreign
pressure and extorting concessions equally from all the competing
powers.

For several reasons, the present analysis is confined to the initial
period of Soviet-Indonesian arms relations, from their genesis until
the beginning of 1960:

1. The history of those years has been practically ignored until
now, general interest focusing on the subsequent era, 1960–1965,
when Djakarta itself publicized Indonesia's military acquisitions,

and Sukarno's West Irian and Malaysian "confrontations" caused major crises and drew world attention to the constant stream of Soviet equipment arriving in Surabaja and other Javanese ports.

2. During the 1960s, Sukarno increasingly limited his own freedom of action by exacerbating relations, first with Washington, then with Moscow, and even with "nonaligned" New Delhi, leaving Djakarta tied to the unprofitable "axis" with Peking, Hanoi, Pyongyang, and Phnom Penh. Thus there was relatively little room, during the later period, for the type of interaction between Soviet leverage and Indonesian counterleverage with which this study is concerned.

The example of Indonesia is of special interest, since a multitude of different conflicts crisscrossed within this particular framework —between East and West, the USSR and China, Sukarno and his adversaries, the Indonesian Communist party (PKI) and the anticommunists, and among the competing Indonesian military services. Because of these various dissensions, the case lends itself to analysis in depth, uncovering layers upon layers of pressures and counterpressures that affect any transaction involving the sensitive defense and security sector.

Part II contains a short survey of the forces at work (Chapter 7), the prehistory of Djakarta's arms link with Moscow (Chapter 8), an examination of the first few years of the new working relationship (Chapter 9), and a glance at the period when the friendship turned sour (Chapter 10, "Aftermath").

Briefly, our analysis suggests that the genesis of the Indonesian arms deal with the communist countries was a prolonged process and that, as in the Egyptian case (and for similar reasons), its inception is to be found at a much earlier date (1956/57) than has generally been supposed. The study indicates that, during this period, Sino-Soviet competition for influence in the archipelago was already vigorous, even though most commentators have claimed that the divergence between Moscow and Peking did not really become serious until the last part of the 1950s. The Indonesians certainly seem to have exploited this and other rivalries between the larger powers and, until the end of the decade, were able cheerfully to pressure the giants rather than to be pressured by them. Since Djakarta doggedly kept all options open, Moscow could exert only a minimum of leverage. However, even when Sukarno himself, during the 1960s, jettisoned his country's diplomatic alternatives in a series of frenzied "revolutionary" gestures, Soviet influence diminished rather than increased, since it was the Chinese and not the Russians who now became the Indonesian President's mentors. As for the Indonesian communist leaders, it appears that they had always resented Soviet military shipments, which, of necessity, benefited their traditional adversaries, the Indonesian armed forces; with the growth of polycentrism in the 1960s, the PKI was quick to adopt a bitterly anti-Russian attitude, one not too different from Sukarno's own stance. It is of considerable interest that, in the face of such Indonesian "ingratitude" (not to speak of the fact that Djakarta frequently permitted itself to insult the Russians), Moscow proved uncharacteristically apathetic, meekly continuing to dispatch economic and military supplies while repeatedly consenting to defer Indonesian repayments for shipments already received. By 1965, it was Sukarno himself and his cronies in the Indonesian air force who took the initiative in severing the country's military links with the USSR. In the aftermath of the September 30, 1965 coup, the Russians were quick to resume full supplies of spare parts and ammunition to Sukarno's antagonists in the Indonesian army, closing more than one eye to the fact that Soviet-made weapons were helping to massacre myriads of Indonesian communists (although by 1968/69 Moscow was beginning to take a tougher line toward Djakarta).

The present study suggests that, confronted by Afro-Asians determined to follow their own independent policies, Soviet military aid has not in itself helped Moscow to exert really meaningful leverage; on the whole, the Russians have merely reacted to events in the recipient countries rather than initiating developments there. (Needless to say, such relative "restraint" on the part of Moscow has owed much to constant Russian awareness that the U.S. Six and Seventh Fleets control the air and sea approaches to the Third World.) However, the Kremlin's tendency to be a somewhat passive partner in these arms relationships is not without its dangers; as our Near Eastern examples indicate (in this Introduction and in Chapter 6), it could well happen that, precisely because they lack full control over their Afro-Asian associates, the Soviet leaders might find themselves being dragged into incalculable adventures.

PART I
GENESIS OF AN ARMS DEAL:
EGYPT, 1955

1 The Situation and Its Requirements, 1954–1955

It is now well over a decade since news of the historic "Czech" arms agreement with Egypt first leaked out, causing consternation in Western capitals. For a development of such dramatic impact, it has attracted surprisingly little academic or journalistic investigation. The aura of secrecy in which such transactions tend to be shrouded no doubt deters scholarly analysis. That is probably why the very best works on the period have been unable to do more than reiterate one, or several, current popular versions of the story of the Arms Deal. From the historian's point of view, this fact is a trifle disconcerting, especially since most of the extant accounts are mutually contradictory, and some are hardly within the realm of credibility.

To list the many permutations and combinations of these themes that have become enshrined in current literature would be tedious. Almost all the accepted stories trace back to three or four different explanations given at various times, and under changing circumstances, by personalities (or their associates) who were believed to be directly involved. Since they could be regarded as authoritative sources, it was not thought that their remarks required microscopic analysis or that there might be objective reasons for them to refrain from revealing all the facts. It may well be objected that inaccurate accounts of a happening of such consequence could hardly have withstood the pressure of a decade of probing and that the event itself is, by now, sufficiently remote in time for the participants to have long since felt able to speak freely. However, throughout the period, the subject has actually evoked extraordinarily few calls for full information; as for authentic revelations being necessarily volunteered just because a few years have elapsed, this argument would hardly seem to be borne out by the analogous case of the 1956 Suez conflict. The antecedents of that event are now almost as distant as the Arms Deal itself and have, moreover, been subjected to the merciless glare of incessant public inquiry, especially in the countries concerned. Yet only recently have any of the participants begun to succumb to pressure for a fuller account, replacing earlier versions. Thus, in investigating why the original pronouncements on the arms agreement have remained unrevised, some thought should be given to the possible effect of a subjective factor: perhaps it is generally true in history that prominent figures tend to become organically linked to their own public statements, of which they cannot then divest themselves short of amputation.

The Political Background

Fortunately, a study of this subject can at least take off from a reasonably firm starting point. There has not, in fact, been much room for controversy over the wider political background of the 1955 Egyptian-Soviet entente, an understanding of which is essential if the Arms Deal itself is to be elucidated. It is generally conceded that Premier[1] Nasser's government resorted to a line of opposition vis-à-vis the West, in 1955, mainly as a reaction to news of an impending military agreement between Iraq and Turkey. These two countries, together with Pakistan, were to constitute the nucleus of what was subsequently called the Baghdad Pact, which added part of the Near East to the Western defensive network against the USSR. By January 12, 1955, not only Egypt, but the rest of the world, had been publicly informed of Turkish-Iraqi plans. For a considerable time prior to that date, London and Washington had been soliciting Cairo's support on the issue of Near Eastern security arrangements. Consequently, it was taken for granted—at least by the Egyptian authorities—that whatever form the military organization of the region finally assumed would be determined by an understanding between Cairo and the West.

---

[1] His assumption of the presidency occurred at a later date.

Although Nasser's government kept pointing to the Arab League's collective security pact (built around Egypt, the predominant Arab military power) as the proper instrument for the defense of the member countries, some indirect link with the West seemed by no means precluded.[2] After all, the 1954 Anglo-Egyptian agreement on the evacuation of the Suez Canal Zone specifically provided for the return of Her Majesty's forces to the former British base in case of external attack not only upon Arab countries but also upon Turkey, a NATO member. Clearly, this clause could be aimed only at the Soviet Union, the one country from which Turkey might fear aggression. Obviously, no doors had been closed, in 1954, to rule out a more definite understanding between Egypt and the West;[3] London and Washington appeared, in fact, to be resigned to the thought that Cairo held the keys to any Near Eastern defense arrangement. The Egyptian Revolutionary Command Council thus believed it was in an excellent bargaining position and need not hurry to accede to Western proposals.[4] This appraisal was of course correct only to the extent to which Egypt could rely upon the solidarity of her sister Arab states in holding out together with her. In view of traditional Near Eastern feuds and rivalries, this was perhaps a pious wish rather than a realistic assumption.

Iraq's elder statesman, the late Nuri a-Said, schooled in decades of intrigue, shrewdly exploited Egypt's delay in coming to terms by striking his own separate bargain with the West. In establishing the Turkish-Iraqi alliance as the nucleus of a regional security network, he could obtain further Western support and arms, catapulting Iraq into a position of hegemony in the Near East. Nuri's

[2] Keith Wheelock, *Nasser's New Egypt* (New York: Frederick A. Praeger, 1960), p. 217: "In private discussions with Western diplomats . . . Nasser did not exclude the possibility of an indirect link between Egypt and a NATO country."

[3] Patrick Seale, *The Struggle for Syria: A Study of Postwar Arab Politics, 1945–1958* (New York and London: Oxford University Press, 1965), pp. 188–190; as late as December 7, 1954, Nasser wrote a warm, pro-Turkish preface for a work on Turkey and Arab policy and, in the same month, Egypt agreed to a statement, which was drafted at the close of a gathering of Arab League representatives in Cairo, suggesting cooperation between the Arab collective security pact and the West, in return for a gift of Western arms.

[4] *New York Times*, August 20, 1954; Nasser stated that "there is nothing standing in the way of our good relations with the West. But . . . until the Arabs realize that there is no longer any hidden domination or control in pacts, any *pressure* to obtain them will be dangerously *premature*" (author's emphasis).

flanking maneuver left the Egyptian military junta outfoxed, isolated, and humiliated.[5] For Premier Nasser, this setback came at a particularly dangerous moment. The previous period had revealed just how shaky the new Egyptian regime was; Nasser had even been temporarily ousted for General Naguib and, upon his restoration to power, was barely able to quench the rebellious Moslem Brotherhood. Widely criticized for his acceptance of British proposals regarding future reactivation of the Suez base and with a blood feud on his hands after executing several Moslem Brothers, Colonel Nasser was simply in no position to swallow public humiliation. To add to his resentment, his own representatives had been adroitly maneuvered by Nuri a-Said into making ambiguous noises that could be interpreted as constituting Egyptian support for Iraq's policies. Nasser's instinctive reaction was to adopt a posture of fundamental opposition to any and all links with the West, simultaneously launching harsh attacks upon Nuri's "betrayal" of Arab solidarity and neutrality. By the third week of January 1955, Cairo was trying its best to establish a new axis of anti-Iraqi states, including nationalist, republican Syria and Wahabbi Saudi Arabia (both traditionally hostile to Iraq's Hashemite dynasty—although for different reasons). What in 1953/54 may, to some extent, have been a tactical display of coolness toward Western defense plans was now elevated to become Egypt's political philosophy of unceasing struggle against any concessions to "imperialism."[6]

The Soviet View

As a result of the Turkish-Iraqi pact, the interests and policies of Egypt and the USSR came to be temporarily deployed along parallel, although not identical, lines. Western moves to close the geographic gap between NATO and SEATO in 1954/55, starting with the Turkish-Pakistani and Turkish-Iraqi pacts, appeared, from the Soviet point of view, to be fraught with unpleasant conse-

[5] Ibid., April 4, 1955; Nasser complained that the West had "violated a gentleman's agreement that Egypt should be permitted to take the lead in constructing a purely Arab defense alliance free from *formal* links with outside powers" (author's emphasis).

[6] Wheelock, *Nasser's New Egypt*, p. 222: "Much of Nasser's original hostility to the Baghdad Pact (and Iraq as the only Arab member) may have stemmed from chagrin at having his ambitions thwarted by the West. . . . Nasser launched a bitter campaign against Iraq and the British, whose covert support he had solicited a few months before."

quences. Admittedly, the two sheet anchors of the projected CENTO[7] system in the Near East, Turkey and Pakistan, already adhered to the Western security network, constituting, respectively, the eastern wing of NATO and the western wing of SEATO. However, no serious defense in depth against a Soviet thrust seemed possible as long as the areas between and beyond the two countries remained aloof. Moreover, the construction of a solid pro-Western military bloc, covering the whole region to the south of the USSR, was regarded by the Russians as the last link in a hostile global chain, leaving no important segment of Soviet territory outside the immediate range of Western nuclear striking power. Added to existing Western naval-air striking forces in the Mediterranean, such a Near Eastern bloc would—so Moscow felt—substantially increase the "threat" from the south.

At that time, several years before the introduction of the ICBM, American "New Look" defense policies still depended largely upon the efficacy of the one existing "equalizer" to the massive Soviet armies, namely, the U.S. strategic bomber force. It was expected that the deterrent posture of the West would improve considerably in the near future, with the gradual addition of West German troops to NATO and the introduction of a truly intercontinental bomber, in the form of the B-52. In the meantime, however, the U.S. strategic air force relied heavily upon planes with somewhat limited range and speed; new refueling techniques still left these aircraft dependent upon the existence of forward bases, within reasonable flying distance of Soviet territory but just outside the immediate reach of Soviet fighter and light tactical bomber units. The Western defense systems in Europe and the Pacific, of course, had created a chain of facilities precisely meeting these conditions; as Moscow saw it, the Baghdad Pact, once fully operative, would help to complete Russia's encirclement.[8] In that case, the south-central USSR might become even more vulnerable than Soviet western and far-eastern territories, since, unlike the latter, it lacked the protection of a buffer zone consisting of junior communist states.[9] Moreover, it seemed unlikely that even the replacement of

[7] CENTO is the name given in recent years to what was earlier called the Baghdad Pact system. Several changes had to be introduced after Iraq, in 1958–1959, withdrew from the pact.

[8] Although Western bases did, of course, exist in Turkey, they were somewhat exposed and isolated until and unless they could be reinforced by military organization of the whole Near Eastern "hinterland," especially Iraq and Iran.

[9] David J. Dallin, Soviet Foreign Policy after Stalin (Philadelphia: J. P. Lippincott Co., 1961), pp. 201 and 388, stresses Moscow's sense of vulnera-

air power by missile systems, on which both sides were working, would nullify the advantages of such a Western global network of forward bases. By virtue of its existence, so policy makers then believed, the West might perhaps be able to go ahead with the development of the cheaper and simpler IRBM, leaving the Russians to pour out their resources on the ICBM, without which they could not create a really massive threat to U.S. territory.[10]

It was obvious that the establishment of the Western security framework was not feasible without the creation of a system of interlocking pacts. Only under the shelter of a full alliance were sovereign nations likely to make their territories and facilities available for military transit and the emplacement of strategic facilities, with the consequent danger of Soviet retaliation. (Since agreements of an earlier "colonial" era, such as the Anglo-Egyptian and Anglo-Iraqi pacts, had been abrogated or were expiring, it was clear that they would have to be replaced by new alliances, if there was to be a legal basis for the presence of Western personnel or installations.) From the Soviet point of view, this aspect of Western policy was politically as well as militarily unpalatable because it threatened to paralyze any further Russian initiative. In an age of declining esteem for ideologies, one tends, perhaps, to minimize the psychological impact upon Soviet leaders of their constant immersion in revolutionary semantics. Of course, Marxism-Leninism can and has been applied "creatively," ex post facto, to justify all kinds of policies actually owing their existence to highly pragmatic considerations. Nevertheless, if there is an irreducible residuum left in the mind of the Soviet practitioner by dialectical and historical materialism, it is the belief that the resolution of one conflict automatically marks the beginning of the next, that the world is an arena for an infinite succession of clashing forces, and that, by the very dynamics of life, he who wishes to stand still, or to withdraw from strife, has already cast himself upon the rubbish heap of history. The influence of this mode of thought upon Soviet political processes was underlined by the relative ease with which Premier G. M. Malenkov and his supporters were defeated in the

bility in this region and concludes that "the importance of the pact was somewhat exaggerated by the Soviet government." See also John M. Mackintosh, *Strategy and Tactics of Soviet Foreign Policy* (New York: Oxford University Press, 1962), pp. 119–123.

[10] Dwight D. Eisenhower, *Mandate for Change, 1953–1956: The White House Years* (New York: Doubleday & Company, 1963), pp. 455–457.

important defense controversy of 1953/54. Malenkov had apparently been prepared to settle for a prolonged East-West stalemate, believing that mutual nuclear deterrence had become an immutable reality; he indicated that major attention and resources could now be devoted to domestic problems. His opponents doubted whether Russia had really achieved parity and, moreover, insisted that it was still feasible, even in a nuclear age, to strive for military superiority—at least to the point where the global adversary might have to stand by and watch idly while unilateral gains were being scored in one region or another. By January 1955, Marshal Zhukov was already expounding the implications of Moscow's new military concepts to a closed meeting of Red Army leaders.[11]

The more militant line had gained adherents precisely because it was felt that the strategic approach of the late Stalin–early Malenkov era threatened to paralyze Russia's global initiative, perhaps irretrievably. Viewed from this angle, the developments of the 1948–1954 period contained ominous implications for Soviet policy makers. Both in Europe and in the Pacific, the lines between East and West had been "frozen," and, for the time being, the USSR was hemmed in by a thermonuclear tripwire in these regions that could be set off, almost automatically, by any forward movement. However, as long as the containment of Soviet power applied only to one section of the globe, namely, the Northern Hemisphere, this situation at least had its compensations: Russian willingness to accept the temporary partition of Eurasia could be bartered for tacit Western recognition that communist gains east of the Elbe and west of the China Sea could not be annulled. Indeed, Soviet policy between the 1954 and 1955 Geneva conferences was pursuing precisely this aim. At the same time, it seems that the more militant[12] Soviet leaders only tolerated such a static approach, even for the briefest periods, because its application was limited to one area; they apparently took it for granted that most of the Southern Hemisphere, at least, would remain fluid, so that a dynamic thrust forward would be possible in that part of the

---

[11] See Raymond L. Garthoff, *Soviet Strategy in the Nuclear Age* (New York: Frederick A. Praeger, 1958), pp. 22–25 and 66–70.

[12] It must be recalled that in the context of the 1953/54 defense debate, and the related controversy over the priorities to be accorded to heavy and light industry, respectively, Nikita Khrushchev's place was with the militants, Malenkov's with the moderates, and Molotov's with the center. For the Near Eastern implications of these differences, see chap. 4.

world. Thus it is hardly a coincidence that the USSR during 1954 had embarked upon a policy of early exploratory probes into South Asia (Afghanistan and India), the Near East (Syria), and Latin America (Guatemala) at the very moment when the first Geneva conference and the creation of SEATO were finally freezing the situation in the Pacific.

The Soviet leadership was bound, therefore, to be seriously perturbed by signs that the West was succeeding in laying down permanent, hardened lines to the south as well as to the east and west of the Soviet empire. The inclusion of the Near and Middle East in a Western network of formal pacts and alliances would not only prevent a Soviet military offensive (which was, in any case, an unlikely proposition just then); what was more serious, it would weaken the political impact of Soviet power upon the region, since the local regimes, sheltering behind the Western defensive shield, could defy Soviet demands with impunity. More important still, an interlocking system of Western commitments would make it almost impossible to implement a forward, dynamic Soviet policy. It would severely inhibit Moscow's freedom of maneuver, since any major change, even from within the area (such as the Russian-sponsored aggrandizement of one Near Eastern state at the expense of another), would almost automatically bring Western forces into play. Thus it could be expected that the extension of the Turkish-Iraqi pact to other Near Eastern countries, and the eventual adhesion of one or more Western powers, would fulfill an important task in relegating Moscow's global role to an essentially passive, static part. Consequently, Russia would have no serious chance of changing the over-all balance of power that, in the early 1950s, was certainly not in her favor. Such a situation was bound to be viewed with abhorrence by most Soviet leaders, however pragmatic their attitude, since the very ethos of the communist state relegates those who stand pat to the scrap heap and those who remain permanently on the defensive to the morgue. For a short while, the Russians attempted to minimize the gravity of their setback by portraying the Turkish-Iraqi agreement as a U.S.-inspired maneuver to wean away Britain's Near Eastern clients.[13] Soon, however, it became apparent that the British were not only prepared to accept this development but were themselves planning to join the new alliance.

13 See, for instance, S. Losev, "Imperialism and the Arab Countries," *New Times,* 1955, no. 2.

The Egyptian Position

It was clear, then, in mid-January 1955, that Moscow, no less than Cairo, would have to act in order to block the train of developments set in motion by news of the impending Turkish-Iraqi pact. From Egypt's point of view, as from Russia's, the freezing of the balance of power and the territorial status quo in the Near East was completely unpalatable. Quite apart from the fear that Baghdad, rather than Cairo, would gain hegemony over the region, Egypt's rulers could discern another major difference between the plans they might have been prepared to consider in 1954 and the direction the Baghdad Pact seemed to be taking. As seen from Cairo, a pan-Arab security framework, even with some indirect link to the West, was one thing; a series of interlocking, but separate, Western arrangements with individual Arab countries, such as Iraq, was quite another. The latter would, de facto, give an automatic, self-enforcing guarantee to the existing states and frontiers in the Near East. However, Egypt's Revolutionary Command Council had, since 1954, increasingly despaired of finding a current solution for its staggering social-economic problems within the confines of a country that was terribly overcrowded and almost bereft of natural resources. Some Egyptian leaders had started to wonder whether the Arab world as a whole, with its vast, lucrative fuel reserves and its control of arable and irrigable, but underpopulated lands (for example, along the Upper Euphrates), might not provide a more suitable unit within which to tackle Egypt's plight. Significantly, the Voice of the Arabs, Egypt's "unofficial" radio station, in 1954 began to expand its flow of broadcasts aimed at the Arab masses rather than their rulers.

It was obvious that no existing Arab regime would voluntarily surrender its power, or its resources, to a wider unit created for the benefit and under the hegemony of a country underendowed by nature, such as Egypt. It was possible, however, that an appeal to the "outs" of the Arab world, both those displaced from power and those bereft of privilege, might place the Egyptian rulers at the head of an irresistible Arab movement. For these, as well as for genuinely emotional reasons, Cairo's tone by early 1955 had grown both "radical" and increasingly "pan-Arab," rather than purely "Egyptian." Nasser's new policy was foredoomed to failure, however, if the West, impelled by purely global and strategic motives, continued to draw individual Arab countries into a security network that would protect their integrity and sovereignty and boost the prestige of their rulers.[14] Clearly, therefore, the interests of Egypt and of the Western powers had become incompatible, for the time being, the former having joined up with the opponents and the latter with the supporters of the status quo. It could be discerned, by January 1955, that Cairo was embarking upon a collision course with the West.

Western Interests

Although the interests of the main Western powers, the United States, Britain, and France, were by no means identical, it is broadly correct to say that the Tripartite Declaration of May 1950 had symbolically confirmed all three together in the role of "custodian" of the Near East. As such, they were politically obliged to support the existing balance of power (and of arms), a factor that in itself made for instinctive identification with nonexpansionist, satisfied elements. (The main difference between May 1950 and January 1955 was that, on the earlier occasion, the West had confined itself to issuing a unilateral declaration which had no formal, binding force as far as Near Eastern governments were concerned; in 1955, on the other hand, the architects of the Baghdad Pact network apparently envisaged a series of full alliances, with firm bilateral and multilateral commitments, as well as military staff arrangements between the great powers and the countries of the region. Thus, from Egypt's point of view, the Tripartite Declaration was relatively innocuous, compared with the implications of subsequent Western policy.)

It was at all times in the natural interest of the "custodian" over the Near East to preserve quiescence and stability within the region under his care and to maintain reasonably good relations with all the local regimes. After all, custodianship inevitably includes responsibility for "fire-brigade" activities, to quench any local conflagration; this is an onerous task that no great power relishes, mainly because it entails punitive action against one or another of the local states. It was, therefore, essential for the "custodian" to

---

[14] See footnote 6 in this chapter. Anthony Eden, in his *Memoirs*, vol. III, *Full Circle* (Boston, Mass.: Houghton Mifflin Company, 1960), p. 245, stressed that his meeting with Nasser on February 21, 1955 left him feeling that the Egyptian ruler opposed the Turkish-Iraqi pact because of jealousy and "a frustrated desire to lead the Arab world."

anticipate and prevent such crises. Consequently, the maintenance of the "pax occidentala" in the Near East required constant vigilance to defuse smoldering local disputes and to prevent dangerous military imbalances that might tempt local rulers to attack their neighbors; at the same time, a consistently evenhanded approach was required toward the mutually antagonistic countries of the area, so as to preserve the Western presence and Western influence in each and every local capital.

Such a complex policy was practicable, however, only as long as the West preserved its monopoly of relations with Near Eastern states, remained able to settle its own internal differences within four walls (for example, by informal tripartite discussions in the Near Eastern Arms Coordinating Committee—NEACC),[15] and was not compelled to start bidding against an irresponsible outsider. Above all, this type of custodianship could be maintained only during the stage at which preventive rather than surgical medicine was required in the region. Such conditions had prevailed during the early 1950s, when all local disputes, including the Arab-Israeli conflict, appeared to be well in hand and no dynamic local force was challenging the West itself. However, the moment an element opposed to the status quo embarked upon a collision course with the West, as seemed to be the case with Cairo in January of 1955, the "custodians" of the area faced a basic dilemma. On the one hand, they could not conceivably offer wholehearted assistance to a force that challenged the precarious regional balance and stability and would probably demand the surrender of the West's "traditional" friends. On the other hand, the Western powers were disinclined to carry their support of the status quo to the point where their future presence in a leading Near Eastern capital, like Cairo, would be completely jeopardized. Thus it seemed that the West neither could acquiesce in Nasser's new course nor, perhaps, would it effectively block his way, at least as long as the Egyptian leader acted cautiously and stopped short of direct military confrontation.

Soviet-Egyptian Convergence

Clearly, such a situation offered great opportunities for Soviet diplomacy. The USSR, as a complete outsider in 1955, did not have

[15] For detailed references to NEACC's work, see Michel Bar-Zohar, *Suez Ultra-Secret* (Paris: Fayard, 1964), pp. 72–143, passim.

an effective presence in even a single Near Eastern capital and thus enjoyed no influence that might be endangered by a dynamic, but one-sided, policy. Consequently, since Russia was attempting to prevent the freezing of the Near Eastern status quo, she was free to ally herself with any local force that, for reasons of its own, opposed the existing balance. In pursuing such an objective, the USSR could, without effort, outbid the West in gaining the favor of a discontented or resentful Near Eastern regime. The West, after all, could hardly lend its hand to undermine its own cherished goal of regional stability, simply to appease a local "have-not" element. The USSR, being basically antagonistic to the Near Eastern status quo, could easily offer support for most of the aspirations harbored by a local opponent of the existing balance. Excluded from participation in the regional custodianship, the Soviet leaders could watch with relative equanimity if their actions caused a flare-up of local crises—short of a full-scale conflagration—making life unpleasant for the Western "fire brigade." At the very least, such a Soviet policy could hope to sabotage the elaborate Western plans for a security network along the southern frontiers of the USSR. There was even a possibility that the West might be sufficiently impressed by Moscow's nuisance value to offer Russia a deal, awarding her a place in the Near Eastern concert of powers so as to induce her to collaborate in the preservation of order and stability. As long as she remained an outsider, Russia, unlike the West, had no particular incentive to pursue an evenhanded approach toward local disputes, since she did not have to be equally friendly with all the states in the area. As a power lacking any major local connections (even the communist parties, outside of Syria and Iran, being fairly insignificant), Russia had nothing to lose if, by befriending one Near Eastern capital, she annoyed another. The final result would still be a plus for Moscow, since its existing diplomatic and material investments in the region amounted to little more than zero.

There were some serious limitations, however, upon the uninhibited pursuit by the USSR of such a forward thrust. Whatever the specific channel chosen for the Soviet offensive, it would have to be conducted with the utmost circumspection. To start with, Moscow would have to ensure that overt provocation of the "enemy" did not reach the point where the West might have to react physically, and Western forces would have cause to reappear in strength throughout the Near East. After all, the USSR wanted to prevent, not provoke, the massive return of Western armed might to the region. Moreover, such a Western counterblow was bound to be directed, in the first place, against whatever Near Eastern states had aligned themselves with the USSR. Such a development would immediately face Moscow with a ticklish proposition. The Soviet leadership would have to decide whether to abandon its newly gained friends in the region, with consequent disastrous loss of prestige and freedom of maneuver, or whether to chance direct military confrontation with the West— clearly an unacceptable risk for Moscow. (Unlike the West, the Russians had no amphibious striking forces commanding the maritime approaches to the region.) In either contingency, the Near East, so far from remaining a fluid area in which Russia could pursue a dynamic policy, would become another "frozen" zone blocking her freedom of action, the very development Moscow wanted to prevent. It was thus essential for Soviet policy to follow a path of indirection, that is, for the USSR itself to avoid overt involvement as far as possible, for Russia's Near Eastern friends to refrain from precipitating a showdown with the West, and for Moscow to remain at all times in a position to disown both its associates and its operations, should an emergency make this action necessary.[16]

There was an additional reason for pursuing such a line. As has already been noted, Western containment of Soviet power in Europe had an obverse side; the establishment of the "frozen" line there could also have the effect of bringing about Western de facto recognition of Soviet rule over the regions east of the Elbe. By 1955, communist power in Eastern Europe had become increasingly precarious, and Moscow was anxious to obtain a breathing spell in order to consolidate its position there. This was one reason for the policy of détente toward the West in Europe that Moscow pursued before and during the 1955 Geneva conference. Although some Soviet leaders desired to start a dynamic thrust to the south, it was obviously essential not to permit such an

[16] For a detailed analysis of Soviet tactical considerations in the Near East, see the author's chapter, "The USSR in the Near East: A Decade of Vicissitudes," in Jack H. Thompson and Robert D. Reischauer, eds., *Modernization of the Arab World* (Princeton, N.J.: D. Van Nostrand Company, 1966); also the author's article, "Tactics in the Third World: Contradictions and Dangers," in *Survey*, no. 57 (October 1965).

offensive to provoke the West to the point of undermining the Geneva policy in Europe.[17]

The temporary coincidence of Soviet and Egyptian objectives in the Near East, from early January 1955 onward, clearly called for some form of joint action that would leave the Turkish-Iraqi pact a stillborn creation, weakening Western influence and isolating Iraq in the Arab world. What seemed to be required were measures that would demonstrate incontrovertibly that the West, in spite of its commanding political presence in the region, did not have a monopoly of control over the balance of forces there. If it could be shown that the USSR, an outsider, was in a position to hand out meaningful rewards or punishments to Near Eastern governments, then the local rulers would have no particular incentive to go along with Western plans. Until 1955, most Near Eastern states had accepted Western predominance and, willingly or unwillingly, had gone along with Western insistence upon regional stability, reinforced by Western measures to preserve the local balance of power and the territorial status quo. These principles were not only underwritten by the Tripartite Declaration of 1950 but were given practical meaning by an informal, yet effective institution owing its existence to the declaration—the Near Eastern Arms Coordinating Committee. The latter, with a considerable measure of success from 1950 to 1955, tried to prevent major fluctuations in the regional arms balance;[18] consequently, most Near Eastern rulers were resigned to the fact that they would neither be able nor be permitted to overwhelm their neighbors. Their only hope of augmenting their power and prestige lay in attempting to win the goodwill and confidence of the West, which, alone, had the power to assist them. Nuri a-Said was not the only one, by any means, to draw this conclusion, although his rivals undoubtedly resented his particular skill and success in playing this game.

Arms Aid: A Political Ploy

If the USSR could put an end to the Western monopoly of arms supplies to the region, and if the three "custodian" powers did not take physical action to interdict Soviet military deliveries and to discipline the recipients (steps the West had successfully initiated

[17] See chap. 4 for a more detailed analysis of this question.
[18] See Bar-Zohar, *Suez Ultra-Secret*, pp. 72–143.

on a previous occasion, during 1954, in Central America), many of the underlying assumptions of Western custodianship over the Near East would disappear. The USSR would then have demonstrated its ability to tamper with the local balance of power and to offer solid inducements to would-be associates; the status quo would no longer be sacrosanct, since some Near Eastern states would now be able to gain a very significant boost in military strength and even conservative rulers would have little incentive left to go along with Western plans. Thus Cairo's rather than Baghdad's policies would receive the accolade of history, and Nasser's humiliation would be avenged. In any case, by giving weapons in large quantities to Egypt, the USSR would enable Nasser to organize a counteralliance in opposition to the Baghdad Pact. As long as Cairo was not in a position to offer military aid to weaker Arab countries, it could hardly persuade them to forgo the advantages of joining a security pact supplied from Western arsenals.[19] If the Russian maneuver succeeded, the West itself might lose heart and abandon its scheme for organizing the region south of the Soviet frontiers, since Moscow would have shown that it was able to "leapfrog" over the immediate physical barrier of the "Northern Tier"[20] and to exercise profound influence over the more remote parts of the Near East. Were that to happen, the West might perhaps decide that, rather than watch the whole elaborate structure disintegrate, it would be preferable to salvage something from the wreckage by offering to accept Russia as a fellow custodian of the Near East so as to gain her cooperation. (In that eventuality, should the Russians consent to such an offer, Moscow and Cairo would come to the parting of the ways; Egypt's interests demanded the dissolution of great-power control over the Arab world, while Soviet interests could be satisfied by the inclusion of the USSR in the local concert of powers.)

Whatever the ultimate reaction of the Western powers, the dispatch of Soviet arms to the region, if carried out adroitly and with finesse, would well meet the basic qualifications of caution

[19] *New York Times*, February 27, 1955, *News of the Week in Review*.
[20] The "Northern Tier" consists of Turkey, Iran, Afghanistan, and Pakistan, the countries of the mountainous northern "roof" of the Near East, adjacent to the USSR. Pro-Western states, like Turkey, Iran, and Pakistan, being non-Arab, could easily be armed without upsetting the delicate Arab-Israeli military balance that was underwritten by the Tripartite Declaration. Iraq could be added to this group since, unlike other Arab countries, it is not contiguous to Israel.

and indirection required by Russian policy in the Near East. Weapons need not involve the Soviet forces themselves, for they could be forwarded gradually and, in the early stages, covertly. The operation might be implemented indirectly and in the name of various intermediaries, and, moreover, it could be stopped at any time and, if necessary, disowned; above all, it could always be treated as a commercial transaction within the realm of the recipient's domestic affairs.

The possibility of utilizing an arms deal as a means of exerting influence over the political situation in a sensitive area was an expedient that would readily come to mind in Moscow, for this had long since become a traditional Soviet gambit. After the military transaction with Egypt finally became public knowledge in the fall of 1955, it was generally treated by Western commentators as a novel and dramatic departure in Soviet policy, certainly as far as Moscow's relations with noncommunist regimes were concerned. In fact, of course, there was a long list of precedents, covering every decade since the October Revolution. Soon after 1917, and during the 1920s, Soviet weapons (and occasionally Soviet military training) were given to the soldiers of Kemal Atatürk, to the troops of Persian and Afghani rulers, to insurgents in the Caspian province of Gilan, and, of course, to the Kuomintang in China; most important of all, military production and training facilities were made available to the German Reichswehr. In the 1930s, Soviet arms and military experts assisted the Spanish Republic and Chiang Kai-shek's forces, as well as continuing to be sent to Iran and Afghanistan, to warlords in northern China and Sinkiang, and, probably, also to Turkey and Yemen. In the 1940s and early 1950s, some obsolete German weapons from Czechoslovak arsenals were dispatched both to Israel and to Syria and, from East German stores, to Egypt; more dramatically, Czech arms were shipped to Guatemala.[21]

There was, however, one essential difference between most of these earlier instances and any prospective arms transaction with a Near Eastern country, such as Egypt, in 1955. Previous Soviet military assistance, however substantial (as it undoubtedly was in Spain and China during the late 1930s), bore an essentially clandestine character. The dispatch of the weapons was meant to

---

[21] For a detailed account of the earlier transactions, see Barton Whaley, "Soviet and Chinese Clandestine Arms Aid," 1965 draft (Cambridge, Mass.: M.I.T., Center for International Studies).

serve a primarily military purpose; they were intended either for immediate use in battles that were being fought at the time or, as in the case of the Reichswehr, for covert accumulation as part of a secret rearmament plan in violation of the Versailles treaty. In all of these earlier instances, it was the arms themselves that were of vital interest to the recipient, and their continued acquisition was best served by keeping the origin and the very presence of the deliveries secret. Clearly, none of the recipients were eager to let the outside world know that they were the beneficiaries of military assistance from a communist source, since there might be unpleasant repercussions. Although, eventually, information concerning the shipments of Soviet arms tended to leak out, this was not usually due to intentional publicity on the part of the Russians or the recipients.

The situation was bound to be very different with regard to a potential arms deal in 1955 between the USSR and a country like Egypt, for the purpose of neutralizing Western hegemony in the Near East. Such a transaction, arranged in the wake of the news concerning the impending Turkish-Iraqi pact, had, by its very nature, to be a demonstrative move intended to serve a specific political aim pursued by both the donor and the recipient. In January–February of 1955, there was no immediate military need for these weapons, since Egypt was not engaged in a fighting war (nor were the great powers likely to tolerate full-scale battles), while the circumstances of Suez-Sinai were certainly not foreseen at the time. (As for the border *guerrilla* that, after February 1955, spread along the demarcation line between Israel and the Egyptian-occupied Gaza Strip, it was to remain essentially a hit-and-run affair, involving, on both sides, mainly light and automatic arms of Western manufacture and some mortars, with only rare resort to heavier items.) Indeed, as has been noted, Moscow could hardly desire to see Egypt actually employing Soviet weapons in a major armed conflict, since that would be bound to provoke forcible Western countermeasures. It is perfectly true that, even where no early military use can be envisaged, regimes led by officers—and, for that matter by civilians—are naturally prone to accumulate as much awe-inspiring hardware as can be obtained. Nevertheless, considering all the factors that have been analyzed, one must conclude that any Soviet-Egyptian arms deal early in 1955 had to serve a primarily political rather than military purpose. Its aim would be to demonstrate that the Western monopoly over the supply of arms to the Near East and, consequently, over the local military and political balance had come to an end; therefore, Near Eastern rulers need no longer go along with Western defense plans or accept the territorial status quo. (On subsequent occasions, Colonel Nasser himself was repeatedly to describe the arms deal in precisely such political terms, as the act that "broke the Western arms monopoly.")[22] This political purpose, however, could hardly be served unless the arms agreement were publicized. That need not, of course, mean an immediate announcement. There could be excellent reasons, as will be seen, for proceeding during the earliest stages with maximal discretion and secrecy and for postponing publication for some limited period. Eventually, there would have to be publicity, however, or the whole transaction would lose its point. In this respect, a Soviet-Egyptian military agreement would differ basically from earlier, clandestine transfers of arms.

This, then, was the situation in early January 1955, and these were the objective considerations dictated by the facts themselves. Given the political lineup of the time, the chances were that Soviet and Egyptian policy makers would almost automatically follow this path of reasoning, and that is precisely what they seem to have done, as is indicated by important evidence (which will be discussed subsequently). One knows of no serious reasons that might have propelled them in a different direction; thus alleged Egyptian and Soviet behavior during this period, as portrayed until now in various published versions, appears all the more illogical and pointless. Actually, during the first weeks of 1955, Cairo had every cause to regard an arms agreement with the Soviet bloc as a current item on the agenda; the subject had come up repeatedly during the previous three or four years,[23] and now Nuri's announcement of January 12 had formally placed Nasser and the West in opposite camps, opening up the immediate possibility of an Egyptian-Soviet entente.

[22] For instance, in his speech to the Egyptian National Assembly, November 25, 1961 (Cairo Radio, domestic broadcast, November 25, 1961), and in his speech in Alexandria, July 26, 1962 (Cairo Radio, domestic broadcast, July 26, 1962).

[23] Wheelock, *Nasser's New Egypt*, pp. 215–216; Dallin, *Soviet Foreign Policy*, p. 389; Bar-Zohar, *Suez Ultra-Secret*, pp. 95–96; *New York Times*, October 23 and 26, 1951, August 11 and 18, 1953, February 11 and 14, 1954; MENA, March 28, 1953; and *Jumhur al-Masri*, October 22, 1951. According to these reports, Moscow had offered Egypt arms for barter as early as the fall of 1951, and the question was discussed again throughout 1953 and in the beginning of 1954.

Logistics

If the preceding analysis is correct and this was the rationale of the situation, one would expect Egyptian-Soviet contacts, sometime in January, to discuss joint action, followed, during subsequent weeks, by an agreement in principle to provide Egypt with credit for the purchase of Soviet arms; once an understanding was reached, there would presumably be a protracted period of preparatory study and discussion concerning the practical data of the transaction (what, how, when, where, and how much), culminating in the signature of more detailed arrangements and crowned by the actual implementation of the deal. Publication was likely to occur only during the last stage, when the transfer of weapons was already well under way. The period between the initial and concluding portions of this complex process could reasonably be expected to extend over many months—almost certainly more than half a year, even if matters proceeded smoothly, and longer if there were delays for political reasons, as, indeed, turned out to be the case. It must be realized that next to no previous military relationship had existed between Egypt and the USSR and that one of the two prospective partners lagged many vital stages behind the other in economic and technical, as well as military, sophistication. In spite of the many earlier arms deals they had implemented, the Russians had not had much experience with a really massive transaction involving the large-scale transfer of modern, highly sophisticated, heavy equipment to a region that climatically and socially, as well as in terms of military doctrine and standardization, was almost on a different planet. (It was, of course, essential that any arms deal with Egypt be of very major proportions, well beyond the confines of the normal military acquisitions tolerated by NEACC, or it would fail to serve its demonstrative political purpose.) The Egyptians could have no clear idea of the equipment the Soviets might be able to provide, while it is improbable that the Russians were really well briefed about Egyptian requirements and capabilities.

A comparison with the situation after the outbreak of the Spanish civil war is of some relevance:[24] at that moment, in the midst

[24] A great deal of material can be found concerning Soviet military aid to the Spanish Republic. Particularly useful, with regard to the chronological questions examined here, are the following studies: Walter G. Krivitsky, *In Stalin's Secret Service* (New York: Harper & Brothers, 1939); Barton Whaley, "Soviet Intervention in the Spanish Civil War, 1936–1939" (Cambridge,

of fierce battles, Soviet military aid to the Republic was a matter of vital urgency for the recipient and of immediate concern for the donor. At the time, Spain's level of military equipment and training lagged behind that of the contemporary USSR, but less so than Egypt's in 1955. Altogether, in the preelectronic 1930s, weapons were still relatively unsophisticated, and the gap between a European military force beginning to undergo modernization, such as Russia's, and an obsolescent European army, such as Spain's, was by no means unbridgeable. (Years later, a small country like Finland could still give a good account of itself in battle against the Red Army.) Consequently, the transfer of arms from one to the other and their subsequent absorption did not constitute a terribly complex process. Moreover, in the case of Spain, the gap between donor and recipient could be narrowed perceptively by channeling part of the Soviet weapons to the International Brigades recruited from more sophisticated parts of the world. As for the transportation of heavy equipment, this depended in 1936, as in 1955, largely upon freighters, the speed of which was not noticeably slower at that time than two decades later. All in all, therefore, compared with Egypt, technical conditions in Spain were

---

Mass.: M.I.T., Center for International Studies, forthcoming, 1969); D. C. Watt, "Soviet Military Aid to the Spanish Republic in the Civil War, 1936–1938," *Slavonic and East European Review,* vol. XXXVIII, no. 91 (June 1960), pp. 536–541; and Claud Cockburn, *A Discord of Trumpets* (New York: Simon and Schuster, 1956), pp. 286–298. Cockburn provides evidence that members of Soviet military intelligence, appearing under Mexican pseudonyms, had already arrived in Spain well before the end of July 1936. The civil war broke out on July 17/18, and Cockburn records four significant military meetings within three weeks of that date, i.e., prior to August 7–8, of which the encounter with one of the "Mexicans" was among the earliest. Cockburn's first meeting with a Republican military leader took place on July 23 and, judging from internal evidence, his encounter with the "Mexican" occurred just a couple of days later. The representatives of Soviet military intelligence had come to survey the capabilities of the Spanish Republican forces and their absorptive capacity for modern weapons. This was an important preliminary step if Soviet military aid was to be given to the Republic. Precisely at the time when Cockburn met the "Mexican," who had probably arrived a few days earlier and managed to send his first reports home, a joint Comintern-Profintern session in Moscow dealt with the question of international volunteers for Spain—an integral part of Soviet military aid. All the essential details were ironed out during the following weeks and, by the first days of September, the Politburo had given final ratification to military assistance for Spain. The first really continuous shipments of Soviet arms to the Republic were arriving by the beginning of November 1936, i.e., nearly sixteen weeks after the start of the civil war. In other words, in spite of the urgency of the situation, it took almost four months from the preliminary military survey to the implementation of the arms deal.

conducive to a quicker rather than a slower weapons transfer process (although, admittedly, the Non-Intervention Committee did pose some political, and the piracy of Italian submarines some logistic, problems). Yet it took almost seven weeks from the outbreak of the civil war to complete the arrangements for the dispatch of Soviet arms to Spain, and just under nine weeks from that stage to the arrival of the first really effective and continuous deliveries in November 1936—altogether fifteen to sixteen weeks, that is, nearly four months. Yet no time was wasted; Soviet military intelligence experts turned up in Spain within a few days of the Nationalist revolt and started to acquaint themselves with the requirements and capabilities of the Republican forces. Consequently, all the essential preparatory studies were well advanced by the time the Politburo had made its final decision to intervene and had concluded the necessary arrangements with the Republican authorities.

If under conditions of such urgency, and in the absence of major technical complexities, almost four months were required in Spain between the first contacts and the arrival of major deliveries, the consummation of an Egyptian-Soviet arms agreement in 1955 could reasonably be expected to take some six to seven months, depending on political obstacles. Not only were the logistics much more involved in 1955, as has been noted, but there was no particular hurry, since the Near East was free of major wars and no conflagration was anticipated. (The incidents along the Egyptian-Israeli demarcation line were, by international standards, hardly more than frontier skirmishes; their frequency and gravity increased only after the Egyptian Arms Deal was already well under way.) Nasser informed the world on September 27, 1955 that he had acquired arms from the Soviet bloc. However, Western sources reported rumors of the transaction as early as the end of August,[25] and it is now known that the first Czech weapons entered the pipeline sometime after the end of July.[26] It may be assumed, therefore, that major deliveries were reaching Egypt at least four weeks before Nasser made his announcement. By subtracting six or seven months from the tentative date of arrival of these ship-

[25] *New York Times,* August 31, 1955, and September 1, 1955.

[26] Seale, *Struggle for Syria,* pp. 234–237, quotes a statement from Major Salah Salem that on July 26, 1955, Egyptian technicians flew to Prague "to check the first consignment of MIG 15s. Arms deliveries had begun although 'Abd al-Nasir did not announce the deal until September."

ments, one may deduce that the initial Egyptian-Soviet contacts on the transfer of arms could hardly have occurred much later than January–February 1955. Since it was precisely at this time —around January 12, 1955—that Soviet and Egyptian interests were temporarily brought into alignment by the impending Turk-ish-Iraqi pact, it would appear that Cairo and Moscow cannot have wasted many days in drawing the logical conclusions.

2 Dubious Versions of History

Viewed against this background, the versions of history given in the accepted, published accounts of the Arms Deal seem to bear little relation to the political and technical requirements of the situation in 1955. Before examining these discrepancies, a cursory glance at a related aspect of the same phenomenon is called for: to a rather remarkable extent, various descriptions of the events in question have caricatured contemporary statesmen, so that their performances seem far more incompetent than is compatible with the laws of probability. For instance, it is rare to find something better than a parody of the serious considerations that, at the time, inhibited any revolutionary departure in America's Near Eastern policy;[1] consequently, the directors of U.S. diplomacy are often portrayed, in sketchy and unsympathetic fashion, as men who stubbornly clung to unrealistic, outdated concepts and failed to grasp repeated chances of preventing the Arms Deal. It follows, then, that they are held entirely responsible for what is alleged to have been a staggering setback suffered by the West.

Chronological Problems

Few critics seem to have paid much attention to the fact that such a harsh verdict must, to a considerable extent, depend upon

[1] The author is merely raising the question of whether practical options were really available to U.S. Near Eastern policy at the time; he is not debating the intrinsic merits, or demerits, of the whole concept of a Near Eastern defense framework.

the acceptance of a particular chronology for 1955. Actually, the judgment can be valid only if it is correct that, several months *before* Moscow and Cairo perceived the similarity of their interests and moved toward a military arrangement, Egyptian statesmen initiated a wholehearted and sustained effort to reach an arms agreement with the United States. (It may be noted, parenthetically, that, considering the stringent legal and diplomatic limitations on American military transactions in 1955, a simple take-it-or-leave-it proposal by a neutralist country to accept arms from Washington, provided there were no "strings," could hardly qualify as an earnest or realistic endeavor. Thus any serious Egyptian bid during that period had to allow the United States sufficient leeway to manage the transfer of weapons in a manner that would not be totally incompatible with current definitions of Western interests, with the joint public commitments of Washington, London, and Paris, and with the binding provisions of congressional enactments.) The timetable on which, essentially, the critics' case rests is taken from sundry reconstructions of the alleged sequence of events during the 1955 struggle for supremacy in the Near East. As presented in almost every one of these scenarios, it was only during the summer of 1955, after months of vainly pleading with Washington, that Cairo resorted to the one possible alternative—an entente with Moscow.

However, if the evidence were to suggest an entirely different chronology, a basic reappraisal of existing interpretations might well be in order. What, for instance, if it were to emerge that sometime before Egypt requested American weapons, at the very outset of 1955, immediately after Soviet and Egyptian interests began to converge, Moscow and Cairo had already been preparing certain essential arrangements preliminary to the full consummation of an arms deal?

It is perhaps not quite so apparent that the same versions of history and the same timetable that place U.S. policy makers in such unfavorable light are also less than flattering in their reflections on the capabilities of Soviet leaders. The directors of Moscow's international operations are portrayed—by inference, at least—as slow to recognize their opportunities in the Near East, reluctant to discard outworn ideological formulations that obscured the true nature of contemporary developments, and fortunate enough to become the beneficiaries of other people's blunders. There, again, so negative a verdict may be justified only if, indeed, the Russians prevaricated until the second half of 1955 before moving to exploit the Near Eastern constellation. What, however, if historical documentation were to indicate a much earlier date?

Although the accepted accounts of the Arms Deal do, of course, recognize the importance of the part played by Colonel Nasser, it would seem that his role, too, has been caricatured rather than accurately portrayed. This fact is not devoid of irony, since most books and articles dealing with the period have drawn heavily upon material from Egyptian sources. A little reflection might suggest some excellent reasons why the political personalities involved in the Arms Deal should have felt obliged to adhere to a particular chronology in describing the course of events to foreign observers. (This aspect of the problem will be analyzed subsequently.) Anyway, as long as no one questions the proposition that the military transaction with the East was arranged only in the latter part of 1955, Egypt's role during the first half of the year must, of necessity, appear to have been that of a mere passive object, buffeted by the whims of the great powers and capable, at the most, of reacting belatedly to their obduracy. It is precisely this mistaken impression that has colored most Western portrayals of Nasser's actions then and afterward; he appears in various descriptions as a man supposedly without clear aims, accumulating resentment at the haughty attitude of the great powers, finally giving vent to his temperament and precipitating a showdown through moves that were as dramatic in their impact as they were dangerous in their consequences. However, could this rather one-dimensional picture still be regarded as authentic if its most prominent features were to prove fundamentally incompatible with the real sequence of events? What, for the sake of argument, if the Arms Deal was already prepared at the very outset of 1955? What if the authors of this hazardous transaction felt impelled by political considerations to maintain a cover of secrecy for some months, while various arrangements for the transfer of weapons were made; and what if it was thought necessary, for tactical reasons, to go through an elaborate round of negotiations with the West in the meantime? In that case, to ascribe to mere impulse what must really have been a deliberately calculated and carefully managed action would hardly be accurate. By any standards, it would have been quite a coup for a self-tutored military man without international experience to have implemented such a "delicate" operation. The very fact that the full story of this manipulation could then remain hidden over a prolonged period, exceeding a decade, would be a measure of its success.

Thus the whole historical interpretation of this important period, as well as the reputations of the statesmen of several countries, would appear to depend on the accuracy, or otherwise, of a few widely repeated accounts.[2] Consequently, there is no escape from the chore of detailed examination to see whether these stories can be squared at all with the known facts or with the logical requirements of the situation in 1955.

Inconsistencies and Misinterpretations

According to the now current, popular versions, neither Egypt nor the USSR initiated serious countermoves, during the first part of 1955, to deter the Western authors of the Near Eastern defense alliance or to neutralize the effects of this project. Yet, as has been noted, the consequences of Nuri's coup threatened both Cairo's interests and Nasser's personal position, while interfering no less with the interests of the USSR. As far as the strange inaction of the Soviet leaders is concerned, it is often said that they were hampered by sheer ideological inertia. They allegedly cleaved to the hidebound Zhdanovite Weltanschauung of early Cominform days, which, it is claimed, oversimplified the world picture and interpreted every event as a mere function of the global conflict between two hostile camps. Consequently, Moscow is assumed to have been incapable of exploiting the fundamental antagonism between Western countries and some of their former colonies and dependencies that, by the 1950s, had turned the whole concept of a noncommunist camp into something of a myth. Most works imply, or state explicitly, that it was only at the time of the Bandung Conference in April 1955 (when the Soviet Foreign Ministry issued a major statement on Near Eastern affairs) that the Russians

---

[2] The versions of the prehistory of the Arms Deal, which are critically examined in this chapter, have been repeated, in countless permutations, by literally hundreds of secondary sources. For the sake of lucidity, the author has summarized the main trends emerging from these accounts, without tediously referring in each case to the specific variations published in individual secondary works. In any case, most of the extant versions in one way or another trace back to the same three or four origins; consequently, apart from examining the objective validity of these stories, the author has confined himself to analyzing the question of whether the personalities from whom the accounts emanated can be regarded as primary sources or, for that matter, as disinterested and reliable witnesses. The reader is asked to refer to the Appendix at the end of this chapter, "A Note Concerning Existing Sources," where these problems are discussed in some detail.

first began thinking in more realistic and opportunistic terms; after that stage had been reached, Moscow started to recognize that there were practical opportunities for a power wishing to launch a political offensive into the region.

None of these assumptions stand up well to closer examination. To start with, it is not correct that the Zhdanovite two-camp theory invariably regarded the rulers of newly independent Afro-Asian countries as hopelessly dependent upon the Western camp and thus foreclosed every opportunity of collaborating with them. His theory was expounded by Andrei Zhdanov in the famous address to the founding convention of the Cominform (September 1947); regrettably, current practice regarding this important speech appears to be: "refer to it always—read it never [at least not in full].''[3] Anyone who troubles to look at the original text, especially the section that never seems to find its way into published excerpts, would discover that, oddly enough, Zhdanov expressed the very opposite of the sentiments usually ascribed to him. He specifically named two Afro-Asian countries as being not only truly independent of the West but "associated with" the Soviet camp (Indochina and Indonesia), and three others as having reached the stage where they "sympathized with" the Soviet bloc (*Egypt* belonging to this category as well as Syria and India).[4] This quotation is hardly consonant with the allegation that he regarded all former colonies and dependencies as mere puppets of "imperialism" with whom no real dialogue was possible. It is true that other Soviet statements of the period were unfriendly to some of the Afro-Asian nationalist leaders, especially those of India, and that in 1948, during the last weeks of Zhdanov's life, a communist campaign of violence was launched against the authorities in South and Southeast Asia. In the Near East, however, general Soviet practice did not diverge too radically from the policies suggested by the Afro-Asian paragraph of Zhdanov's address; in Stalin's day there were several attempts to find a common language with the Wafd leadership in Egypt, and, as has been noted, both at that time (late in 1951) and in 1953 and 1954 (after Stalin's death), Soviet and Egyptian representatives seem to have discussed the

[3] Thus the treatment of Zhdanov's speech constitutes a complete reversal of the old French adage concerning the loss of Alsace-Lorraine: "think of it always—speak of it never."
[4] A. A. Zhdanov, "Report on the International Situation," *For a Lasting Peace, For a People's Democracy,* November 10, 1947.

possibility of a military transaction.[5] Direct evidence (covering the months from July 1953 until August 1954) is now available, showing that the Fourth (Near Eastern and Asian) Directorate of Soviet military intelligence (GRU) was, in fact, intensely interested in the idea of using Egypt "as an anticapitalist military power in the Near East."[6] (As leading defectors from its ranks revealed in the 1930s, the GRU had for many years been in charge of military assistance to noncommunist countries, especially during the initial, clandestine stages of such transactions.)[7] More overtly, Malenkov's first major foreign policy review, in August 1953, devoted special attention to Russia's desire for friendly relations with all the Arab and other Near Eastern countries.[8] Admittedly, the signs of Moscow's growing interest in Cairo were interspersed with brief periods during which the Soviet media sharply criticized Egyptian leaders—for instance, in 1952, when the military junta came to power and, again, in the second half of 1954, when Nasser reached a compromise agreement with Britain on the evacuation of the Suez Canal Zone.[9] However, as the next chapter will show, during the first days of 1955 Moscow had already overcome its temporary annoyance and was beginning to woo Egypt very persistently, both in words and in deeds. It is true, as will be seen, that there appear to have been some serious differences of opinion within the Kremlin, at the beginning of 1955, concerning the disadvantages and risks that a Soviet leap into the Near East would entail; however, the opponents of an entente with Egypt were clearly unable to veto Moscow's new line, although, subsequently, they managed sometimes to reduce the momentum of Russia's thrust into the region. Altogether, therefore, the facts would hardly seem to bear out the view that for many years, right up to April 1955, ideological preconceptions had somehow chained the Russians to a totally inactive policy in the Near East. Even this brief

---

[5] See chap. 1, footnote 23.

[6] Oleg Penkovskiy, *The Penkovskiy Papers* (New York: Doubleday & Company, 1965), p. 52.

[7] Walter G. Krivitsky, *In Stalin's Secret Service* (New York: Harper & Brothers, 1939), passim, and Barton Whaley, "Soviet and Chinese Clandestine Arms Aid," 1965 draft (Cambridge, Mass.: M.I.T., Center for International Studies).

[8] *Pravda*, August 9, 1953.

[9] "Observer," in *Pravda*, September 8, 1954; even at that time, however, Moscow paid particular attention to the question of military assistance to Egypt, warning the military junta against accepting U.S. arms aid and mentioning past indications of Soviet "sympathy for the national aspirations" of Egypt.

survey shows that, in reality, Moscow was very much concerned with the affairs of the region and, at least from 1953 onward, was perfectly prepared to take a pragmatic view and exploit every possible opportunity of gaining local allies. Thus one is bound to react skeptically to the claim that, early in 1955, the Russians simply lay dormant for several vital months before taking any counteraction whatever against the new Western defense arrangements in the Near East. This interpretation is all the more incredible because the Soviet media were full of unmistakable signs that the Soviet leadership was intensely exercised about the probable consequences of the Western project.[10]

Yet the traditional accounts still maintain that, during the initial months of 1955, in spite of their obvious dismay at the events in Baghdad, the Russians and Egyptians alike contented themselves with purely verbal assaults upon Iraq, Turkey, and the West. Cairo is said to have followed up on this useless exercise with but a single diplomatic gesture, in the form of a transparently inoperable anti-Iraqi agreement concluded with Syria and Saudi Arabia. Not unnaturally, this failed to convince other Near Eastern leaders that their future lay with the anti-Baghdad group—not to speak of deterring Nuri himself, who calmly proceeded to sign the Turkish-Iraqi pact on February 24, 1955. In spite of this serious setback, Nasser is alleged to have continued ignoring the one obvious, practical move[11] that could enable Egypt to neutralize the consequences of the pact, about which there was so much apprehension in Cairo. Although the young leader was anything but timid or unimaginative, most commentaries simply assume that he went on resolutely averting his eyes from Russia's beckoning hand.

Instead of taking the path that seemed clearly indicated by the conditions prevailing at this time, Egypt is portrayed as having done the very reverse. With Nuri's pact about to be completed, Cairo appealed for arms . . . to Washington. Yet, as has been noted, the new Western security system in the region not only threatened to transfer Arab hegemony from Cairo to Baghdad but to "freeze" the Near Eastern territorial status quo and balance of power in

---

[10] To take a single example: of the first nine issues of *New Times* in 1955 (covering January–February of that year), only one (no. 5) did not contain a complete article (or "International Note") devoted to Soviet attacks upon the Near Eastern defense project. David J. Dallin, *Soviet Foreign Policy after Stalin* (Philadelphia: J. P. Lippincott Co., 1961), pp. 201 and 388, stressed that Soviet leaders exaggerated the importance of the Baghdad Pact project.

[11] As was noted in chap. 1 (footnote 23), a Soviet-Egyptian arms deal had been repeatedly on the agenda between 1951 and 1955.

such a way as to contain Egypt at a time when, demographically and economically, she appeared to be bursting at the seams. Cairo's one feasible countermove was to deprive the West of its most practical lever for maintaining the local equilibrium, namely, its monopoly of arms supplies to the region. By taking this step, Cairo would cause the Western "custodians" of the Near East to lose a uniquely serviceable instrument that had been constantly used to adjust the delicate balance between the larger of the local states, such as Egypt, and their weaker neighbors. Unless this monopoly was broken, the West would continue controlling the machinery that ensured regional tranquillity by inhibiting the instinctive urges of the more powerful local leaders. It was precisely this aspect of the situation that caused irredentist forces in the Near East to search for ways of compelling the West to relinquish its "sphere of influence." In view of these considerations, almost any Egyptian leader could be expected to challenge Western military and political tutelage over the Near East the moment the West threw its support behind Baghdad, Cairo's traditional rival. Colonel Nasser's own testimony clearly implies that these were, indeed, his major objectives at that time:

In 1954 and 1955 . . . we did not hesitate to break up the arms monopoly. . . . Brothers, this was a big and ferocious battle, but it did not frighten us—we believed in . . . our right to do away with the spheres of influence.[12]

His reference to 1954 provides a significant clue to the date when this policy was adopted. It could, at any rate, have been no later than the turn of the year 1954/55; indeed, this deduction is fully compatible with the political requirements of the situation. The announcement of the forthcoming Turkish-Iraqi pact was published on January 12, 1955, but indications of this development had reached Near Eastern capitals several weeks earlier. By the end of December 1954 it was almost certainly realized in Cairo that counteraction would have to be taken. At any rate, Nasser's dates leave little doubt that the objectives he outlined had been adopted well before the second half of February 1955, when Egypt asked the United States for weapons.[13]

[12] Nasser's speech in Alexandria, July 26, 1962 (Cairo Radio, domestic broadcast, July 26, 1962).
[13] President Eisenhower, in *Waging Peace, 1956–1961: The White House Years* (New York: Doubleday & Company, 1965), has testified that "as early as February of that year [1955] Nasser had attempted to obtain arms from

The historian is therefore confronted with a positively bizarre situation: according to the evidence, the Egyptian government decided, for perfectly logical reasons, to challenge the arms monopoly and the "spheres of influence" of the West; it then proceeded to implement this policy by requesting arms from the United States, the leading Western power, the initiator of the 1950 Tripartite Declaration, the guarantor of the Near Eastern equilibrium, and the author of the Near Eastern defense project. Moreover, the request was submitted at a time when, because of congressional and diplomatic restrictions, American military assistance was conditional upon the recipient's undertaking to use American weapons only for internal security and for legitimate defense or upon his willingness to support regional defense arrangements.[14] In terms of Egypt's policy guidelines, as they had been defined at the time, such provisions were utterly unacceptable. Nor was there any likelihood that American political conditions could be bypassed entirely, since Egypt required some form of U.S. governmental assistance, at least in the shape of long-term

---

the United States" (p. 24). It is true that President Eisenhower then goes on to say that Nasser submitted a list of armaments, "$27 million worth," because the Egyptians were "apparently alarmed over the ferocity of an Israeli reprisal raid in the Gaza Strip." This seems to present some difficulty, since the Israeli raid only occurred on the night of February 28–March 1 and thus could hardly have been the cause of an Egyptian arms request presented earlier in February. However, as will be seen later in this chapter, the contradiction may be more apparent than real. Cairo hinted in the last days of January 1955 that it might conceivably be interested in American weapons; consequently, the United States and Britain gave intensive study to the whole question of Near Eastern armaments during the first week of February. Shortly thereafter, probably in the second half of February, the possibility of extending some form of U.S. military assistance to Egypt reached the stage of active discussions. This is apparently the reason why President Eisenhower named the month of February as the correct date for this development. The original Egyptian arms request was valued at nearly twice as much as the $27 million mentioned by the president. However, the amount involved was reduced to $27 million, at the insistence of the United States, when talks between the two countries were resumed in the spring. Active consideration of military shipments to the area had been interrupted by the Gaza incident; the ensuing tension between Egypt and Israel caused Secretary Dulles to impose a temporary embargo on arms supplies. When this ban was lifted and, subsequently, intensive negotiations began, Colonel Nasser undoubtedly utilized the Gaza incident as an argument to explain why Egypt's need for arms was more urgent than ever. President Eisenhower confirms that, indeed, the discussions were held in two stages (i.e., presumably before and after Gaza), when he says that Egypt had "dropped the matter temporarily." The question of Premier Nasser's motivation during this episode is analyzed later.

[14] These conditions are described more fully later in this chapter; see "Political Motivations."

military credits repayable in soft currency, and was not prepared to consider the outright purchase of arms for dollars. It is hard to resist the conclusion, therefore, that, in requesting arms from the United States, Egypt had consented to a dialogue that was highly unlikely to produce any results; nor, from Cairo's point of view, was the success of this move even theoretically desirable, since it would reinforce rather than liquidate the arms monopoly and "spheres of influence" of the West. The facts would suggest one possible way of resolving this paradox: for very sound tactical reasons, which will be examined later, Colonel Nasser's aim may have been simply to establish for the record that, months before the arrival of Soviet arms was announced, Egypt had made the effort of going through a round of negotiations with the West. Thus it was probably the impact of this demonstrative move that interested the Egyptian government, rather than the outcome of the talks, which, indeed, could be considered a foregone conclusion. Moreover, as will be seen, ongoing talks with Washington were undoubtedly useful to Cairo as a way of convincing Moscow that Egypt had alternate options and should, therefore, be treated with great respect.

The fact that the whole episode, with its apparent logical inconsistencies, presents historians with serious problems has been ignored in the traditional accounts of this period; they sidestep this question and compound the confusion by suggesting that, in approaching the United States, Egypt may have been impelled by an entirely different motive, one of a purely military rather than political nature. Egypt, it is said, had fallen badly behind current arms levels in the Near East, because the West had deprived her of military supplies during her protracted struggle with Great Britain over the Canal Zone. Even after this problem had been resolved, deliveries were allegedly made in such a tardy and niggardly fashion that Colonel Nasser's army was left almost without spare parts and its equipment reduced to a nonoperational state.

The Course of Arms Negotiations

Many accounts claim that the urgency of this situation was brought home by a dramatic event that forced Cairo to take action: they explain that Premier Nasser received an unpleasant jolt when Israeli forces, in the course of a punitive raid on the night of February 28–March 1, 1955, surprised an Egyptian military encampment near Gaza, inflicting considerable casualties. The incident reportedly caught the local garrison both ill equipped and unprepared; it is said to have obliged the Egyptian leader to redeem his army's prestige, as well as his own, by taking steps to obtain impressive modern hardware, including fighter planes, bombers, and tanks. There is, of course, no reason to dismiss considerations of this kind, which might well have weighed heavily with Colonel Nasser, who had personally exploited the memory of similar military shortcomings during the Palestine War in order to rouse Egyptian officers against King Farouk. The question remains, however, whether this was really a relevant factor in Cairo's decision to approach the United States for arms.

The actual timetable of events would seem to militate against such an assumption. A few days after the agreement on the Canal Zone ended Egypt's conflict with Britain, in October 1954, the U.S. ambassador, Jefferson Caffery, offered Cairo military assistance, although the United States had never previously been a main arms supplier to a member of the Arab League. At the time, Cairo cold-shouldered this suggestion, since, in accordance with the provisions of the U.S. Mutual Security Act, such aid was conditional upon Egypt's willingness to support regional defense arrangements.[15] More than three months later, at the very end of January 1955, when Ankara and Baghdad were already preparing for the signature of their new security pact (which was being accompanied by sizable U.S. military shipments to Iraq), Egypt began to indicate some measure of interest in Ambassador Caffery's offer.[16] Perhaps it was thought that such a hint might raise Western hopes and, consequently, induce Washington to delay the completion of the Turkish-Iraqi pact and the delivery of American arms to Nuri a-Said.

The West, indeed, responded immediately, and intensive Anglo-American consultations took place, early in February 1955, on the whole question of military supplies to the region.[17] However, at that late stage, the United States and Great Britain could hardly call off all their Near Eastern defense arrangements, nor, it seems, did Egypt offer sufficient inducements for them to consider such

---

[15] Arnold Wolfers, ed., *Alliance Policy in the Cold War* (Baltimore, Md.: The Johns Hopkins Press, 1959), p. 256, and John C. Campbell, *Defense of the Middle East: Problems of American Policy*, rev. ed. (New York: Harper & Brothers), p. 180.
[16] *New York Times*, January 29, 1955.
[17] Ibid., February 6, 1955.

action. On the other hand, the West apparently was not unwilling to give Cairo arms while, at the same time, proceeding with preparations for the Baghdad Pact, in the hope that Premier Nasser might use such an arrangement as an elegant excuse for abandoning his vociferous opposition to the Turkish-Iraqi alliance.[18] Since it was precisely the liquidation of this pact that interested the Egyptian leader, the thought of such a compromise was hardly realistic.

It is significant, however, that, although he failed to prevent the Turkish-Iraqi alliance (which was finally signed on February 24), Colonel Nasser did not withdraw his bid for arms from the United States; on the contrary, during the second half of February, a request to that effect was apparently forwarded to Washington.[19] Thus there would seem to have been some development in the earlier part of February causing Egypt to feel that a useful purpose could be served by persisting with this effort, regardless of the fact that the West refused to abandon its Near Eastern security arrangements (and in spite of the legal and diplomatic limitations on U.S. military aid that seemed to rule out any major transaction on political terms acceptable to Egypt). The event that made Cairo react in this manner could hardly have been the Gaza raid, for the simple reason that it only took place on the night of February 28–March 1 and, coming as a complete surprise, could neither have been foreseen in Egypt nor have motivated actions that had already been initiated some weeks earlier. (The next chapter will attempt to answer the question of what development did occur, earlier in February 1955, that caused Premier Nasser to persist with an apparently pointless approach to Washington.)

Actually, the Gaza incident, so far from being the catalyst that precipitated Egypt's request for arms, proved, if anything, to be a temporary obstacle. Because of the regional tension that followed the raid, Secretary Dulles felt impelled to impose a brief embargo on shipments to both Israel and Egypt of even those minor items of equipment that the United States had sold since the fall of 1954.[20] Only when the immediate crisis had subsided could the Egyptian request receive practical consideration. By that time,

---

[18] Ibid., February 23, 1955.
[19] See footnote 13 in this chapter.
[20] United Press dispatch from Washington, March 10, 1955.

of course, Gaza was imprinted on the general consciousness as a dramatic incident of the recent past and could be conveniently cited in public as the cause of Egypt's quest for arms. In recent years, some commentators have indeed come to feel that the Gaza raid, while it no doubt shocked the Egyptian leader, also proved to be tactically useful afterward in justifying moves that had probably been initiated for somewhat different reasons.[21]

Militarily speaking, the incident could hardly have been of much direct relevance to Cairo's bid for heavy armaments. Neither at Gaza nor during the subsequent series of Egyptian forays and Israeli punitive raids did the two sides seem to have the intention or the opportunity of resorting to heavier hardware, such as planes, tanks, or large-caliber artillery. Indeed, it is difficult to find instances in 1955 when such weapons were utilized; the border *guerrilla* was generally fought out with light automatic arms and occasional mortars. (The two countries were already beginning to manufacture their own automatic weapons—in Egypt, under Swedish license.)[22] Both sides increasingly relied on picked commando formations, using the traditional light equipment of such small, mobile units. Since Egypt's military request to the United States referred almost entirely to heavy armaments,[23] it could have had little direct connection with the Gaza situation. What the Gaza garrison conspicuously lacked was adequate modern training, but it was precisely in this field that Egypt rejected U.S. assistance, insisting that foreign training missions impeded the exercise of national sovereignty.[24]

Whatever the actual motive, during the first quarter of 1955 Egypt presented the United States with a shopping list of heavy armaments, valued originally at over $40 million.[25] Pleading a shortage of foreign currency, Cairo asked that the weapons be

---

[21] Keith Wheelock, *Nasser's New Egypt* (New York: Frederick A. Praeger, 1960), p. 233, states that Gaza constituted a "convenient excuse"; Robert St. John, *The Boss: The Story of Gamal Abdel Nasser* (Toronto: McGraw-Hill Book Co., 1960), p. 204, makes a similar observation.

[22] *New York Times*, March 11, 1956.

[23] Wheelock, *Nasser's New Egypt*, p. 229; MENA, April 2, 1955.

[24] Wheelock, *Nasser's New Egypt*, pp. 225–228; Elizabeth Monroe, *Britain's Moment in the Middle East, 1914–1956* (Baltimore, Md.: The Johns Hopkins Press, 1963), p. 186.

[25] *Jewish Observer & Middle East Review*, October 14, 1955. The United States subsequently insisted that this request be scaled down to about $27 million, still a considerable amount by Near Eastern standards in 1955.

provided in the least painful manner possible, that is, if not as a grant, then at least for long-term credit repayable in soft currency.[26]

However, so the traditional versions of history claim, the United States at first made difficulties over the type and amount of arms requested by Egypt; then Washington allegedly refused to consider payment in anything but hard currency, insisting, moreover, that American weapons be accompanied by a U.S. training mission in a supervisory capacity and that Egypt give a commitment not to use the arms except under certain specified circumstances. Cairo is said to have turned down these conditions, regarding them as a threat to Egypt's independence, and to have pleaded for easier repayment terms, asserting that the Egyptian army's equipment was already markedly inferior to the armaments of neighboring competitors.

The same versions of history allege that Washington proved obdurate and that, in desperation, Premier Nasser then turned his glance toward Moscow, determined, however, to give the West a last chance. The U.S. and British ambassadors were duly warned, in June 1955, of the possibility of an Egyptian-Soviet arms deal, but—so the traditional stories claim—the United States remained shortsighted and treated Egyptian warnings as a bluff. Consequently, it is said, Egypt had no choice but, reluctantly, to accept Soviet offers.

Military Implications

Neither the military nor the political implications of this portrayal of events really stand up well to closer examination. To take the military argument first: Egypt is said to have fallen behind in equipment because the West had deprived her of arms supplies during the years of struggle against Britain over control of the Suez base. Even when this conflict was resolved, in the fall of 1954, the West allegedly failed to resume full-scale deliveries, the United States insisting upon participation in a regional defense network, the British sending few items and fewer spare parts, and the French refusing to help because of Egyptian interference in Algeria. Consequently, it is claimed, by the time of Gaza, Egypt's position had become deplorable, with only 6 planes proving air-

---

[26] Wheelock, *Nasser's New Egypt*, p. 229.

worthy and few tanks being operational because of the need for repairs.[27] Egypt's Arab rivals and Israel, on the other hand, are said to have continued receiving armaments without serious interruption.

Fortunately, as a result of the spate of studies on the Suez-Sinai conflict, the military lineup in the Near East prior to the Egyptian Arms Deal is now fairly well known and can easily be checked.[28] In the years immediately after the 1948 Arab-Israeli war (that is, just prior to the military junta's rise to power), Egypt had well under 100 light tanks and a mere 50 obsolete propeller planes (Spitfires and a handful of bombers and transports). By the late summer of 1955, however, Egypt already possessed some 200 tanks and over 80 jet fighters (as well as some 20 older Halifax and Lancaster bombers). This was Western equipment that had been delivered partly since Naguib and Nasser took over (and, in any case, since 1950), while some important items had arrived even more recently, that is, in the months after the Suez Canal Zone agreement with Britain (October 1954). Thus, for instance, Egypt's armored strength consisted partly of Shermans (Mk III) but also of a much better tank, the Centurion, which was supplied to only one other country of the Arab League, namely, Iraq, an ally of the West. Altogether Egypt had received well over 40 Centurions from Britain, of which at least 32 were delivered during the first half of 1955, the very period under discussion here.

By that time, Egypt's jet fighter force was made up of Meteors, Vampires, and Fury night fighters, which, by contemporary Near Eastern standards, were considered reasonably modern planes; in 1952, Cairo was even given a license to produce Vampires and Venoms, while in 1953, at the time of the conflict with Britain over the Canal Zone, the Egyptian air force was able to acquire well

[27] This claim was made by Major Salah Salem; see Patrick Seale, *The Struggle for Syria: A Study of Postwar Arab Politics, 1945–1958* (New York and London: Oxford University Press, 1965), pp. 234–237.
[28] The material for the military analysis presented in the following paragraphs is derived from Colonel Robert Henriques, *A Hundred Hours to Suez* (New York: Viking Press, 1957), pp. 26–27; Jules Menken, "Problems of Middle Eastern Strategy," *Brassey's Annual: The Armed Forces Year Book,* 1956 ed. (New York: Frederick A. Praeger, 1956), chap. XIII; Major-General Moshe Dayan, *Yoman Ma'arekhet Sinai* [Sinai Campaign Diary] (Tel Aviv: Am Hassefer Publishers, Ltd., 1965), pp. 10–12, 72–73, and 180–193; A. J. Barker, *Suez: The Seven Day War* (London: Faber & Faber, 1964), pp. 59–61; Michel Bar-Zohar, *Suez Ultra-Secret* (Paris: Fayard, 1964), pp. 72–120; and Monroe, *Britain's Moment in the Middle East,* p. 185.

over a score of Vampires indirectly, via Italy and Syria. In 1955 Egypt also received two destroyers from Britain, as well as a first consignment of French 150 mm. guns and 120 mm. mortars. Earlier, Egypt had bought two Hunt class frigates from Britain; two Colony class frigates arrived from the United States in 1952, in spite of all the limitations that have been analyzed, and 600 American military vehicles were acquired even later, in 1953. (These transactions were implemented before Cairo and Washington clashed over the question of the Turkish-Iraqi alliance.) Moreover, in 1954 and 1955, Egypt was handed a considerable proportion of the 600,000 tons of supplies and equipment stored at the Suez Canal Zone base, which Britain was beginning to evacuate.[29]

By Near Eastern standards of that time, these were substantial reinforcements, both in quantity and in quality. Even Iraq, an ally of the West, did not receive more favorable treatment during the period in question, except, perhaps, for the number of Centurions delivered. Up to 1955, Iraq was not permitted to forge ahead of Egypt with regard to the total number of either jets or tanks acquired. The West granted only small amounts of arms to other Arab countries, with the possible exception of Jordan (which, however, lagged considerably behind both Egypt and Iraq). Moreover, comparing military deliveries to Egypt and Israel, striking parallels can be found between the policies adopted by the Western powers toward these countries. After 1948, Israel, like Egypt, had fewer than 100 light tanks and only 40–50 propeller-driven, obsolete planes. By 1955, Israel, like Egypt, had acquired about 200 tanks (although, unlike Egypt, Israel was refused the Centurion at that time); compared with some 80 Meteor and Vampire jets in Egypt's possession, Israel, in mid-1955, had some 50 jets (including a single squadron of Ouragans, which, however, had not yet been fully delivered); like Egypt, Israel received two destroyers in 1955. It is correct, as Colonel Nasser later stated when presenting his Arms Deal to the world, that Israel, in 1955, was negotiating for additional French and other Western equipment. So, however, was Egypt, which by early 1956 was to receive 20 additional French 150 mm. guns and 40 French AMX-13 tanks, as well as 200 Valentine (Archer) tank destroyers dispatched from Britain via Belgium.[30]

It would thus seem that the Western powers, up to the time when the Egyptian-Soviet Arms Deal was announced—and even six months later—had by no means discriminated or deprived Cairo of essential weapons; on the contrary, they had sent whatever was required to maintain a reasonable military equilibrium throughout the region, especially between Egypt and Israel. Precisely the same treatment was extended to other states in the area; at the same time great care was taken to avoid a Near Eastern arms race. Consequently, all recipients in the region were permitted a limited flow, rather than a flood, of weapons.

That this was a matter of conscious policy can be seen from an analysis of military transactions negotiated during the period, showing with what deliberation and caution the West approached any and all Near Eastern requests for hardware. A fairly detailed recent survey of the history of arms talks between a Western and a Near Eastern country indicates that it was not at all unusual for many months to pass before even a limited quantity of weapons was permitted to reach any state in the area.[31] According to that study, Israel's Chief of Staff Moshe Dayan visited Paris in August 1954 to request equipment, including one of the less sophisticated prototypes of the Mystère fighter plane—the Mystère 2. Shortly afterward, the French authorities consented to deliver a single squadron of these planes, in two separate shipments of six each. However, the implementation of this transaction was repeatedly delayed by political considerations, in spite of the very small size of the order. Again and again, misgivings were voiced at meetings of NEACC, which had been duly informed by Paris of the impending shipment. Finally, when the Mystère 2 had become entirely obsolete, the order was replaced by a request for the Mystère 4. However, the same considerations caused further delays, and it was not until April 12, 1956, well over eighteen months after the original order, that the first delivery of eight Mystères took place. (The situation was to change radically, of course, in the weeks preceding the Suez-Sinai conflict; however, by that time, a full year after the announcement of the Egyptian-Soviet Arms Deal, the whole area was already smoldering, and hope that the regional military balance could be maintained was largely being abandoned.)

During the 1950–1955 period, these obstacles and delays were

[31] Bar-Zohar, *Suez Ultra-Secret*, pp. 72–120.

encountered in equal measure by Egypt and Israel and, no doubt, by the other countries in the region. The West had little choice but to follow such a course if it wished to maintain stability in the Near East and prevent an unbridled arms race. That this was a primary consideration for the "custodians" of the Near East is suggested by the statistics. As was seen earlier, Western arms shipments to Egypt and to Israel tended to cancel each other out qualitatively and, to a lesser extent, quantitatively. This policy was, of course, based on the assumption that the two countries could be balanced against each other in isolation and that, militarily speaking, one could ignore the symbolic alignment between Egypt and the other Arab countries under the Arab collective security pact. Although Egypt theoretically had a slight edge with her Centurions and her somewhat larger number of jet fighters, the Western powers probably felt that Israel's advantage in training, organization, and modern skills would easily compensate for any lag in matériel.

Thus even a cursory glance at changes in Near Eastern armaments during the early 1950s indicates that the "custodians" of the region were achieving a carefully planned military equilibrium. In no way do the facts substantiate the view that Egypt was singled out by the West for different or inferior treatment. Nor does the evidence bear out the claim that Egypt's military condition, at the time of Gaza, was particularly deplorable, at any rate as far as the availability of equipment and spare parts was concerned—the training and the preparedness of men being an entirely different matter. A mere four and a half months after the Gaza incident the Egyptian command held its annual military parade. During this brief period the general condition of Egyptian equipment could hardly have improved in a very revolutionary manner, nor has anyone ever suggested that it did. Yet, according to reports from the parade, more than 50 of Egypt's 80 jets were sufficiently airworthy to participate in the acrobatics of the flypast, which would appear to contradict the claim that, only a few months earlier, a mere 6 planes were capable of taking to the air. (Even a year later, just prior to Sinai, although attrition had presumably taken its toll and Egypt had not bought additional Vampires and Meteors or spare parts, two squadrons, numbering 27 of these Western planes, were still fully operational, one squadron of 30 planes was being converted and considered partly operational, and one squadron of 15 was just being organized.) Similarly, during the 1955 parade, over 120 tanks, nearly two thirds of the total, were reportedly in good enough shape to participate, which does not bear out the proposition that, at the time of Gaza, most of the tanks had been unusable and needed repair.[32]

The facts, therefore, would hardly seem to sustain the view that there were serious military factors in 1955 urging Egypt on in her quest for a massive arms transaction. The shopping list submitted by Cairo to the United States does warrant the adjective "massive," since it was disproportionately large, at least judged by the military standards of the time. Great Britain, a major source of arms for the Near East, during a five-year period (1951–1956) supplied all the Arab League countries with hardware officially valued at less than $80 million;[33] although this sum undoubtedly constitutes a considerable underestimate of the equipment actually handed over, it does show, by comparison, the real magnitude of Egypt's original request for more than $40 million of arms in 1955. If granted, it would have given to a single country, in one year, possibly one half of the total amount received by the whole area over five years. A transaction of this size, far from being required to restore the balance, was bound to upset the regional equilibrium. That such a military balance did exist at the beginning of 1955, before Egypt submitted her request, was indicated by Colonel Nasser himself; he told a prominent visitor, at the time, that Israel did not constitute a military threat to Egypt,[34] in other words, that the two countries were roughly in equilibrium.[35]

[32] Dayan, *Yoman Ma'arekhet Sinai*, pp. 192–193; *Jewish Observer & Middle East Review*, July 29, 1955. This does not mean that Egyptian standards of maintenance, in 1955, were particularly high; it would simply indicate that spare parts, ammunition, and other equipment were available in rather larger quantities than has been supposed. Some observers have been misled by the fact that, during the Suez-Sinai conflict, Egypt seemed unable to bring a great proportion of her equipment into operational use. This was largely due to the fact that the crisis caught Egypt in the midst of conversion from Western to Soviet arms. Consequently, her military personnel, especially in the air force, had not completed retraining, and both operational and maintenance statistics suffered accordingly.

[33] Henriques, *A Hundred Hours to Suez*, pp. 26–27.

[34] By the time of Suez-Sinai, of course, the military situation in the Near East was completely transformed.

[35] The visitor was Mr. Richard Crossman (see *New Statesman and Nation*, January 21, 1955); see also St. John, *The Boss*, pp. 205–206, who indicates that at this time (January 1955) Arab representatives were told that Egypt's military strength was quantitatively superior to Israel's.

Political Motivations

To repeat: a closer examination does not bear out the claim that there were substantive or cogent *military* reasons in 1955 for a large-scale Egyptian arms deal. The purpose of such a transaction had to be *political;* however, the only rational political goal that an Egyptian arms deal could have at that time was, as Premier Nasser himself indicated, bound to be in diametric opposition to contemporary Western aims in the region. In the words of the Egyptian leader, Cairo was attempting to "break up" the Western "arms monopoly" and, consequently, "to do away with" the Western "spheres of influence"; that is, Egypt's goal was to liquidate Western tutelage over the Near East and thus "unfreeze" the territorial and political status quo in the area. In 1955, the United States could not seriously be expected to collaborate in such an effort; for one thing, in the 1950 Tripartite Declaration, the United States had guaranteed both the territorial integrity of the Near Eastern states and the maintenance of the military and political balance in the region.

Moreover, Nasser could have no illusion about Washington's probable reaction if requested to give military aid, or military credit repayable in goods, to a country actively opposing the Western security network in the Near East. The United States could hardly be expected to consent, especially if the country in question would not give the required commitment to refrain from employing American arms against its neighbors or permit a U.S. military mission to supervise the use of these weapons. There was no room for error in this matter, for the simple reason that U.S. decisions on military assistance were not left entirely to the personal choice of individual policy makers but came within the purview of U.S. public law and official international commitments.

Congress, in 1949–1951, had voted stringent provisions concerning the grant of military aid, whether as a gift or in other forms; the Mutual Defense Assistance Act and the Mutual Security Act contained fairly strict instructions on the precise conditions under which such aid might be given. Participation in regional defense arrangements was one way of gaining eligibility for U.S. military assistance; another possibility was the development of a country's defensive strength as a direct contribution to the security of the Free World as a whole. If arms, under whatever provision, were given to a government, it was incumbent upon the latter to make binding commitments that such weapons would be used only for legitimate defense and for internal security (that is, not for an attack upon neighboring countries). The same condition was also imposed under the terms of the 1950 Tripartite Declaration, by which the United States, Britain, and France solemnly committed themselves to support their jointly formulated policies. In addition, Congress required that U.S. arms be accompanied by a military assistance advisory group that, to some extent, could supervise the proper use of American weapons and, consequently, would be able to ensure that the recipients kept their promises. The only practical way for a potential recipient to sidestep all of these conditions was to buy U.S. arms for hard cash, as a regular commercial transaction, without any form of U.S. governmental assistance. Even then, however, it was clear that the type and amount of weapons requested would have to conform to the stipulation in the Tripartite Declaration that called for the preservation of the regional arms balance.[36]

These facts were perfectly well known to every Near Eastern government, even if they had not been reemphasized, time and again, by U.S. representatives. Colonel Nasser himself had no illusions whatever on this matter; as he told his officers on March 29, at the very time when negotiations on his arms request were proceeding in Washington, although the West had previously "offered us military aid," no agreement had proved possible and, therefore, "I believe that it would be a miracle if we ever obtained arms from this source."[37] It seems fairly clear, then, that Egypt, when it turned to Washington and asked for arms under conditions that were not really compatible with U.S. domestic law and international commitments, realized that American consent could hardly be expected under those circumstances. Obviously, Premier Nasser's representatives were not going through such an apparently pointless exercise simply to pass the time. What the actual purpose may have been will be examined subsequently, but, under the circumstances, it could hardly have been the acquisition of arms from the West.

This assumption was confirmed when the United States attempted, in some measure, to accommodate Cairo during subsequent months. The demand that Egypt should cease opposing the Baghdad Pact was dropped, and Washington offered to *sell* Cairo

---

[36] Eisenhower, *Waging Peace*, pp. 24–25.
[37] Cairo Radio, domestic broadcast, March 31, 1955.

weapons to the tune of $27 million;[38] this was still a substantial proposal, compared with the amounts that had been customary in the Near East prior to 1955. However, there were some serious problems with regard to the quality as well as the quantity of the arms in question. Admiral Radford later pointed out that Egypt had demanded types of weapons that the United States just could not send to the area if the regional military balance was to be maintained.[39] Nevertheless, the $27 million package seems to have contained at least some of the items requested by the Egyptians, although probably not as many and of as sophisticated a category as they had desired. Yet Cairo failed to accept this offer, pleading a shortage of foreign exchange, and suggested instead that the United States should give Egypt a long-term credit, repayable in goods or soft currency. This would have amounted to military assistance under a different name, while circumventing all the conditions imposed by U.S. domestic law and international commitments. Such a proposal was unlikely to prove acceptable to Washington, especially since Egypt's foreign exchange position at that time was not really critical. At the end of 1955, Egypt's gold and foreign currency reserves amounted to well over $641 million, a little lower than in King Farouk's day but still a highwater mark of Colonel Nasser's rule (by 1956, the reserves had declined to $566 million and, by 1957, to $511 million).[40] Since the sum involved in buying arms from the United States was only $27 million, it does not seem very likely that a shortage of hard currency could have been the real reason for rejecting Washington's offer of a transaction in dollars.

Altogether, therefore, the episode leaves observers with a distinct impression that Premier Nasser requested arms from the United States under conditions that were unlikely to be granted and then shifted his position when the United States attempted to move closer toward it. Consequently, it is difficult to avoid the conclusion

[38] *New York Times,* October 26, 1955.

[39] U.S., Congress, Senate, *Hearings before the Committee on Foreign Relations and the Committee on Armed Services,* 85th Congress, 1st session (Washington, D.C.: Government Printing Office, 1957), pt. I, p. 438. President Eisenhower, in *Waging Peace,* pp. 24–25, stressed that the United States was "obliged to abide by our standing agreement with the French and British to maintain a rough balance between the military strength of Israel and the neighboring Arab states, a balance that this arms sale would have drastically disturbed."

[40] *International Financial Statistics* (Washington, D.C.), vol. XV, no. 4 (April 1962), pp. 260–261.

that Cairo's dialogue with Washington may, to some extent, have been calculated to create the impression that the West was rejecting Egypt's approaches and thus was leaving her no choice but to look elsewhere for help.

To sum up: the accepted accounts of Egypt's military negotiations with the West in 1955 are extremely difficult to square with the known facts and with the simple demands of logic; clearly, a different interpretation is needed.

Additional Questions

Very much the same can be said about the traditional portrayals of Egypt's initial contacts with the communist countries, which, allegedly, led to the Arms Deal after Cairo had become totally disillusioned with the West. Upon closer examination, the stories dealing with the genesis of the Egyptian-Soviet entente turn out to be both confused and mutually contradictory.

According to one widely publicized version, when Premier Nasser realized that his discussions with the United States were leading nowhere, he asked Chou En-lai, at the Bandung Conference, for Chinese arms. Chou regretfully pointed out that China was militarily incapable of meeting the request, being still dependent upon Soviet supplies, but would be prepared to approach the USSR on Egypt's behalf. (Another variation has it that the Egyptians did not request Chinese arms, but simply asked Chou to act as mediator between Cairo and Moscow, and that this discussion took place in Rangoon a few days before the Bandung Conference.)[41] Chou is then said to have contacted Moscow, and the Soviet ambassador to Cairo, D. S. Solod, promptly went to inform the Egyptian leaders, upon their return from Bandung, that the USSR would be happy to oblige. However, Colonel Nasser is alleged to have put the offer on ice, being anxious to give the West a last chance before proceeding to take the irrevocable step of signing a military agreement with Moscow.

This portrayal of events must be regarded with grave reservations. The simple fact is that the first Chinese-assembled (not Chinese-manufactured) jet was not flown until September 1956,

---

[41] The first story emanated from Major Salah Salem (see Seale, *Struggle for Syria*, pp. 234–236), while the author of the second was Muhammad Hasanayn Haykal, "Political Enquiry," pt. 4 (Cairo Radio, domestic broadcast, December 25, 1958).

seventeen months after Bandung, while other sectors of China's armaments industry were hardly in much better shape at the beginning of 1955.[42] Yet, as far as Egypt was concerned, the very purpose of an arms deal in 1955 required a massive transfer of jet fighters and bombers, as well as modern tanks and guns; unless Cairo could obtain these items in considerable quantities, such a military transaction would have no demonstrative political value, since it would leave the Near Eastern balance of power unaltered. To approach the Chinese, therefore, when they were notoriously incapable of producing such hardware would have been quite pointless. While Peking did have a fair number of obsolescent Soviet weapons of Korean War vintage, these were useless for re-export, since the Chinese themselves had few spare parts.[43] (The situation was quite different in the case of Czechoslovakia; although the Czechs were unable to supply the total quantity of matériel required by Cairo, they had an impressive war industry at the Skoda works and could turn out a sufficient number of modern planes by 1955 to provide a plausible cover for additional items of Soviet manufacture.)[44]

Being military men, it is hardly credible that the Egyptian leaders had to be educated by Chou En-lai about the basic facts of China's dependency on the Red Army, or that they should have approached him without first taking the elementary precaution of checking into the matter. Nor can it just be taken for granted, without any attempt at explanation or analysis, that Colonel Nasser really needed Premier Chou as an "intermediary" to obtain Soviet arms. The observer has every right to ask why it would not have been much simpler to approach Solod, the Soviet ambassador in Cairo, whose personal standing in Moscow was believed to be considerably higher than that of any ordinary Soviet career diplomat, as the Egyptian leaders had undoubtedly discovered. Indeed, the question must arise why Colonel Nasser should have believed that Chou was the proper catalyst to initiate a novel and intimate relationship between Cairo and Moscow or that Chinese inter-

---

[42] Raymond L. Garthoff, "Sino-Soviet Military Relations," *Annals of the American Academy of Political and Social Science*, September 1963, pp. 84–88. It was only "beginning in 1955" that "the Soviets did in fact begin gradually to render assistance to the development of a modern Chinese military industry."

[43] Ibid. Up to 1955, the Russians held China "on a leash" as far as military supplies were concerned.

[44] Asher Lee, *The Soviet Air Force*, rev. ed. (New York: John Day, 1962).

ference could help rather than hinder in this task. (As the next chapter will show, only when placed in the context of an entirely different timetable does the Chou episode assume a meaningful shape.) Whatever the correct interpretation, it is unlikely that Nasser could have approached Chou in the hope that China might provide a channel for the covert transfer of Soviet weapons to Egypt. Since the Egyptian leaders were deeply concerned about possible Western reactions to any military agreement with the East (as will be seen subsequently), they could hardly have thought that a "Chinese" arms deal would be regarded as more innocuous than a direct transaction with the USSR. After all, Washington, at that time, probably regarded Peking with greater aversion than Moscow.

In any case, as it stands, the Chou episode is partially contradicted by Colonel Nasser's own statements. The Nasser-Chou conference at Bandung took place on April 19, 1955 (and their meeting in Rangoon a few days earlier). Moscow's alleged reply to Chou's intervention was given by Ambassador Solod soon after Premier Nasser's return from Bandung (apparently, the reference is to May 21, when a publicized one-hour meeting between Nasser and Solod took place).[45] According to Colonel Nasser's statements, however, he himself took the initiative and approached Solod directly without any intermediaries; moreover, Nasser's words indicate that his discussion with the Soviet ambassador did not take place until June, after the Western ambassadors in Cairo had been given a last warning to come up with a favorable reply to Egypt's military requests. "I pleaded with them, but to no avail. So I turned to Russia and told the Soviet Ambassador frankly that I wanted to arm quickly. . . ."[46] It is known that Premier

---

[45] ANA, Cairo, May 21, 1955. According to Salah Salem, who has persistently claimed a direct part in the genesis of the Arms Deal, it was not Nasser but Salem whom Solod first came to see, on May 6, 1955, in order to transmit Moscow's good news (Seale, *Struggle for Syria,* pp. 234–236). However, the earliest publicly reported meeting between Solod and Salem took place on June 9, 1955, and it so happens that one of the journalists afterward asked Solod whether this was the first time they had ever met. Solod replied that it was (Cairo Radio, domestic broadcast, June 9, 1955). There is no reason why Solod should have told a deliberate untruth; even if he had wanted to evade questions about earlier meetings, he could easily have done so by making vague and general statements. No one expects an ambassador to reveal the contents of diplomatic discussions to the press. It would seem, therefore, that Solod's reply throws grave doubt on the reliability of Salem's account, which was recorded a full five years after the events in question.

[46] Wheelock, *Nasser's New Egypt,* p. 230.

Nasser confronted U.S. Ambassador Henry Byroade[47] with an ultimatum to this effect on June 9, 1955;[48] consequently, the Egyptian leader's purported approach to Ambassador Solod could only have taken place sometime in the second or third week of June. Moreover, Colonel Nasser made a special point of stressing that, when he did approach Solod, the latter was able to come back with a favorable reply from his government within a mere "four days."[49]

This account is hardly compatible with the Bandung–Chou En-lai version, according to which (a) the Nasser-Solod discussion took place weeks before Egypt's ultimatum to the West, not afterward, (b) Solod offered Egypt arms because of Chou's intervention, not because Nasser approached him, and (c) the Soviet ambassador took several weeks to bring a favorable reply (from April 19 until sometime between May 6 and May 21), not "four days." Clearly, both stories cannot be accurate; the question remains whether either can be correct. The shortcomings of the Bandung-Chou version have already been pointed out. Premier Nasser's presentation contains an even more serious weakness; it would leave a mere six or seven weeks for the whole complex transaction, from the purported initial discussion with Solod, sometime in mid-June, to the time the first shipment of arms is known to have entered the pipeline, immediately after the end of July.[50] On technical grounds alone, this portrayal of events could hardly be accepted.

Moreover, the confusion is compounded by conflicting stories concerning developments after Solod had informed the Egyptian authorities of his government's willingness to supply weapons. According to one version, Solod's offer was placed on ice for several weeks so that Cairo could make absolutely certain whether the West remained adamant in its refusal to supply arms. Another story has it that Solod was rebuffed, but approached the Egyptian

[47] Ambassador Henry Byroade replaced Ambassador Jefferson Caffery in Cairo early in 1955.
[48] Wheelock, *Nasser's New Egypt*, pp. 229–230; Seale, *Struggle for Syria*, pp. 234–236. W. W. Rostow, in *The United States in the World Arena* (New York: Harper & Brothers, 1960), p. 355, indicates that this ultimatum gave the West its first inkling that Egypt might be turning toward the East: "In June . . . Washington received word that a deal to exchange Communist arms for Egyptian cotton was in the making." President Eisenhower, in *Waging Peace*, p. 25, states that when Nasser finally implemented the Arms Deal, "he made good his threat of the previous June. . . ."
[49] Wheelock, *Nasser's New Egypt*, pp. 229–230.
[50] Seale, *Struggle for Syria*, pp. 234–237.

government again and suggested that Dimitri Shepilov, then editor of *Pravda*, be invited to visit Cairo. The Egyptian leaders followed this advice, and Shepilov duly appeared in Cairo during the second half of July; however, he is said to have been ignored, in spite of being the government's guest, until he himself took the initiative and volunteered the information that he had come to take care of Egypt's military needs. According to a third version, Solod's offer was immediately taken up by the Egyptian authorities, and Shepilov was specifically invited in order to put the finishing touches on the transaction; there was certainly no question of ignoring him. The same story adds that Egyptian officers took off for Prague at the end of July, while Shepilov was still in Cairo, to bring the transaction to its operative stage.[51] Yet another version claims that, soon after Nasser had returned from Bandung, and before Shepilov came to Cairo, representatives of the Egyptian military junta negotiated the technical details of the deal with the Soviet military attaché in the Egyptian capital.[52]

The contradictions are endless. Thus, if Solod's offer was really made in May and the Egyptian authorities immediately proceeded to negotiate the transaction with the Soviet military attaché in Cairo, then by June, when Ambassador Byroade was threatened with the "possibility" of a Soviet arms deal, it was, in fact, already becoming a fait accompli.

Moreover, in addition to the discrepancies between them, none of these stories are basically compatible with Premier Nasser's claim on September 27, 1955 (when he announced the "Czech" Arms Deal) that he had signed the military agreement only during the previous week. This pronouncement has been widely accepted, and some authors have even alleged that September 20 or 24 was the date of the signature. Yet the first consignment of arms had entered the pipeline soon after the end of July, and, by the end of August, reports of the transaction were beginning to reach the media.[53] It is hardly conceivable that the agreement itself was only signed weeks later. The normal, logical procedure is that two countries reach an agreement in principle, then negotiate the more technical details and sign a protocol, and, finally, go on to implement the transaction. It would be very odd, indeed,

[51] Ibid.
[52] Cairo Radio, domestic broadcast, December 25, 1955.
[53] See Seale, *Struggle for Syria*, pp. 234–237; also *New York Times,* August 31 and September 1, 1955.

to see this process reversed and find implementation preceding the signature of the agreement.

There are thus many reasons, technical, logical, and circumstantial, why the accepted, traditional versions of the prehistory of the Arms Deal cannot be regarded as serious history. This applies in equal measure to the existing accounts of both Egyptian-Western and Egyptian-Soviet dealings in 1955. Almost all of these versions are incompatible with the requirements of the situation (as analyzed in Chapter 1), the technical prerequisites of a complex military transaction, and the rationale of Egyptian and Soviet behavior at the time. What is equally serious, the various stories contradict one another and raise many more questions than they attempt to answer. It is essential, therefore, to reexamine the developments of the year 1955 in the light of new, overlooked, or misinterpreted information and to reconstruct the genesis of the Arms Deal accordingly.

Appendix to Chapter 2:
A Note Concerning Existing Sources

The traditional versions of the prehistory of the Arms Deal, which are analyzed in Chapter 2, may be found in numerous books, articles, and newspaper dispatches. Over the last decade, the gist of these accounts has been reproduced, in one form or another, literally hundreds of times. While the present study hopes to show that there are sound reasons for reopening the file on this subject and for taking issue with currently accepted verdicts, it would be quite unfair even implicitly to criticize the authors of the publications in which the conventional versions appear. To single out one work for correction, rather than another, when all have drawn sustenance from the same spring, would be invidious. Moreover, it must be remembered that none of the authors in question set out to investigate the Arms Deal as such but merely came to touch upon it, tangentially, in their pursuit of other topics. Thus they were not obliged to devote special research to this problem; since seemingly authoritative accounts could be found, which were not being challenged, they were entitled to take them at face value. In view of these considerations, Chapter 2 has simply summarized the main hypotheses upon which currently accepted histories of the period rest, while generally omitting reference to the secondary sources in which separate versions of these themes appear. Where a specific work is quoted, the purpose is to refer the reader to an early and articulate statement of a particular view (or to retrace the path to a primary source), but not to take issue with an individual author. Both fairness and readability may be served in this fashion, since it would be tedious and irrelevant to enumerate the endless permutations and combinations of the main themes that have found their way into print.

With a few minor exceptions, all the familiar accounts trace back to the same two or three authorities, who have generally been regarded as primary sources of authentic information. Some reports originated with Major Salah Salem, former Egyptian minister of national guidance, others with Muhammad Hasanayn Haykal, editor of *al-Ahram*, who has revealed details about this period in his articles and in conversation. Salem is portrayed, in his own accounts, as a man who played an important role during the initial stages of the Arms Deal and should, therefore, be considered as a firsthand source. His claim cannot be accepted without serious reservations. Salem is generally believed to have forfeited Colonel Nasser's full confidence after certain political indiscretions in the fall of 1954 and the beginning of 1955, some of them reportedly committed while carrying out sensitive missions on the Egyptian leader's behalf. There are even indications that Salah and his brother, Gamal Salem, expressed anxiety about the consequences of Egypt's incipient entente with the USSR; both were suspected, at the time, of favoring the West. It is a fact that the Salem brothers were gradually eased out of their positions in the latter part of 1955. Under such circumstances, it is doubtful whether Nasser, during that period, would have regarded Salah Salem as an ongoing member of the innermost circle that was briefed on top-secret operational matters, not to speak of entrusting him with the task of arranging delicate transactions with the East. It is true that Salem was selected to accompany the Egyptian Premier to the Bandung Conference in 1955, but that was precisely the occasion when the technical services of a public relations officer, such as the national guidance minister, would be required.

Haykal, on other hand, has not suggested that he was personally involved in the Arms Deal. It has merely been taken for granted that, since Nasser holds him in high regard and has frequently resorted to him as a private channel of communication, his would inevitably be the authoritative version of events. In reality, however, Haykal's personal stock seems to have fluctuated considerably in Nasser's estimation from one period to another. It is therefore a matter for speculation just when Haykal is testifying in his capacity as Nasser's well-informed confidant and when he is merely speaking as one of the editors who customarily assist the government in its external public relations, without necessarily having received a complete and frank briefing. Moreover, in this particular context, Haykal has never claimed that his accounts are based on details told to him by the Egyptian leader. Thus it just cannot be taken for granted that either Salem or Haykal is really a primary source of full and precise information; nor, for that matter, is there any way of verifying whether the versions they have made available to foreign observers are entirely identical with the facts in their own possession. After all, they are in a delicate position, since the authorities apparently still treat the full story of the Arms Deal as a confidential matter.

Of the Egyptian and Soviet personalities who undoubtedly do qualify as primary sources, Premier[54] Nasser himself has spoken on the topic, both in public and to visitors. However, he has usually been unwilling to go into detail, other than in fragmentary fashion, and several of the particulars he has mentioned are full of ambiguity and, sometimes, mutually inconsistent. While frustrating for the analyst, this should be a familiar problem for observers acquainted with the region. It is not, of course, the function of political speeches or statements in any part of the world to reveal the precise facts of history. This is especially true of the Near East, where, for several millennia now, orators and scribes alike have regarded history not as an exact science but, rather, as a treasure chest in which, for every given situation, a fitting parable may be found. Thus on different occasions, the same historical episode may serve to provide the speaker or chronicler with entirely different analogies to suit the tactical needs of the day. Western analysts, who are not accustomed to think that an event of the past contains various morals for various moments, are usually puzzled to find one person referring to three mutually incompatible details of a particular incident in three consecutive statements. Much confusion might be avoided if it were realized that, in many parts of the planet, historical fact is not viewed as

---

[54] He was premier in 1955 and assumed the presidency subsequently.

a rigid and unalterable landmark on the vistas of man's past but as a kind of genie that can be conjured up in any shape useful to the speaker's present needs. What, in the West, is treated as a science is deemed, in other regions, to be one of the creative arts.

Thus some of the difficulties in interpreting the Egyptian leader's more detailed references to the Arms Deal may have been caused by the influence of Near Eastern traditions of rhetoric; on the other hand, there would seem to have been political and tactical considerations that convinced Colonel Nasser of the need to present the over-all context of this delicate topic in a particular light and in a rather more consistent manner. (The following chapter will, hopefully, clarify this aspect.) In fact, cultural habits and political calculations have pulled in different directions, confronting analysts with complex problems in evaluating Premier Nasser's statements as a source of material about this episode: on the one hand, the fragmentary details cited by him are tantalizingly vague and, to some extent, incompatible with statements from his own entourage; in addition, they seem to vary somewhat with the occasion and with the audience. As against this tendency, Colonel Nasser has, for a whole decade, portrayed both the wider international context of the Arms Deal and its deeper causes in a fairly uniform and constant fashion. As will be seen in the course of the present study, he had excellent reasons at the time for wanting news of this transaction to emerge in a particular way, juxtaposed against a carefully chosen background, and with a strong suggestion that the sequence of events had conformed to a specific chronology. Moreover, the Egyptian leader probably found that his presentation of the episode conveyed an image of his conduct of affairs that was diplomatically useful not only then but on subsequent occasions. The widespread assumption, after 1955, that he was impulsive and that allowances had to be made for this trait enhanced his freedom of maneuver. In view of this fact, he seems to have been prepared to minimize the role played by careful calculation during this enterprise so as to enlarge his diplomatic options, since a full release of the detailed prehistory of the Arms Deal might actually have shown him to be somewhat more adroit and shrewd, and rather less temperamental, than is generally believed. Thus practical considerations may have caused him to persist with his original portrayal of the reasons for the transaction; there is the additional possibility that, like most statesmen, he may gradually have become attached to his own official attitudes, in which case he would hardly be inclined to encourage the release of material at odds with the orthodox view.

In any event, it is apparent that scholars are confronted by highly complex problems in their attempts to interpret and utilize Colonel Nasser's references to the Arms Deal; at the same time, they have to bear in mind that his statements constitute one of the few available primary sources of material on the topic. Although it is natural to make the most of what there is, literal and uncritical reliance upon such data, without prior painstaking analysis, seems more likely to create profound misconceptions than to elucidate history. All in all, one can but sympathize with scholars who have tried to reconstruct the story of this episode from evidence that, in two instances, has not turned out to be really firsthand, while, in the third, proper evaluation has proved so difficult as to discourage correct and meaningful use of the material.

Moreover, these obstacles have been compounded simply because historians have labored under the misapprehension that the second partner in the Arms Deal, the USSR, has consistently failed to speak up on the subject. Consequently, there has appeared to be no choice but to rely on the other available sources, whatever their shortcomings. In reality, this supposition was not well founded, even in earlier years. The truth is that Nikita Khrushchev himself has repeatedly reminisced aloud, dropping significant hints about the real background of the historic military transaction between the two countries. Admittedly, the place where some of these statements have been recorded is *al-Ahram*, the editor of which has been an occasional recipient of Khrushchev's confidences. The question may be posed why Haykal's evidence should be accepted with fewer reservations in this instance than in another context, which was mentioned earlier. The fact is that, in publishing his conversations with Khrushchev, Haykal was directly quoting the leader of a very powerful foreign state whom he had just seen and who, in one case, was actually visiting Egypt at that moment. Moreover, on two occasions that are relevant here, late in 1957 and early in 1964, their meetings coincided with a period of particular friendship between the two countries, when Haykal would certainly not have wished to arouse Khrushchev's ire by misquoting him. The Russians never gave the slightest indication of regarding Haykal's versions of these chats as anything but precise—not to speak of repudiating his reports; on the contrary, they always treated him with respect, granting him further interviews, although, during the 1959–1961 Moscow-Cairo dispute, he had attacked the USSR as much as any of his colleagues. Thus there is no good reason for analysts to doubt that Haykal's accounts of his conversations with Khrushchev are accurate. Haykal's role, in this case, was simply that of the straightforward reporter. As such, he was fulfilling an entirely different function than in those of his articles that, without naming sources, gave details about a topic his government was known to regard as confidential; in the latter instance, there is room for doubt, since it may be assumed that the appearance in print of such references would have been actively discouraged unless the authorities thought that publication was serving a tactical purpose.[55] Statements by Khrushchev, on the other hand, belong to a very different category of material, the dissemination of which could hardly be controlled by anyone other than the Russians themselves. Thus, had Haykal refrained, for any reason, from printing an account of his conversations with Khrushchev, the latter would undoubtedly have taken offense.

The question still remains: Why should Khrushchev's own words necessarily be accepted as an accurate portrayal of history rather than dismissed as yet another unsupported, subjective, and possibly propagandistic version of events in the mid-fifties? There may well be some elements of distortion in his statements on the topic; however, by and large, his accounts are far more compatible with the logical requirements of the situation in 1955, as well as with facts that have been established through independent evidence, than are descriptions from other sources (as the present study will show). Moreover, precisely because the Russians maintained complete silence about the antecedents of the Arms Deal (at least at the time of its announcement and immediately afterward), they never became wedded to any particular version of its history. Consequently, Khrushchev and the Soviet media were not inhibited, later on, from dealing with the subject somewhat more frankly and accurately than other sources. Generally, the Russians, as donors of military assistance, have faced rather fewer problems and embarrassments in admitting the facts than many of the recipients, who try to maintain a precarious balance between East

[55] That does not mean that, even in the latter case, his articles in *al-Ahram* are devoid of significance; they can be treated as useful source material, provided the accepted criteria of academic criticism are applied and each revelation is carefully interpreted in the light of other evidence.

and West. Indeed, fairly recently, a Soviet journal for the first time mentioned the precise chronology of the Egyptian Arms Deal; the dates in question, which (as will be seen subsequently) are fully corroborated by other evidence, leave the historian little choice but to conclude that the popularly accepted versions of the episode are not and could not be correct. Moreover, it does not appear that the Soviet editors who were responsible for the publication of this information necessarily acted with any specific political aim in mind; the reference was tucked away obscurely in a rambling historical introduction to a three-part analysis of conditions in developing regions. Actually, it was so unobtrusive that it has been completely overlooked until now, although the rest of the article received considerable attention in the West. It seems entirely possible that the Soviet author was not even particularly conscious of the fact that, from some points of view, publication of the precise date constituted a problem; after all, as far as the Russians themselves are concerned, there is no longer any particular reason for regarding this as a delicate question.

To sum up: the sources that gave rise to the traditional views of the Arms Deal must be considered to have very serious shortcomings, while more relevant and better-corroborated material has either been overlooked or appeared recently. Moreover, the latter fundamentally contradicts the former. Consequently, there is no escape from the need for a complete reappraisal of this topic and of its implications for much of the history of that important period.

3 New Light on the Subject

As has been noted (in Chapter 1), the logic of the Near Eastern situation at the outset of 1955 demanded some form of joint Soviet-Egyptian initiative; given Moscow's and Cairo's respective goals, it was almost incumbent upon the two governments to take urgent measures to neutralize or liquidate the incipient Western defense network in the region. Moreover, there were objective reasons, which have been analyzed earlier, why joint action should take the form of an arms deal between the two countries. Such a possibility had been discussed repeatedly between 1951 and 1954;[1] during that period an Egyptian mission, led by Major-General Hassan F. Ragab, had suggested acquiring Soviet arms under the guise of "agricultural machinery."[2] This and similar proposals did not prove to be productive at the time, since political delays were encountered on both sides; only after the turn of the year 1954/55 did the Western defense project in the Near East assume forms that were likely to alarm Moscow and Cairo into taking speedy countermeasures. Nevertheless, Egyptian feelers during the previous three years had served to arouse the attention of the organization traditionally concerned with military and other clandestine

[1] See chap. 1, footnote 23.
[2] David J. Dallin, *Soviet Foreign Policy after Stalin* (Philadelphia: J. P. Lippincott Co., 1961), p. 389; a Soviet Near Eastern broadcast, in Persian, on February 21, 1955, drew attention to the fact that the Egyptian trade delegation to East Europe in the previous year had been headed by Major-General Ragab.

relations between the USSR and noncommunist states—the GRU (Soviet military intelligence).[3]

Indications of Clandestine Contacts

There is evidence that, sometime between July 1953 and August 1954, the Fourth (Near Eastern and Asian) Directorate of the GRU became intensely interested in "the potential of Egypt as an anticapitalist military power in the Near East."[4] In rather characteristic fashion, this interest appears to have generated activities along two very different lines: the first "was directed against Egypt";[5] the second, apparently, included an attempt to collaborate with some branches of the Egyptian government for limited and mutually beneficial purposes. According to one account, at the very outset of 1955 this initiative produced a project for cooperation between Ali Sabri, who at that time reportedly directed Cairo's clandestine activities, and his Soviet counterparts to organize triangular trade in strategic raw materials interdicted by the U.S. Battle Act. Apparently, the object of the scheme was to purchase copper in Chile and transport it with the aid of Swiss intermediaries to the USSR.[6] Whatever the full significance of these details, the report does provide some indication of the degree of operational intimacy achieved during the first days of 1955 between the two governments, bypassing the normal diplomatic channels.[7]

This information has some bearing on the genesis of the Egyp-

---

[3] See Walter G. Krivitsky, *In Stalin's Secret Service* (New York: Harper & Brothers, 1939), passim, and Barton Whaley, "Soviet and Chinese Clandestine Arms Aid," 1965 draft (Cambridge, Mass.: M.I.T., Center for International Studies).

[4] Oleg Penkovskiy, *The Penkovskiy Papers* (New York: Doubleday & Company, 1965), p. 52. While several commentators have criticized the particular manner in which *The Penkovskiy Papers* were presented to the public, there does not appear to be any valid reason for doubting the authenticity of their contents. Whatever may have been the actual form in which this material reached the West, many of its details have already been verified from independent sources. An incisive analysis of this question may be found in Barton Whaley, "Soviet Clandestine Communication Nets" (Cambridge, Mass.: M.I.T., Center for International Studies, forthcoming, 1969), chap. III–D, "Military Intelligence (GRU)."

[5] Penkovskiy, *Papers*, pp. 52 and 273–274.

[6] *L'Aurore* (Paris), July 16, 1964, p. 2a, which reproduces a long interview with Captain Dmoukhovsky, who is reported to have been one of Ali Sabri's subordinates.

[7] Ibid.

tian-Soviet military agreement: precisely the persons who were reported to have been involved in the clandestine copper transaction have also been directly linked to the Arms Deal. Thus Ali Sabri figures in an important account as the man who, during the operational stage, negotiated the Egyptian army's detailed shopping list with the Russians and arranged for implementation of the agreement with one of the military representatives at the Soviet embassy in Cairo.[8] The reference most likely is to a member of the Cairo *Rezidentura* of the GRU, the agency that would normally be in charge of Soviet military shipments to other countries.[9]

If these were the channels through which the Arms Deal was prepared, the prevailing reticence about the prehistory of the transaction becomes very understandable. The activities of such organizations would normally remain outside the ken of the rest of the government apparatus, and publicity would usually be discouraged even after prolonged periods. (In the case of the Soviet Union, of course, this does not mean that "diplomatic" representatives would necessarily have been excluded from participation in transactions of this kind. A considerable proportion of Soviet diplomatic personnel, including counselors, ministers, and even ambassadors, apparently belonged to the GRU, or to its nonmilitary "neighbor," the KGB, rather than to the normal roster of the Soviet Foreign Ministry itself. Members of the clandestine organizations naturally had their own channels to Moscow, bypassing the Soviet Foreign Ministry, which frequently seems to have been left in the dark.[10] Among Soviet representatives in the Near East, the number of persons performing other than normal diplomatic functions appears to have been particularly high, especially in Cairo and Ankara.[11] The Soviet ambassador to Egypt, D. S. Solod, may conceivably have belonged to this category, judging by his exploits in Syria and Lebanon during the late 1940s, in Egypt at the time of the Arms Deal, and in Guinea during the notorious penetration episode of 1960/61.)

In view of these various considerations, the sudden flurry of joint Soviet-Egyptian activities early in 1955 could, perhaps, be regarded as a natural development of relations established be-

---

8 Cairo Radio, domestic broadcast, December 25, 1958.
9 Penkovskiy, *Papers,* passim, especially pp. 64–101; Whaley, "Soviet Clandestine Communication Nets," chap. III–D.
10 Whaley, "Soviet Clandestine Communication Nets," chap. III–D.
11 Ibid.

tween the clandestine organs of both governments rather than as an initiative necessarily planned or even approved by the Soviet Foreign Ministry and its head, V. M. Molotov. This hypothesis may provide an answer to a puzzling problem: the Soviet Foreign Minister, as will be seen, apparently did not share the sanguine expectations of the benefits to be derived from a Near Eastern adventure that seem to have been fashionable in the GRU and among some of his colleagues in the Presidium of the CPSU (Communist Party of the Soviet Union). In normal times, Molotov's status as a senior member of the Presidium would have more than compensated for his essentially subordinate and technical position as foreign minister; in his former, thought not in his latter, function, he would have been both "in the know" and able to determine policy decisions. However, by early 1955, his most important rival in the Presidium, CPSU First Secretary N. S. Khrushchev, was successfully undermining his position and gradually shunting him aside. Khrushchev's domination of the Central Committee apparatus, his control of the KGB through his former subordinate Serov, and his close alliance with leading Red Army cadres undoubtedly gave him a decisive voice over GRU and other clandestine activities.[12] It is by no means certain that Molotov was even kept informed of all developments in this field. (The complexities of the Khrushchev-Molotov struggle will be examined later.)

That the contacts between the two governments, during January and February 1955, did have a characteristically clandestine flavor can be seen from contemporary descriptions of Egyptian-Soviet activities in Ankara. At the end of January 1955, it was reported that members of the Soviet and Egyptian embassy staffs in the Turkish capital had been conferring together continuously since January 20. A denial was issued, but on February 6 the Egyptian ambassador and the Soviet chargé d'affaires were observed driving separately to the Cubuk Dam in Ankara's outskirts, conferring at length while walking together in the fields, and then departing separately. Again a denial was issued, but subsequently a very circumstantial report appeared, quoting a former chef de cabinet of the Turkish president, who stated that he had been an accidental eyewitness to one of these gatherings:

---

[12] For the question of political control over GRU activities, see ibid., chap. III–A.

This was definitely a pre-arranged meeting. When the Russians, thinking that I too was a member of the Egyptian embassy, started to come towards us, the Egyptian Ambassador became red in the face and, leaving me hastily and excitedly, joined the Russians and hurriedly plunged into the woods with them.[13]

Commenting on these reports, Turkish observers accused Egypt of concerting measures with the USSR to undermine the incipient Turkish-Iraqi pact.[14] There is little reason to quarrel with this interpretation; the question remains, however: What precisely was the nature of these steps and why should Ankara have been chosen as the locale? It is possible only to venture a hypothesis in answer to this problem. There is strong evidence, as will be shown, that, by January–February 1955, Bloc military aid for Egypt had become a priority item on the agenda of possible measures to counteract the effects of the Western defense project. Questions of logistics must have been encountered at this point: Soviet and Czech military supplies could be dispatched to Egypt from ports on the Baltic, the Black Sea, or the Adriatic. The route from the Baltic around Europe into the Mediterranean was unduly long and cumbersome and, moreover, wide open to foreign observation. (In 1956, after the Arms Deal had already been made public, this sea-lane was used occasionally for the transfer from Gdynia to Alexandria of large naval units, which could not have been hidden in any case.) The route from the Black Sea, on the other hand, was far more simple and direct. However, it suffered from one particular weakness—passage through the Straits of the Bosporus and the Dardanelles. The Russians were presumably aware, by then, that Soviet and foreign vessels which passed through the narrows with military supplies for Spain in 1936–1938 had been thoroughly surveyed by the German military attaché in Ankara, who managed to report on their contents in amazing detail. The Germans appear to have derived their information from Turkish records,[15] although Turkey officially did not take sides in the Spanish civil war. It

---

[13] *New York Times*, January 28, 1955; Ankara Radio, domestic broadcast, February 9, 1955, quoting the Anatolia (News) Agency; Paris Radio, domestic broadcast, February 10, 1955; and *Jewish Observer & Middle East Review*, February 25, 1955.

[14] Ibid.

[15] D. C. Watt, "Soviet Military Aid to the Spanish Republic in the Civil War, 1936–38," *Slavonic and East European Review*, vol. XXXVIII, no. 91 (June 1960), pp. 536–541.

must have been clear to Moscow that Soviet military shipments passing through the Straits in 1955 would be exposed all the more to hostile surveillance, since the Turks themselves had now joined "the other side." It seems probable, therefore, that Egyptian-Soviet activities in Ankara during the first weeks of 1955 were connected with the problem of security measures to protect the contents of future shipments through the Straits from premature exposure.

A Yugoslav Role?

In view of these problems of logistics, it is conceivable that Moscow and Cairo were also giving attention at this time to the alternate possibility of utilizing the supply route from Czechoslovakia through the Adriatic to Alexandria. In practice, this could only mean using Yugoslav ports. Belgrade's foreign policy, at this stage, consisted of a precarious tightrope act between East and West. During the previous year, Yugoslavia had actually strengthened her ties with the West by joining the Balkan alliance. It is now known, however, that there were, at the same time, important developments in the direction of a full-scale rapprochement with the Soviet bloc. As Peking has revealed, in the summer of 1954, "Khrushchev proposed to improve relations with Yugoslavia . . . to treat it as a fraternal socialist country for the purpose of winning it back to the path of socialism." This proposal was approved by the Chinese and even by Yugoslavia's old enemy, Albania.[16] Belgrade's reaction, not unnaturally, was one of caution, and the Yugoslavs made quite sure of keeping all their Western options open. Nevertheless, Khrushchev's overtures appear to have had some impact upon Marshal Tito's policies, long before the Soviet leader staged his dramatic reconciliation pilgrimage to Belgrade in May 1955. Being aware, no doubt, that the question of relations with Yugoslavia was an object of contention in the Moscow power struggle, Tito probably felt that it might be tactically advisable to strengthen the hands of the pro-Belgrade faction, led by Khrushchev himself.

These considerations may explain why the Yugoslavs, early in

---

[16] "Third Comment on the Open Letter of the Central Committee of the CPSU," *The Polemic on the General Line of the International Communist Movement* (Peking: Foreign Languages Press, 1965), p. 176. (This document refers to the contents of a letter from the Central Committee of the Chinese Communist Party to the Central Committee of the CPSU, June 10, 1954.)

1955, sponsored an arrangement implying a fair measure of intimacy and mutual trust in the relations between Belgrade and the Bloc. While negotiating a Czech-Yugoslav trade agreement, it was agreed that, in future, Czechoslovak overseas exports would be shipped from the Yugoslav port of Rijeka (Fiume) on the Adriatic.[17] Since, in effect, this gave the Yugoslavs a stranglehold on landlocked Czechoslovakia's Afro-Asian trade, it is obvious that the Czechs, before consenting, must have received adequate reassurances regarding Belgrade's future policies. Clearly, the arrangement worked out to Prague's satisfaction, because Rijeka subsequently (up to 1958) came to serve as the main port of entry and exit for the Afro-Asian commerce of several East European countries. The Yugoslav-Czech trade agreement was signed in mid-February 1955, after Marshal Tito had left on an extended overseas tour; however, the importance and implications of the Rijeka project were such that it could hardly have been settled in his absence. It seems likely, therefore, that Tito had already given his assent several weeks earlier, before leaving Belgrade, and that agreement in principle had been reached with the Czechs by the time the Yugoslav leader met Premier Nasser at Suez on February 5, 1955.[18] Thus Nasser may well have discovered, in the course of this meeting, that, in future, it would be feasible to send shipments from Czechoslovakia to Egypt via a Yugoslav port.

The possibility of using the Adriatic route, in addition to the Black Sea, for the transport of Bloc arms to Egypt is likely to have been viewed by the Egyptians with considerable enthusiasm. Rijeka-Alexandria constitutes the most direct line linking Czechoslovakia and Egypt; since Yugoslavia was considered a neutral country and Yugoslav-Egyptian relations were known to be friendly, it was improbable that an increase of movement between the two ports would arouse any particular comment. By resorting to this sea-lane, one could relieve the pressure of traffic along the Black Sea route and thus help to avoid drawing undue attention to Alexandria-bound vessels passing through the Straits. In any case, on the assumption that Czechoslovakia would have to fill the ostensible role of arms supplier to Egypt, it was clear that more than one supply route would have to be used. The Czech armaments industry could supply only part of the hardware for a really massive transaction, so that it was necessary to supplement ship-

---

[17] Prague Radio, domestic broadcast, February 18, 1955.
[18] TANYUG (Belgrade), in English, February 5, 1955.

ments from Prague with weapons from Soviet stores, using a "Czech" arms deal as a cover. Therefore, it was useful to know that, potentially, two alternate sea-lanes might be available, one from Odessa for Soviet weapons and one from Rijeka for Czech arms. The Yugoslav-Czech arrangement was reached at too convenient a moment for Moscow and Cairo to have overlooked this possibility. If the USSR and Egypt did consider taking advantage of the newly available Adriatic route, preparations for an arms deal must, almost certainly, have become entangled with the delicate problem of Soviet-Yugoslav relations, which played so significant a part in the Moscow 1954–1957 power struggle.

Toward a Revised Chronology

The indications that contacts between Egypt and the communist countries in the period from January 20 to February 6, 1955 may have had some bearing on the logistics of a future arms transaction are reinforced when these dates are placed in their historical context. The fact is that a mere one or two weeks later—sometime between February 14 and 21—a decisive development in the genesis of the Arms Deal took place. This was not known at the time when previous accounts of the Arms Deal were published; however, a recent Soviet revelation in *International Affairs* (*Mezhdunarodnaya Zhizn,* the semiofficial organ of the Soviet Foreign Ministry)[19] leaves analysts little choice but to revise the generally accepted chronology of the period. This authoritative Soviet source stated flatly that "Nasser's government concluded *in February 1955* a commercial agreement with Czechoslovakia for the delivery of arms" (author's emphasis).[20] If that was the case, it is entirely understandable that a preliminary search for secure supply routes should have preceded this event and prepared the way for it. The same article contained a favorable review of Egyptian policies since Nasser's rise to power, and, in view of the very warm tone of the appraisal, there is no good reason to suspect Moscow of printing this revelation in order to implement some devious tactical maneuver likely to embarrass Cairo. In fact, the date of the

[19] *Mezhdunarodnaya Zhizn* is the Russian-language edition of the Foreign Ministry's monthly; the English- and Russian-language editions are not necessarily identical in content.
[20] K. Ivanov, "National-Liberation Movement and Non-Capitalist Path of Development," *International Affairs,* 1965, no. 5, p. 61 (in the English edition), p. 66 (in the Russian edition).

Egyptian-Czech agreement was buried in a rather rambling historical survey, which constituted merely one segment of a three-part series on politics in the developing areas. The reference was so obscurely tucked away that it seems to have passed without notice, even though the series as such received a fair amount of attention in the West.

Moreover, there is no reason for assuming that the date mentioned in the article owed its existence to an error or slip of the pen. Both the Russian and English editions of *International Affairs* contain the identical text, although the English edition appeared some days later, so that any mistakes could easily have been corrected. Furthermore, the very next sentence opens with the words "In March 1955, . . ." so that a consistent time sequence is presented; the Egyptian-Czech agreement of February is mentioned first and, immediately afterward, an event of the following month is described. What is also noteworthy, the article explains that one reason for Egypt's decision to conclude the Arms Deal was her fundamental objection to the "Middle East (*later* Baghdad) Pact" (author's emphasis). The phraseology employed here is almost pedantically consistent with the statement that February 1955 was the date of the Egyptian-Czech agreement; at that time, Western security projects for the region had no official title and could, at most, be given an informal geographic name, such as the Near Eastern (or Middle East) Pact, for the simple reason that no formal defense agreement existed prior to February 24, 1955. It was only on this date that the "Turkish-Iraqi Treaty" was finally signed; even that name was rapidly superseded, however, by the better-known appellation "Baghdad Pact," which was adopted some time after Britain adhered to the treaty, at the beginning of April 1955. The nomenclature used by *International Affairs*, therefore, indicates that the author was consciously ascribing the Egyptian-Czech agreement to the period when neither the term "Turkish-Iraqi Treaty" nor the name "Baghdad Pact" could yet be applied, that is, some date prior to February 24, 1955.[21]

The article in question appeared under the byline of K. Ivanov, a prominent Soviet journalist who in recent years has been increasingly associated with Afro-Asian affairs. It should be noted, however, that important questions of foreign relations are rarely entrusted to the hands of a single Soviet writer unassisted by expert

[21] Ibid.

officials. Whoever the authors may be, it can be assumed that all such contributions to *International Affairs* are prepared on the basis of official source material provided by the Soviet authorities. (Even excerpts from the Western press would otherwise be unavailable to the writers.)[22] It seems probable, therefore, that the date of the Egyptian-Czech agreement given in Ivanov's article is, in fact, the date recorded in Soviet government documents.

Fortunately, it is not necessary to rely on deductive processes alone in appraising the reliability of the revelation made by *International Affairs*. The Soviet statement is heavily corroborated by independent information from public, non-Soviet sources. Sometime in the second week of February 1955, a rather enigmatic Czechoslovak delegation did, in fact, appear in Cairo.[23] It was said to have come to discuss a possible expansion of trade relations between the two countries, with specific references to a barter agreement whereby large quantities of Egyptian cotton might be exchanged for Czechoslovak "heavy machinery."[24] The delegation left—as noiselessly as it had arrived—sometime during the fourth week of February, without announcing whether an agreement had been reached or whether further talks would be held.[25] In June 1955, another Czech trade delegation arrived in Cairo, and this time went through the normal routine of negotiating a new trade and payments agreement, which was then duly signed and published.[26] There was nothing mysterious about the activities of the June delegation, for the simple reason that the existing trade and payments agreement between the two countries was due to expire in the subsequent quarter and thus had to be renewed or renego-

[22] In the USSR, excerpts from the Western press constitute restricted material, which is made available to privileged cadres; for this purpose, TASS publishes separate bulletins, printed in different colors indicating successive degrees of classification, containing increasingly detailed translations from Western publications.

[23] Cairo Radio, domestic broadcast, February 13, 1955, stated that the Czech delegation had arrived "recently" and would meet the minister of trade and industry, Hassan Mari, the following day. See also *Egyptian Economic and Political Review*, vol. 1, no. 7 (March 1955), pp. 34–35.

[24] Ibid.

[25] The last public reference to its visit appeared on February 22 (Cairo Radio, domestic broadcast, February 22, 1955), stating that the delegation had informed Egypt of its intention to import large quantities of cotton in exchange for Czech products; however, no agreement to that effect was published at the time.

[26] *Egyptian Economic and Political Review*, vol. 1, no. 11 (July 1955), p. 31, and vol. 2, no. 1 (September 1955), pp. 24–26; also Cairo Radio, domestic broadcast, June 1, 7, 9, 14, and 27, and July 9, 1955.

TOWARD A REVISED CHRONOLOGY   79

tiated at about that time. The question arises, therefore, why was it necessary to dispatch a previous Czechoslovak delegation to Cairo as early as February? Its mission could hardly have been to deal with normal trade questions when an over-all agreement was due to be negotiated during the summer in any case; nor is it likely that the discussions of February were intended somehow to smooth the way for the subsequent negotiations. No one has suggested that serious difficulties were anticipated, and the June talks, in fact, proceeded without a major hitch; moreover, why was it not stated in February that the Czechs had come for this purpose? It is true that any barter agreements involving Egyptian cotton had to be arranged ahead of time; however, the Alexandria cotton export season starts in the fall of each year, and February was a distinctly early date for such discussions, unless it was intended to divert a really large segment of the cotton crop to Czechoslovakia. This, in itself, could have only military implications, since Prague's nonmilitary exports to Alexandria at the time (and during the subsequent year) neither did nor could reach proportions that would have warranted shipping a very sizable percentage of Egypt's cotton to Czechoslovakia by way of payment.[27]

Actually, it is unnecessary to indulge in speculation about the real purpose of this enigmatic mission. A correspondent of one of the best informed European news agencies was able to report on February 14, 1955:

It is learned from a well-informed source that Czechoslovakia is ready to exchange heavy arms for Egyptian cotton. A Czech mission headed by Dr. Otakar Teufer, Director General of the Prague Foreign Trade Department arrived in Cairo and had its first conference on February 14 at the Foreign Ministry with Egyptian Under-Secretary for Foreign Affairs, Sami Abu al-Futuh and General Hassan Ragab, Under-Secretary of the War Ministry.[28]

For some reason, this item did not arouse the attention of Western editors and received little or no play in the Western press at the

[27] In the year immediately following the Arms Deal, Egyptian cotton exports to Czechoslovakia rose from the previous 250,000 cantars annually to almost 1 million cantars (one sixth of Egypt's total exports). In the subsequent year, however, when the bulk of repayments was sent directly to the USSR (which had provided most of the arms after the initial Czechoslovak shipments), Egyptian cotton exports to Prague declined again almost to the earlier level (less than 400,000 cantars).

[28] AFP, Paris, February 14, 1955.

time. Only a decade later was the organ of the Soviet Foreign Ministry to confirm, in effect, that the dispatch had been correct.

Major-General Ragab, the official who was reported to have negotiated with the Czechs in February 1955, was actually under-secretary for armament factories.[29] As noted earlier, Ragab, during the previous year, had led an Egyptian delegation to Bloc countries, including Czechoslovakia, and had proposed bartering Egyptian cotton for Bloc weapons under the guise of "agricultural machinery." On February 21, 1955, while the Czech mission was still in Cairo, a Soviet broadcast to the Near East found occasion to refer to Ragab's 1954 visit as the symbol of a new era of large-scale barter between Egypt and the Bloc.[30] Almost immediately after the Czech delegation left the Egyptian capital, Major-General Ragab was again sent to Eastern Europe, including Prague,[31] presumably to follow up on the new agreement. At that very time, Czech refugees arriving in Austria reported that a considerable number of Soviet armament experts, including research, control, and supervisory personnel, had arrived in Czechoslovakia in order to step up local military production to full capacity.[32] It appears that a sudden increase was expected in the demand for Czech weapons.

The cumulative weight of the evidence examined would seem to indicate, therefore, that sometime between February 14 and 21, 1955 an agreement concerning future arms deliveries was, in fact, reached between members of the Egyptian government and the Czechoslovak delegation visiting Cairo.

If so, it becomes necessary to inquire whether the arrangements of February 1955 may be identified with *the* famous Arms Deal itself. To some extent, this is a matter of definitions. If it is asked whether the Egyptian-Czech talks in February resulted in a final and irrevocable commitment, a point of no return from which both sides proceeded without delays or evasions to the stage of implementation, then the answer would appear to be negative. As will be seen, the developments of February 1955 seem to have constituted an essential preliminary stage rather than the culminating

[29] *The International Who's Who*, 28th ed., 1964–1965 (London: Europa Publications Ltd., 1964), p. 887.
[30] See footnote 2 in this chapter.
[31] Dallin, *Soviet Foreign Policy*, p. 391. The author is obliged to Mrs. David Dallin for making available her late husband's "D Papers" insofar as they relate to this study.
[32] *Volkszeitung* (Klagenfurt), March 5, 1955.

point in the long process to which historians refer as "the Arms Deal." For instance, there is no indication whether the Czech delegation to Cairo even included military experts. Indeed, Major-General Ragab's subsequent departure for East Europe, apparently to investigate precisely what hardware the Bloc arsenals had to offer (as well as other developments, which will be analyzed later), must lead one to conclude that the February agreement could not have contained any provisions concerning the precise amounts and types of weapons, unit prices, or schedules of transfer.

It seems probable that the initial Czech-Egyptian discussions produced only a very general arrangement of a primarily financial character, whereby Prague promised Cairo credit, within certain limits, for the purchase of an unspecified amount of arms, repayable in goods.[33] If that was the case, K. Ivanov's description would appear to have been reasonably accurate, since it referred to the arrangement of February 1955 as "a commercial agreement . . . for the delivery of arms."[34] Actually, there were to be prolonged investigations and deliberations, not to mention serious delays of a diplomatic nature, before more detailed and definitive protocols could be drawn up; even then, as will be seen, the gap between agreement and implementation seems to have been considerable. (This ought to be a familiar picture for any observer acquainted with Soviet military and economic aid practices since 1955. In the majority of instances, the USSR and the recipient country initiated the aid process by concluding a credit agreement that was drawn up in very general terms; often many months elapsed until more detailed protocols were signed, and even more time intervened before the stage of implementation was reached.)

In any event, a major Czech-Egyptian arms agreement in 1955 could hardly have amounted to much more than a cover for military shipments from Russia herself. Czechoslovakia alone was not in a position to provide all the matériel required for a really mas-

[33] It seems that Western observers subsequently failed to distinguish between the February 1955 arrangements and the final protocols of the arms agreement; thus it has been asserted that the Arms Deal contained no itemized lists of weapons or unit prices. Apparently this was true of the February agreement, but subsequent protocols (negotiated, in all probability, with the Russians rather than the Czechs) almost certainly filled in the necessary details. For western interpretations, see Dallin, *Soviet Foreign Policy*, p. 394, and idem, "D Papers."

[34] See Ivanov, "National-Liberation Movement," p. 61 (in the English edition), p. 66 (in the Russian edition).

sive transaction; clearly, therefore, the particulars of such a deal had to be arranged directly with the power that would actually supply a large portion of the hardware, namely, the USSR. In view of the vast disparity between the military, economic, and technical levels prevailing in Egypt and Russia, respectively,[35] the very process of relating the requirements of the recipient to the surpluses of the donor was bound to be protracted. It was necessary to establish, at the very outset, exactly what types and amounts of arms could be acquired directly from Czechoslovakia and what categories of weapons would have to be transferred from the USSR; it seems probable that Ragab's mission to the Bloc, in the spring of 1955, was primarily intended to serve this purpose. Naturally, it would have been much simpler for Cairo to deal only with Moscow. However, because of the cogent tactical considerations analyzed earlier,[36] the Russians undoubtedly felt that they had to act through an intermediary who could, if necessary, be disowned. Czechoslovakia was bound to be Moscow's first choice for this role, since it was the only communist state, except the USSR itself, whose military industry was advanced enough at that stage to constitute a plausible source of arms shipments containing reasonably modern planes and tanks. Several years earlier, Czechoslovakia had already performed a similar task by supplying weapons to several Near Eastern countries[37] and, even more significantly, a mere nine months prior to the Cairo agreement, the Czechs had been involved in the notorious Guatemalan arms deal.[38]

Early Signs of Soviet-Egyptian Rapport

In view of the essentially subordinate role played by Prague in all these arrangements, it is obvious that major developments must have occurred in the relationship between Egypt and the Soviet Union herself, at the outset of 1955, in order to bring a Czechoslovak delegation to Cairo for armament negotiations during the second week of February. Even an examination confined to the purely overt communications between Moscow and Cairo reveals indications of sudden warmth as early as the opening days of the

[35] See chap. 1, "Logistics."
[36] See ibid., "Soviet-Egyptian Convergence."
[37] See ibid.
[38] Dwight D. Eisenhower, *Mandate for Change, 1953–1956: The White House Years* (New York: Doubleday & Company, 1963), pp. 424–425.

year. Thus, during the first week of January 1955, it was announced that the Soviet Red Cross and Red Crescent had taken the unusual step of donating money to Egypt in connection with a minor natural disaster; Ambassador Solod then called on the Egyptian foreign minister, ostensibly to convey his government's sympathies as well as the gift but, actually, to initiate a long conversation.[39] However, such sporadic signs of a new atmosphere were merely surface phenomena reflecting a much deeper trend toward Soviet-Egyptian intimacy. As was shown earlier in this chapter, several significant clues indicate that the real change in the relations between the two countries occurred in the field of clandestine operations. The complex arrangements concerning covert triangular trade in strategic metals that are reported to have been made at this time, as well as the sudden flurry of surreptitious meetings in Ankara, hint at the nature of the new Moscow-Cairo entente. As was also noted, it was precisely the GRU, the institution normally entrusted with operations of this kind, that also revealed an early and intense interest in the possibility of providing Egypt with Soviet weapons. It is quite possible, therefore, that the alleged clandestine trade arrangements produced a flow of goods that led logically to the idea of repaying Egypt for her efforts through a complementary barter deal in arms.

The various covert strands of the new Soviet-Egyptian intimacy appear to have been tied together, sometime in January 1955, during an unpublicized mission to Moscow of an Egyptian emissary, reported to have been the "Red Major," Khaled Mohieddin.[40] At

[39] TASS, in Russian, January 8, 1955; Cairo Radio, domestic broadcast, January 8, 1955.

[40] For some interesting references to Khaled Mohieddin's career, see Anouar Abdel-Malek, *Égypte: Société Militaire* (Paris: Éditions du Seuil, 1962), especially pp. 98–101, 120, and 126. Khaled Mohieddin had been involved in an attempt to oust Colonel Nasser from power during the spring of 1954; however, since he was a blood relation of Nasser's associate Zakharia Mohieddin, Khaled received no punishment other than comfortable exile in France, Switzerland, and Italy. The "Red Major" had been an important member of Nasser's Free Officers, but had apparently also maintained a close association with Egyptian communist groups. His career in Egypt, subsequent to the Arms Deal, became something of a barometer of Soviet-Egyptian relations: during the heyday of friendship between the two countries, in the mid-fifties and again in the mid-sixties, he was given fairly prominent tasks in the Egyptian press, but in 1959, when Khrushchev and Nasser quarreled, Khaled Mohieddin was dismissed. It is possible that, during the period of his 1954–1955 exile, Mohieddin may have earned his way back into the good graces of his former associates by performing services connected with Ali Sabri's operations; he was a suitable candidate for a mission to Moscow be-

that time, there were practical reasons why high-level communications between the two capitals should not be conducted through normal diplomatic channels: Egypt, since late in 1954, had not been represented in Moscow by a senior diplomat, the previous Egyptian ambassador having concluded his tour of duty and no suitable replacement having been sent to the Soviet capital;[41] moreover, the nature of Soviet-Egyptian relations was such that clandestine organizations were apparently involved, and operative details, therefore, were not likely to be entrusted to the respective foreign ministries. Under these circumstances, it does, indeed, seem plausible that, during January 1955, Cairo should have considered it necessary to dispatch a special Egyptian mission to Moscow to prepare the ground for an arms deal between the two countries. If so, it could hardly have been an accident that, within a very brief time, active contact between Egyptian and Soviet personnel should have been noted in Ankara and, immediately afterward (in mid-February), the Czechoslovak "trade" delegation should suddenly have turned up in Cairo. It appears logical to assume that a cause-and-effect relationship linked these consecutive developments.

In that case, one must ascribe particular significance to evidence indicating that, during the very period (January–February 1955) when the foundations of the Soviet-Egyptian military relationship were being established, at least one Soviet leader had reservations about a Near Eastern adventure—the man who, theoretically, was in charge of Moscow's foreign policy. On February 8, 1955, as the Czechoslovak "trade" delegation was on the point of leaving for Cairo, Soviet Foreign Minister V. M. Molotov delivered a major address on the international situation, which, in its Near Eastern and other sections, contained several remarkable features that were almost unprecedented in Soviet practice. Careful analysis of this speech, its background, and its subsequent history can help to

---

cause of his procommunist posture and because, as a private individual resident in Europe, his movements were less likely to arouse attention than was the journey of an official delegation from the Near East. Whatever Mohieddin's true role in the prehistory of the Arms Deal may have been, it is a fact that he was permitted to return from exile soon thereafter. For an additional interpretation of some of the problems connected with this stage of Soviet-Egyptian relations, see a forthcoming study by Linda Groff of the Fletcher School, "Foreign Aid as an Instrument of Foreign Policy: A Comparative Case Study of U.S. and Soviet Bloc Foreign Aid Programs to the UAR, 1952–65," pt. II, "Historic Survey."

    [41] ANA, in Arabic, April 21, 1955; Baghdad Radio, domestic broadcast, April 16, 1955.

shed light on the interplay during 1955 between the Moscow power struggle and specific international issues (such as Russian policy in the Near East). Since the contest between the various factions in the Soviet capital seems to have had considerable bearing on the Arms Deal, it is necessary to subject the available evidence to detailed reexamination.

4 Internal Struggles and Soviet Foreign Policy

By the winter of 1954/55, the "collective leadership" that had taken over in Moscow after Stalin's death and had appeared to be surviving its first traumatic experience—the execution of Beria—was in disarray. A coalition between N. S. Khrushchev, N. A. Bulganin, and certain marshals of the Red Army had initiated attacks on policies identified with Premier G. M. Malenkov, especially his drive for a reallocation of resources in favor of consumer industries and his advocacy of a minimalist defense policy based upon mutual nuclear deterrence (that is, his acceptance of a global stalemate). Malenkov's opponents challenged the view that the Soviet Union had already achieved a strategic balance with the West, and they demanded a further concentration of investments in heavy industry, so that the USSR might become capable of reaching and overtaking Western military might.[1] Judging by their

[1] Analyses of this period may be found in H. S. Dinerstein, *War and the Soviet Union*, rev. ed. (New York: Frederick A. Praeger, 1962), passim; Arnold L. Horelik and Myron Rush, *Strategic Power and Soviet Foreign Policy* (Chicago: University of Chicago Press, 1966), pp. 17–31; Robert Conquest, *Power and Policy in the U.S.S.R.: The Study of Soviet Dynasties* (New York: St Martin's Press, 1961), chap. 10; Raymond L. Garthoff, *Soviet Strategy in the Nuclear Age* (New York: Frederick A. Praeger, 1958), passim, and especially chap. 4; David J. Dallin, *Soviet Foreign Policy after Stalin* (Philadelphia: J. P. Lippincott Co., 1961), pt. 2 and pt. 3, chap. 1; John M. Mackintosh, *Strategy and Tactics of Soviet Foreign Policy* (New York: Oxford University Press, 1962), chaps. 7 and 8; and Myron Rush, *The Rise of Khrushchev* (Washington, D.C.: Public Affairs Press, 1958), chaps. 1 and 3.

actions immediately after Malenkov's overthrow, Khrushchev and Bulganin apparently also believed that a resolute political offensive, at least outside Europe, could enable Russia to chalk up new gains even before catching up with the United States,[2] and that Malenkov was, therefore, doubly wrong in wishing to settle for a stalemate. V. M. Molotov seems to have occupied a position somewhere between these rival views; his statements, while generally in line with the sentiments of the anti-Malenkov group, indicate that he favored a less exuberant foreign policy, Europe-centered[3] and limited to maintaining the gains of Stalin's period, and that he deplored Khrushchev's penchant for bold but risky offensives. Basically, of course, each faction was concerned far less about policy than about personal power. The various groups usually took good care to relate their policy platforms to their immediate tactical requirements.

Realignment in the Kremlin

By the beginning of 1955, Malenkov was under such heavy fire that his position had become untenable; his authority had been undermined by the execution, in December 1954, of his erstwhile accomplice in the "Leningrad affair," V. S. Abakumov, and his demotion was apparently "approved" at a plenum of the CPSU Central Committee, January 25–31, 1955.[4] On February 8, 1955, Malenkov was forced to announce his "resignation" in humiliating terms. A new government was set up, headed by Bulganin and including Marshal Zhukov, the hero of the Red Army; in fact, however, the regime was now dominated by CPSU First Secretary N. S. Khrushchev. The new leader had forged his way to power by shrewdly playing off his competitors against one another; thus he undoubtedly used Molotov to undermine Malenkov. With Malenkov's decline and fall, Molotov clearly became dispensable as far as the victorious Khrushchev-Bulganin coalition was concerned. Although he was temporarily permitted to continue in his government post, there were increasing attempts to treat Molotov as the

[2] Dallin, *Soviet Foreign Policy*, p. 228 (Khrushchev's address to the July 1955 Central Committee Plenum).
[3] Molotov's foreign affairs address at the joint session of the Supreme Soviet (*Pravda*, February 9, 1955). He stressed that, however much emphasis might be placed upon Asian affairs by some people, in his opinion Europe should not "be relegated to the background."
[4] Address by F. R. Kozlov (*Pravda*, July 3, 1957).

mere incumbent of an essentially technical position (as most Soviet foreign ministers have tended to be) rather than as a veteran member of the CPSU Presidium and a one-time associate of Lenin.

The attempt to cut Molotov down to size had actually started some months previously. Khrushchev, whose domination of the CPSU Secretariat (especially its Foreign Department), control of the secret police (through his accomplice I. A. Serov), and alliance with the Red Army had given him vital access to external channels of communications, tried to bypass Molotov in the conduct of international affairs from mid–1954 onward. This tendency was especially marked in the area of Soviet relations with the other communist states. By July 1954, it could already be noted that members of the CPSU Central Committee *apparat* (subject to the authority of Secretary Khrushchev) were gradually replacing career diplomats and secret police functionaries as Soviet representatives to various countries of the Bloc (for example, Hungary, Poland, and China).[5] Moreover, at the same time, Khrushchev and Bulganin were prominently touring such neighboring states as Czechoslovakia and Poland and exploiting these visits for the purpose of delivering significant statements on the international situation.[6]

By September 1954, Khrushchev, A. I. Mikoyan, Bulganin, and D. T. Shepilov (who eventually replaced Molotov as foreign minister) were visiting Peking for what turned out to be a summit meeting with Mao Tse-tung, covering the whole gamut of Sino-Soviet relations; yet both Foreign Minister Molotov and Premier Malenkov were left at home. Their standing and influence could not but be damaged by this omission, especially since Stalin's death had left Mao in the position of being the one remaining communist veteran of truly international stature; personal endorsement by Mao could, therefore, have significant prestige value for any contestant in the Moscow power struggle. This fact had been well and truly noted as early as March 10, 1953, immediately after Stalin's demise, when *Pravda* published a retouched group photograph, with the faces of most of the original participants carefully

[5] Edward Crankshaw, *Khrushchev: A Career* (New York: Viking Press, 1966), p. 196; see also Radio Free Europe, Munich, "Molotov and the Ministry of Foreign Affairs," Background Information papers, January 26, 1956.
[6] Prague Radio, domestic broadcast, June 15, 1954; *Pravda*, June 16, 1954; and *Izvestia*, July 22, 1954.

expunged so that Malenkov might be portrayed standing alone between Stalin and Mao, receiving, as it were, the political blessings of both. Khrushchev's September 1954 pilgrimage to Peking appears to have been exploited in similar fashion. Ten months later, at the July 1955 CPSU Central Committee Plenum, which was devoted largely to a concerted onslaught upon Molotov, Mikoyan attacked the Soviet Foreign Minister for having allegedly advocated the subjection of China's economy to the so-called "Joint" (Soviet-Chinese) Companies. Mikoyan revealed Mao's bitter objections to this practice; he left little doubt that during the 1954 Peking meeting, in Molotov's absence, the other Soviet leaders had wooed Mao at the Soviet Foreign Minister's expense by placing all the onus for past wrongs upon Molotov and by accepting China's demand to dissolve the "Joint" Companies. (To give the widest possible distribution to their self-portrayal as Mao's true friends, Khrushchev, Mikoyan, and Company thoughtfully dispatched confidential transcripts of the July Plenum proceedings to the various "fraternal" communist parties, including, no doubt, the Chinese Communist Party.)[7] As will be shown, Molotov, on his part, was forced to resort to ingenious tactical devices in the hope of neutralizing any Chinese tendency to support his rivals.

Precisely as he attempted to exclude Molotov from control over Soviet-Chinese relations, so Khrushchev, from the summer of 1954 onward, increasingly took charge of Soviet efforts to effect a rapprochement with Tito's Yugoslavia, apparently on the formal grounds that this was a question of interparty rather than interstate affairs.[8] In February 1955, at the very time when Molotov was publicly voicing his disapproval of Tito's international posture, the Czechs, clearly with the encouragement of someone in Moscow, concluded the agreement with Belgrade that gave Tito a stranglehold over landlocked Czechoslovakia's Afro-Asian trade by channeling it through the Yugoslav port of Rijeka.[9] For such an arrangement to have received Soviet backing it must be assumed that Khrushchev had surreptitiously brought relations with Bel-

[7] For details of the July Plenum, see testimony of Seweryn Bialer in U.S., Congress, Senate, Committee on the Judiciary, *Scope of Soviet Activity in the U.S.*, Internal Security Subcommittee Hearings, pt. 29, June 8–29, 1956, 84th Congress, 2nd session (Washington, D.C.: Government Printing Office, 1957), pp. 1155–1174 (hereafter cited as Bialer testimony); also Dallin, *Soviet Foreign Policy*, pp. 227–233.

[8] Ibid.; see also chap. 3, "A Yugoslav Role?"

[9] See chap. 3, "A Yugoslav Role?"

grade to the point where Tito could be regarded as a reliable friend. By May 1955, Khrushchev felt sufficiently in control to stage his famous reconciliation pilgrimage to Belgrade without Molotov, taking, instead, the men who had accompanied him to Peking in the previous fall (Bulganin, Mikoyan, and Shepilov). Two months later, during the July 1955 Plenum, Molotov was accused of having obstructed the rapprochement with Yugoslavia, allegedly because he was blinded by his personal involvement in Stalin's feud with Tito; the Soviet Foreign Minister retorted that he had not opposed a normalization of relations between the two countries but had only rejected proposals to grant ideological rehabilitation to the Yugoslav League of Communists.[10] (It should be pointed out that exercise of the former option, unlike the latter, would have left Soviet-Yugoslav relations at least partly in Molotov's, rather than Khrushchev's, bailiwick.)

In all probability, the incipient Soviet-Egyptian relationship constituted yet another arena in which Khrushchev was usurping some of Molotov's functions. It has already been noted that the partly covert nature of the various activities in which the two countries seem to have been jointly involved may have resulted in the Soviet Foreign Ministry being bypassed altogether,[11] at least during the initial stages of the Moscow-Cairo entente. Khrushchev, as was pointed out earlier, had ultimate control over clandestine operations from the end of 1954 onward,[12] and it is unlikely that his rivals were permitted to know precisely what was going on. Thus Molotov may well have been unaware of both the full implications and the details of the Soviet-Egyptian activities during January 1955. If that was the case, he must suddenly have discovered, sometime at the beginning of February, that a major international coup was being prepared. Since the Czechoslovak "trade" delegation was to arrive in Cairo during the second week of February, the Prague authorities could hardly have been informed of their prospective part in the Arms Deal later than the first week of the month; at that stage, the Soviet Foreign Ministry and its formal head could not very well be kept from knowing what was happening. Moreover, precisely at that time (February 5, 1955), the Suez meeting between Nasser and Tito took place, which, as has

---

[10] See Bialer testimony and Dallin, *Soviet Foreign Policy.*
[11] See chap. 3, "Indications of Clandestine Contacts."
[12] Ibid.

been noted previously,[13] may have had some bearing on the Cairo-Prague deal, in view of the part assigned to the Yugoslav harbor of Rijeka in the transshipment of Czech goods to Afro-Asia. Any involvement of Yugoslavia in Moscow's Near Eastern projects meant adding a fourth partner to an already complex international scheme, at which point the Soviet Foreign Minister could not but hear echoes of all these manifold activities. If a Yugoslav ingredient was included in the scheme, Molotov's reaction was bound to be all the more unfavorable, since he certainly had no wish to support operations that might help Khrushchev prove that his pro-Tito line was producing useful results.

Whether it was the question of Soviet relations with Belgrade, with Peking, or with Cairo that exacerbated the relations between Molotov and Khrushchev, there is little doubt that by early 1955 the Soviet Foreign Minister was motivated mainly by the need to make a stand against insidious attempts to shunt him aside. Under these circumstances, the need to draft a foreign policy platform for the new government that was on the point of replacing the Malenkov administration could not but precipitate a confrontation between Molotov and his opponents. Between January 25 and 31, 1955, the plenum of the CPSU Central Committee was told of Malenkov's shortcomings[14] and undoubtedly "ratified" his removal. It may be assumed that the top leadership, working within the narrower confines of the Central Committee's Presidium, had hammered out policy guidelines for the occasion, to provide the Central Committee with indications of the political posture that would be considered proper under Malenkov's successors. This is known to have been the situation as far as agriculture and industry were concerned, and it is hardly conceivable that global strategy and world affairs would have been excluded, since these were central issues in the power struggle. If so, it becomes necessary to take a closer look at the balance of forces within the Presidium during that period and to evaluate the effect of power relationships upon political decisions in the Kremlin.

In 1954/55, the supreme organ of the CPSU Central Committee consisted of nine men, of whom Mikoyan, Saburov, and Pervukhin appear sporadically to have supported Malenkov (at least over such issues as consumer goods versus heavy industry and the

[13] See chap. 3, "A Yugoslav Role?"
[14] Address by F. R. Kozlov (*Pravda*, July 3, 1957).

viability of the nuclear stalemate), while Khrushchev, Molotov, Voroshilov, Bulganin, and Kaganovich seem to have coalesced against him.[15] Malenkov's opponents, however, had little in common beyond their desire to demote him, while his supporters, and especially Mikoyan, were by no means firm in their allegiance to the Soviet Premier. Moreover, the adherents of the Malenkov group were weakened from the beginning by the fact that, except for their chief, they were regarded as junior members of the "club."[16]

Consequently, even though his adversaries found it difficult to join forces against him, Malenkov's position in relation to the senior leaders of the party Presidium was always distinctly precarious; the support of a Saburov or a Pervukhin could hardly suffice to cancel out the opposition of veterans like Molotov or Khrushchev. Moreover, there are indications that, from 1954 onward, senior members of the Red Army (whose power had increased because of their successful intervention in 1953 against Beria and the paramilitary units of his secret police) were increasingly bringing their influence to bear against the "capitulationist" elements in Malenkov's policy.[17] Thus the opponents of the Soviet

[15] For some analyses of this period, see the references cited in footnote 1 in this chapter, especially Conquest, *Power and Policy;* see also Werner Scharndorff, *Moskaus Permanente Saüberung* (Munich: Günter Olzog Verlag, 1964).

[16] In the first months after Stalin's death, Soviet newspapers invariably printed the names of Mikoyan, Saburov, and Pervukhin after those of the other CPSU Presidium members, and, even when the traditional procedure was changed and party leaders began to be listed in alphabetical order, ways were found to denote the inferior status of these three men. Thus, while other Presidium members concurrently holding government posts were given the title of Chairman or *First* Deputy Chairman of the Council of Ministers, Mikoyan, Saburov, and Pervukhin alone were relegated to the inferior position of Deputy Chairman; moreover, the ceremonial seating order of the elite on public occasions (a characteristic way of indicating precedence within the hierarchy) revealed the weakness of this group. On the dais of the Supreme Soviet, a central box, or loge, of honor (consisting of ten seats, arranged in two rows of five each) was reserved for the party leadership; however, prior to 1955 only seven of these ten seats were occupied by the CPSU Presidium, three being left empty, while the two junior members of the top party organ, Saburov and Pervukhin, were pointedly relegated to adjacent rows, together with Candidate Members of the CPSU Presidium, junior members of the CPSU Secretariat, and other lesser fry. As for Mikoyan, he invariably sat in the inferior second rather than in the prominent front row of the loge of honor. (This ceremonial box, reserved for the party Presidium, should not be confused with the seats on the edge of the dais occupied by the Presidium of the Supreme Soviet, a "parliamentary" organ of no real political importance.) See *Pravda,* August 6 and 9, 1953, December 3, 1954, and February 9, 1955.

[17] See footnote 1 in this chapter.

REALIGNMENT IN THE KREMLIN   93

Premier were unlikely to encounter insuperable obstacles in removing him from his position; their real problem was to reach
agreement on a realignment of power after his dismissal. At least
two alternatives presented themselves: one was to remove Malenkov and the whole of his group and pack the Presidium with new
appointees subservient to the victors; the other was to win over
some or all of Malenkov's supporters, thus isolating him and
creating an entirely new constellation of power.

On this issue, the interests of Malenkov's various opponents
were bound to differ radically. It is known from later revelations
that the adversaries of the Soviet Premier were aligned in two distinct factions:

1. Molotov's foreign policy views were usually supported (prior
to the summer of 1955) by Kaganovich,[18] and Voroshilov, gradually approaching senility, tended to tag along with these two
men,[19] to whom he was bound by personal ties extending over
several decades.

2. Party First Secretary Khrushchev was generally supported by
Bulganin, a wily opportunist who could not be depended upon in
an emergency (as he proved two years later).

It follows that Khrushchev could derive little benefit from any
attempt to remove not only Malenkov but his followers as well.
A wide purge along these lines was likely to leave the First Secretary in a minority of two against three among the remaining five
senior members of the Presidium; moreover, any packing of that
organ with new members was likely, under such circumstances, to
reflect the status quo and freeze the minority in a position of dis-
advantage.

Thus the logic of the situation dictated Khrushchev's tactics: it
was in his interest to win over some or all of Malenkov's supporters
as a way of multiplying his options. With the backing of Mikoyan,
Saburov, and Pervukhin and with the aid of Bulganin, the First
Secretary could build up a majority group within the Presidium,
isolating Malenkov on the one side and Molotov and Kaganovich
on the other. Indeed, Khrushchev's moves from the fall of 1954
onward clearly reflected such tactical considerations: together
with his ally Bulganin and his client Shepilov, Khrushchev em-

[18] See "Resolution of the Central Committee of the CPSU, June 29, 1957,"
Pravda, July 4, 1957.
[19] See address by A. I. Mikoyan to the Twenty-second CPSU Congress
(ibid., October 22, 1961).

barked upon several significant international visits (such as the trip to Peking and, subsequently, the pilgrimage to Belgrade) in the company of Mikoyan, who was thus singled out as a key personality in international affairs, undermining Molotov's position.[20] The most logical interpretation of Khrushchev's behavior is that he was deliberately wooing Malenkov's supporters to rid himself, at one fell swoop, of both his main rivals—Foreign Minister Molotov and Premier Malenkov.

It is all the more noteworthy then that, on the opening day of the Central Committee plenum that ratified Malenkov's demotion, *Pravda*, twenty-four hours after printing a vitriolic attack on the policies with which the Soviet Premier was associated, announced that Mikoyan had been relieved, "at his own request," of his position as Soviet minister of trade.[21] No reason was given, nor was it stated that he would be assigned another post; since Malenkov had been attacked primarily for his advocacy of consumer industries, the growth of which depended on the development of foreign trade (Mikoyan's primary field of endeavor), the obvious implication of *Pravda*'s announcement was that Mikoyan was being demoted for his support of Malenkov's policies. Subsequently, it became known that the decree concerning Mikoyan's dismissal had actually been signed by the Presidium of the Supreme Soviet on January 22,[22] but another three days passed before publicity was given to this fact by *Pravda*, whose editor Shepilov was Khrushchev's satellite. It is likely, then, that Khrushchev resisted Mikoyan's demotion, which, for the tactical reasons just mentioned, was bound to weaken the position of the First Secretary and to boost Molotov's chances. Presumably, the Molotov group was not prepared to give its final consent to Malenkov's ouster until Khrushchev acquiesced in the simultaneous demotion of Malenkov's whole group, including Mikoyan. If so, it is probable that the Central Committee plenum took place within the framework of an uneasy truce between Molotov and Khrushchev, with the former occupying a distinctly stronger position; otherwise, Mikoyan would not have lost his ministry. In that case, one should not exclude

[20] During the Stalin period, Mikoyan had been a member of the Politburo's four-man subcommittee on foreign affairs, together with Molotov, and thus was a natural candidate for the task of encroaching upon the Foreign Minister's sphere. See Merle Fainsod, *How Russia Is Ruled* (Cambridge, Mass.: Harvard University Press, 1958), p. 282.

[21] *Pravda*, January 24 and 25, 1955.

[22] Ibid., February 8 and January 25, 1955, respectively.

the possibility that the Presidium's original candidate to succeed
Malenkov as premier (Chairman of the Council of Ministers) was
the man next in rank, namely, the senior First Deputy Chairman,
Molotov himself.

There are several indications that this may have been the case
and that the Presidium subsequently reversed its decision and gave
the post to Bulganin. Thus Malenkov's announcement of his "resignation" at the February 8 session of the Supreme Soviet made very
little sense as an explanation for his replacement by Bulganin;
however, the note does fit the circumstances perfectly if one assumes that it was prepared with Molotov's accession to the
premiership in mind. The statement spoke of Malenkov's alleged
"lack of experience" for the post of premier;[23] such a remark was
entirely pointless unless it was intended that Malenkov should be
replaced by someone who *did* have previous experience in this position. The only member of the Presidium to whom this applied was
Molotov, who had been premier (as well as foreign minister) for
a decade prior to World War II, while Bulganin had had no more
experience in heading the government than Malenkov himself.
Obviously, Moscow wanted its official explanation for the change
to sound reasonably convincing, and only a last-minute substitu-
tion of Bulganin for Molotov can explain the publication of a statement that did not fit the circumstances at all. Many foreign
observers remarked at the time how ludicrous it was to replace
Malenkov with Bulganin if "experience" was the criterion for the
post.

Moreover, the agenda for the forthcoming session of the Supreme Soviet, which was announced immediately after the conclusion of the January Central Committee plenum of the CPSU,
provided for only one major political event—an address on the
international situation (apart from routine items devoted to the
budget and various administrative matters).[24] Important speeches
on international affairs at the Supreme Soviet were normally delivered by the head of the government. This held true during both
Molotov's and Malenkov's premierships. It was known at the beginning of the session that the address would be delivered by
Molotov, and the agenda made no provision for major statements
by other leaders; this, in itself, would seem to imply that Molotov

[23] Ibid., February 9, 1955.
[24] Moscow Radio, domestic broadcast, February 3, 1955.

was the party's prospective candidate for the post of Chairman of the Council of Ministers.

As the session proceeded, however, the agenda was suddenly altered, and the routine "confirmation" of interim decrees by the Supreme Soviet was pushed ahead of the foreign affairs address.[25] Clearly, unforeseen developments had necessitated last-minute changes; when Molotov's turn finally came to deliver his speech, yet another delay occurred, and a note of "resignation" was read out on Malenkov's behalf, couched in terms that, as has been noted, seemed to be tailor-made for Molotov's candidacy. However, immediately after the announcement was heard, Khrushchev rose and proposed that Bulganin should become premier.[26] This step created an awkward situation, which obviously had not been envisaged when the agenda of the Supreme Soviet was published a few days earlier. Molotov was already scheduled to speak, and it was now necessary to provide room for another address, by Bulganin, the new head of government. Since Molotov was scheduled to cover foreign relations and Khrushchev had already exhaustively dealt with a major aspect of domestic affairs at the Central Committee plenum (in a survey of agriculture published by *Pravda*), there was hardly anything left for the new premier to say. On the following day, therefore, Bulganin delivered a dull, brief statement that merely went over ground already preempted by others.[27] It is hardly conceivable that affairs would have been handled in this fashion had Bulganin actually been the candidate sponsored by the Central Committee plenum of January 25–31.

There are other indications that a major change in the power structure was taking place during the first days of February. On January 25, 1955, as has been noted, Mikoyan's dismissal from the Ministry of Trade was published, showing that Khrushchev's tactic of allying himself with this and other former supporters of Malenkov had been temporarily foiled and that Molotov's influence therefore prevailed at the time. A few days later, on January 29, while the party plenum was still in session, prominent American journalists, who had requested interviews with leading Soviet personalities, were granted a meeting with Molotov; the text of the conversation was published immediately in the Soviet press, and

[25] Ibid., February 7, 1955.
[26] Ibid., February 8, 1955; *Pravda*, February 9, 1955.
[27] Moscow Radio, domestic broadcast, February 9, 1955; *Pravda*, February 10, 1955.

his words were clearly treated as the final and authoritative pronouncement.[28] Only a week later (on February 5) were the journalists allowed to see other Soviet leaders, including Khrushchev, Bulganin, and Marshal Zhukov; these interviews, however, were not published for several days, a clear indication that they were subject to internal review.[29]

Up to that time, the agenda of the Supreme Soviet had remained entirely consistent with the assumption that Molotov would be the head of the new government and would deliver the official pronouncement on its policies. However, Khrushchev's February 5 meeting with U.S. newspapermen indicated that the anti-Malenkov coalition was breaking up, even though the Soviet Premier had not yet been formally dismissed. Khrushchev exploited the interview to deliver himself of certain comments that could not but reflect upon Molotov's reputation while, at the same time, giving a boost to Mikoyan—who badly needed support after his recent demotion. Khrushchev seemed to go out of his way to stress that Mikoyan must be regarded as the Kremlin's best authority on a very important international question, namely, the situation inside the United States. Surprised, his interlocutors asked Khrushchev whether it was not a fact that the Soviet leader who had visited the United States most frequently and most recently was Molotov; in a distinctly derogatory manner, Khrushchev brushed off Molotov's trips as having occurred at unpropitious times and kept insisting that Mikoyan was the man who really understood the situation.[30] This was particularly odd since Mikoyan had been in the United States only once, and that, moreover, had been a full two decades earlier, during the Depression, whereas Molotov's repeated visits had taken place during the 1940s.

Nor could the attack on Molotov's grasp of affairs be regarded as unpremeditated for the simple reason that *Pravda,* a few days later, printed this passage in all its glory, in what was otherwise a mere paraphrase of the interview; since *Pravda*'s report did not pretend to be a verbatim text, the paper was under no particular obligation to reproduce such personal comments unless, indeed, they were more than simple slips of the tongue. By the time the story appeared in *Pravda* on February 11, the premiership had al-

[28] Moscow Radio, domestic broadcast, January 30, 1955.
[29] The interview with Khrushchev was given on February 5 and published in *Pravda,* February 11, 1955.
[30] Ibid.

ready been awarded to Bulganin, so that Molotov, an obvious loser, could be regarded as fair game. However, on February 5, when Khrushchev first met the American journalists, Molotov still appeared to be a very serious contender for power; the attack upon his competence, therefore, had to be regarded as an overt sign of a turning point in the power struggle.

Thus it would seem that, sometime during the first week of February 1955, Khrushchev was able to bring about drastic changes in the political arrangements that had been made at the time of the Central Committee plenum in January. One can only speculate about the factors that made this possible, but Marshal Zhukov's increasing prominence at this very moment, including his meeting with Western journalists, is highly suggestive. Any agreement to elevate Bulganin to the premiership was likely, at the same time, to entail his removal from the post of defense minister in order to avoid concentrating too much power in one pair of hands. Consequently, the Red Army leadership, by supporting his candidacy, could help to create a vacancy in the key Ministry of Defense; in that case, career officers like Marshal Zhukov might be able to capture a vital position that previously had been monopolized by "political" marshals, like Bulganin himself. Thus, paradoxically, the regular soldiers, although disliking Bulganin (the prototype of the political commissar), had sound selfish reasons for supporting him and his ally, Khrushchev, against Molotov.

The fact remains that, two days after Khrushchev's interview with the American journalists, the agenda of the Supreme Soviet was suddenly altered, and, the next day, Bulganin's elevation to the premiership was announced, followed by Marshal Zhukov's appointment as minister of defense.

Other indications of the kind of factors that had been involved in the complex process of altering the balance of power became apparent during this session of the Supreme Soviet; thus the ceremonial seating order of the main Soviet leaders was altered in a meaningful manner. The characteristic public symbolism of the Kremlin revealed that, with the support of Malenkov's former adherents (two of whom—Pervukhin and Saburov—were unexpectedly upgraded rather than being dismissed together with their chief), Khrushchev had, at one and the same time, outmaneuvered both Malenkov and Molotov and was now proceeding to pack the party Presidium (by promoting personal retainers like Kirichenko).[31] Starting out with the "arithmetic majority" in the Presidium against him, Khrushchev, as on several previous and subsequent occasions, had used outside pressure (in this case, apparently, with Zhukov's assistance) to overawe his opponents; consequently, he was able to insist on a solution clearly harmful to the interests of the Molotov group, namely, that Malenkov should be demoted but that his three adherents should not suffer. The latter, owing their political survival to Khrushchev, then provided him with an automatic majority. In effect, Molotov's ascendancy of late January suffered a sharp reversal sometime between February 5 and 8, leaving the Soviet Foreign Minister in an exposed and isolated position.

This fact received vivid public demonstration a few hours after the Supreme Soviet session at which Malenkov was demoted, Bulganin was nominated, and Molotov delivered his foreign affairs address. With a single exception, the whole Presidium, as well as its Candidates and members of the Secretariat, staged a joint appearance that evening at the Bolshoi; since the formal occasion was a thoroughly unremarkable performance by amateur artists from various factories, it was clear that the elite had not been attracted to the theater by its love of art. The real reason for the gathering was to be found in Malenkov's "resignation" note, which had stressed that certain circles abroad would inevitably interpret

[31] *Pravda's* front page on February 9, 1955 showed that Molotov had been relegated from his customary corner seat in the front row of the Supreme Soviet's box of honor to a place in the distinctly inferior second row (to be exact, the photograph revealed that this was the only seat left vacant for Molotov to occupy upon completing his address from the rostrum). On the other hand, Malenkov's former supporters, Pervukhin and Saburov, who during earlier sessions, because of their junior status, had not been allowed to enter the loge of honor at all (see footnote 16 in this chapter), were now seated in that box, together with Khrushchev's Ukrainian satellite, Kirichenko, who had been only a Candidate Member of the Presidium and whose appearance in the coveted enclosure was, therefore, significant. The implications of these changes could hardly be mistaken: Khrushchev and Bulganin, apparently backed by certain marshals, had overridden Molotov and rescued Malenkov's former supporters, thus gaining a majority on the Presidium; Khrushchev seems to have exploited his advantage immediately by foisting Kirichenko on his colleagues. (Although Kirichenko was not officially elevated to full membership in the Presidium until five months later, at the July Plenum of the Central Committee, *Pravda's* photograph indicates that he had already been promoted in February, without the formal ratification of the Central Committee. The other two Candidates, Shvernik and Ponomarenko, remained seated outside the loge of honor, according to *Pravda's* picture, so that Kirichenko was definitely singled out for treatment implying higher status.)

the Soviet government changes as evidence of disunity within the collective leadership. Consequently, the Kremlin felt that some public display of unity was essential. It was all the more surprising, therefore, that one single leader ostentatiously absented himself from this occasion, namely, Molotov.[32] Under the circumstances, it can hardly be assumed that the new leadership excluded him and thus willfully precipitated a demonstration of internal dissension (after all, even Malenkov was brought along to the Bolshoi). It seems far more likely that Molotov, in staying away, was staging a characteristically lone and stubborn stand, a demonstration of protest foreshadowing his rather remarkable refusal in subsequent years to submit meekly to the majority.[33] Since the Bolshoi performance took place a mere couple of hours after the conclusion of the Supreme Soviet's afternoon session on February 8, and since Molotov's behavior seems to have been the result of last-minute developments (otherwise the leadership might well have canceled its whole "unity" display rather than stage an appearance without him), it may be assumed that something occurred during the session to exacerbate relations within the elite. The event in question, as will be seen, must have been Molotov's foreign affairs address.

Molotov's refusal to entertain thoughts of a premature surrender seems to have been based upon his awareness that the Soviet political situation still remained quite labile. The alterations in the USSR's governmental structure announced during the Supreme Soviet session of February 8 did not last three weeks. On February 28, the composition of the Bulganin government was changed, Mikoyan, Saburov, and Pervukhin being promoted from Deputy Chairmen to First Deputy Chairmen of the Council of Ministers.[34] This act was no doubt intended to undermine still further the

[32] Moscow Radio, domestic broadcast, February 9, 1955; *Pravda,* February 9, 1955.

[33] Repeatedly, and almost uniquely among CPSU leaders, Molotov refused to "play the game" and clung to his role of lone dissenter, publicly displaying his opposition to the policy of a hostile majority. When Khrushchev, in June 1957, answered his opponents' coup d'état by staging a countercoup and ousting them from the Presidium, Molotov was the only member of the defeated "anti-Party group" who dared to refuse the demand that he support his own condemnation and to insist that his vote be recorded as an abstention. Years later, he went so far as to criticize Soviet foreign policy in a memorandum submitted to the Presidium, in spite of the fact that most of its members were his opponents.

[34] *Pravda,* March 1, 1955.

prestige of both Malenkov and Molotov. The former, who had been demoted two full grades, from Chairman to ordinary Deputy Chairman, was now the only full member of the CPSU Presidium to hold so undistinguished a rank in the government *apparat.* Molotov, who had been the senior of two First Deputy Chairmen (ranking first in order of succession to the chairmanship of the Council of Ministers), now found himself in a crowd, being merely one of five First Deputy Chairmen, including persons who were indubitably his juniors in the party Presidium. Moreover, Bulganin had been promoted over his head to the post of Chairman.

A few days later, *Pravda* added insult to injury, allowing itself to print what was, in effect, an unprecedented direct attack upon an incumbent Soviet cabinet member. Molotov's February 8 foreign affairs address to the Supreme Soviet had contained distinctly unfriendly references to Tito's Yugoslavia. Tito retaliated and publicly censured Molotov by name; to the great amazement of outside observers, Tito's attack was reprinted, almost verbatim, in *Pravda,* whose editorial board did not see fit to add a single word of reservation, dissent, or comment.[35] Only after a few days did a mild rejoinder to Tito appear in *Pravda.*[36] Two months later, Molotov was pointedly excluded from Khrushchev's reconciliation pilgrimage to Belgrade and, at the subsequent July Plenum of the CPSU Central Committee, Khrushchev, Mikoyan, and Company extended the range of their attacks from Molotov's views on Yugoslavia to the whole of his international policy.[37] The Soviet Foreign Minister was assailed over such issues as his delays in concluding the Austrian State Treaty, his support for the economic exploitation of China and Eastern Europe (through the "Joint" Companies), and his neglect of the Third World. These questions had to a considerable extent been resolved in Khrushchev's favor some months earlier, and the last occasion on which Molotov had dared publicly to voice contrary opinions had been on February 8, in his address before the Supreme Soviet.[38] Thus, as time went on, it began to look increasingly as if that speech itself had constituted Molotov's real offense. *Pravda's* action in reprinting Tito's attack upon the

[35] Ibid., March 10, 1955.
[36] Ibid., March 12, 1955.
[37] See Bialer testimony and Dallin, *Soviet Foreign Policy.*
[38] Although there is reason to believe that, behind the scenes, Molotov continued to wage a stubborn campaign against what he considered to be a mistaken policy.

February 8 address had already indicated the degree to which the Soviet Foreign Minister's words had angered his opponents in the Kremlin. By the fall of 1955, little doubt could be left that the Molotov speech had, indeed, been an unusually significant and controversial document. In September 1955, Molotov was coerced into signing a letter of "apology" concerning certain ideological definitions contained in the February 8 address; in fact, it was perfectly clear that his recantation applied to the speech as a whole. To drive the point home, the authoritative CPSU organ *Kommunist* accompanied the letter with an editorial blast against Molotov's very concepts of policy.[39] Again, two years later, the Central Committee's resolution of censure against Molotov, following his ouster from the Presidium in June 1957, abounded in polemics against his basic approach to world affairs, as outlined in his February 1955 address.[40] As late as the Twenty-second CPSU Congress, in 1961, Mikoyan again returned to this theme.[41]

Molotov's February 8 Speech: An Autopsy

Obviously, then, for its echoes still to reverberate years afterward, Molotov's February 8 speech must have been an event of major significance in the Moscow power struggle. This is perhaps not too surprising, as the preceding analysis has indicated, since the first part of February, when the address was being drafted, appears to have been a period of kaleidoscopic realignments within the Kremlin; thus Molotov's programatic document could not but have been a factor in the Moscow tug of war at that important moment. If the evidence cited here has been interpreted correctly, the speech was originally drafted by the man who expected to be head of government (Molotov), at a time when he appeared to be holding the upper hand (that is, at the very end of January and during the first days of February). However, his prospects were apparently dimmed and his position seriously weakened a day or so—perhaps only a few hours—before the address was actually delivered on February 8. Since the struggle with his opponents was largely fought out over questions of international policy, the preparation of a statement on this very subject, drafted

[39] *Kommunist,* no. 14, September 1955.
[40] See "Resolution of the Central Committee of the CPSU, June 29, 1957," *Pravda,* July 4, 1957.
[41] *Pravda,* October 22, 1961.

MOLOTOV'S FEBRUARY 8 SPEECH: AN AUTOPSY   103

at a moment of such instability, could not but result in a curious and contradictory document.

Molotov's extensive and detailed survey of the global situation and of Soviet policy (some 15,000 words) could hardly have been written anew in the brief hours between the sudden alteration of the Supreme Soviet's agenda (which was apparently caused by the Kremlin's decision to switch candidates for the premiership) and Molotov's appearance on the rostrum.[42] Needless to say, a document prepared by the Soviet Foreign Minister at a time when he regarded himself as the authoritative voice on global affairs was bound to prove less than satisfactory to the victorious Khrushchev-Bulganin coalition on February 8. In view of the pressure of time, it may be presumed that Molotov's opponents could do no more than insist upon textual alterations in those parts of the speech that dealt with the most important controversial questions. However, since the Foreign Minister was to demonstrate only a few hours after making the address that he was still stubbornly resisting the pressure of his adversaries,[43] it seems more than likely that every request for a change of words prior to delivery must have set off a full-scale battle of attrition. Under such circumstances, a thorough reediting of the speech was out of the question; thus the final result could hardly amount to more than a patchwork of contradictory concepts—a Molotov text, in fact, with gems of Khrushcheviana superimposed upon it. Consequently, it is not surprising that the document contained enough objectionable matter to require piecemeal repudiation, section by section, during the subsequent period.

The contents of Molotov's address do, indeed, appear to bear out these assumptions. Such a collation of inconsistencies, nonsequiturs, and contradictions would be surprising in any official statement; emanating from the USSR, where definitive and programatic documents are known to be edited with particular pedantry and preciseness, it is nothing less than remarkable. This holds true especially of a speech with major international and domestic implications. Moreover, the author happens to be the same V. M. Molotov whose particular clerical aptitude and competence had

[42] Moscow Radio, domestic broadcast, February 7, 1955; less than twenty-four hours separated the change of agenda from the delivery of Molotov's speech.

[43] By boycotting the Bolshoi "unity" appearance of the Soviet leadership; see "Realignment in the Kremlin" earlier in this chapter.

been (somewhat patronizingly) noted by Lenin and others, and who was notorious for his thoroughness and persistence. Such a statement simply could not have issued from his pen; it could have resulted only from last-minute corrections, hastily inserted after a stormy confrontation between the Soviet Foreign Minister and his opponents.

At first sight, it might appear as if the document had simply been pieced together as part of a normal compromise between two opposing factions. Thus separate passages dealing with different issues can be shown to reflect the political views of Molotov and Khrushchev, respectively, which are sufficiently well known to historians from testimony concerning the July 1955 Plenum and from other evidence that has been noted earlier.[44] For instance, Molotov's statement that any Soviet steps to effect a rapprochement with Tito would have to depend "no less . . . on Yugoslavia herself" and that the Belgrade regime was largely to blame for the rift, since it had "departed from the position" of orthodoxy, reflected his own personal approach toward this question. It could not be considered compatible with Khrushchev's attempt, ever since June 1954, to woo Tito back into the Bloc.[45] In this matter, therefore, it would seem that Molotov's view prevailed temporarily (until Pravda, a couple of weeks later, disowned the Foreign Minister's line by reprinting Tito's attack upon his speech). No doubt, Molotov regarded relations with Belgrade as a central issue, vitally affecting his own prestige, and stuck grimly to his guns. Perhaps Khrushchev was not prepared to pressure Molotov unduly in this matter, at any rate until he could finally dispose of Malenkov and appoint Bulganin in his place, that is, until such time as Molotov would become entirely dispensable.

As far as accepting a State Treaty with Austria was concerned, on the other hand, Molotov's speech clearly went far toward accommodating the policies of his opponents. The signature of such a treaty meant the abandonment of the Soviet Occupation Zone in Austria; Moscow's reward would be the neutrality of Austria as a whole. To the surprise of most observers, Molotov's address contained a definite indication that Russia was now prepared to proceed in this direction; indeed, the Austrians immediately took the hint and explored the situation. Very soon, intensive East-West

---

[44] See footnotes 1 and 2 in this chapter; Bialer testimony; and Dallin, Soviet Foreign Policy, pp. 227–233.

[45] See chap. 3, "A Yugoslav Role?" and especially footnote 16 in chap. 3.

negotiations started, which were quickly crowned with success. Yet as late as the July Plenum, some five months later, when Molotov was accused of having obstructed the treaty, he not only refrained from denying this charge but insisted that he had been entirely right to argue against the needless surrender of the Soviet Zone in Austria. Significantly, he did not refer to his February 8 address as proof that he was being unfairly accused of opposition to a treaty that his own speech had helped to initiate.[46] Apparently, it was well known at the plenum that this and other sections of his address had not emanated from him but had been inserted in spite of his disapproval and against his better judgment. Since the future of Austria was not as central in his eyes as relations with Yugoslavia and other communist states, which involved major jurisdictional conflicts between him and Khrushchev,[47] it may have been relatively easier to override his misgivings about a State Treaty with Austria than his objections to a wholehearted rapprochement with Tito.

Thus an analysis of the Austrian and Yugoslav passages in Molotov's February 8 speech undoubtedly does convey the impression that the two opposing factions had waged a seesaw struggle, resulting in a patchwork document, with the views of one party prevailing on some issues and the opinions of the second group being accepted on other questions. However, in reality, the history of this address appears to have been far more complicated.

The speech delivered on February 8 was by no means a straightforward compromise between rival politicians. A closer look reveals that certain key issues were treated in a most chaotic manner, not one but several mutually incompatible passages being devoted to each, so as to set forth the views of *both* factions on a single issue—even though they flatly contradicted one another. In terms of Soviet practice, this was a palpable absurdity that could not have been the result of a simple deal between the two competing groups. The only hypothesis that can explain what brought about such an unusual phenomenon has already been noted:[48] Khrushchev, sometime on February 6 or 7, after he had lined up his forces to coerce the Presidium into endorsing Bulganin's candidacy for the premiership, apparently exploited the favorable constellation to try and impose his whole concept of policy on the Soviet leader-

---

[46] See Bialer testimony and Dallin, *Soviet Foreign Policy*, pp. 227–233.
[47] See "Realignment in the Kremlin" earlier in this chapter.
[48] See the opening paragraphs of this section.

ship. Since the international platform of the new regime was scheduled to be presented by Molotov to the Supreme Soviet in a matter of hours, Khrushchev must have concentrated his energies on an effort to reshape the text of the Soviet Foreign Minister's address, which almost certainly had reached final draft form at that late stage. In the face of Molotov's stubborn resistance, it seems that Khrushchev had to content himself with a limited number of additions and corrections, reflecting the views of his group on some, although by no means all, of the disputed questions. With so little time remaining, the changes appear to have been hastily inserted, and there was simply no opportunity to reedit the document as a whole to iron out inconsistencies and eliminate outright contradictions.

Consequently, the February 8 address contains significant traces of the respective viewpoints of both groups in the Kremlin on several matters of key interest around which a particularly sharp struggle was waged. Whereas the Khrushchev approach is presented in the passage concerning the Austrian question and Molotov's policy is spelled out in the paragraphs dealing with Yugoslavia, the attitudes of both factions are given expression in the sections of the speech that outline relationships within the communist bloc and Soviet attitudes toward the Near East. These rival opinions, printed, as it were, side by side, are of particular value to the analyst since they reflect a dispute within the Kremlin that can be dated, with a reasonable degree of assurance, sometime between February 5 and 8, 1955 (a few days, it will be recalled, before the Czechoslovak "trade" delegation arrived in Cairo to negotiate the grant of a loan to Egypt for the purchase of arms). Moreover, a couple of days later, Soviet translations of the Molotov address (for distribution abroad) introduced subtle but significant changes in the text, particularly in the paragraphs containing the mutually contradictory opinions of the two competing leaders, thus throwing further light on the nature of the "debate." As has been noted earlier, there are several indications of serious setbacks suffered by Molotov between February 8 and the second week of March. It is likely, therefore, that these additional, ex post facto, alterations in the tone of the Foreign Minister's statement were made at the behest of his opponents; indeed, the changes are entirely consistent with the hypothesis that Khrushchev's followers were attempting to water down passages which retained too much of a Molotovian flavor.

The first piece of mute testimony to the character of the policy debate within the Kremlin concerns the problem of relations between Moscow, Peking, and other communist capitals. It is to be found in the same part of the speech that contains the ideological error for which Molotov, seven months later, was forced to publish a letter of apology. The Foreign Minister, it will be recalled, was accused of having mistakenly stated in his February 8 address that only "the *foundations* of a socialist society" (author's emphasis) had been built in the USSR, whereas, Molotov's critics pointed out, every schoolchild knew that *socialism itself* had already triumphed in the Soviet Union prior to World War II. Molotov admitted this error and was duly denounced in an editorial in *Kommunist*.[49]

Interestingly enough, however, no historian seems to have noticed that, only a few paragraphs earlier in Molotov's speech, the "correct," orthodox formulation was also given, stating that "socialism had already triumphed in our country in the period before the Second World War."[50] No junior apprentice in the school of Marxism-Leninism, not to speak of a veteran Bolshevik leader noted for his pedantry, would include, in one and the same document, two contradictory statements claiming, respectively, that only the "foundations of socialism" had been built and that socialism itself had triumphed. If a mere clerical error had really been responsible, a stubborn, seasoned campaigner like Molotov would have been quick to point to the passage containing the orthodox formulation to demonstrate that he had not intended to challenge the accepted view. However, the Soviet Foreign Minister did not make use of this fact, any more than, during the July Plenum, he made reference to the paragraph in his February 8 address that opened the way toward the Austrian State Treaty. It is likely that he abstained from doing so in both instances because many members of the Soviet elite knew very well that the "correct" passages had been inserted in the speech at the behest of his opponents.

Needless to say, the question was not one of mere semantics, of purely historical interest. Molotov's formulation appeared in the section of his address dealing with the relationships between the various communist governments and with the future of the Bloc as a whole. The Soviet Foreign Minister insisted that the communist states were all "on different levels of development, on dif-

---

49 See *Kommunist*, no. 14, September 1955.
50 *Pravda*, February 9, 1955.

ferent levels of social transformation," and that, "side by side with the Soviet Union, where the foundations of a socialist society have been built, there are Peoples' Democratic Countries which have so far taken only the first, though very important, steps toward socialism." He proceeded to warn that "for all the significance and special role of the USSR," the other communist countries would have to "rely increasingly also on the support they render one another." Moreover, he went out of his way to emphasize that the other governments of the Bloc were approaching their tasks "with no little difficulty and not without great shortcomings in their constructive work." He concluded this passage by cautioning that, in assessing the relative strength of the two principal world forces, one should not "overestimate" the positive aspects of past and present trends; one must keep in mind that this is "a long historical period of which, so far, we have lived through only a little more than thirty-seven years."[51]

Obviously, in downgrading the stage of socialist construction reached both by the USSR and by the other communist countries and in underlining the serious shortcomings and weaknesses existing throughout the "socialist camp," Molotov was warning against ebullient foreign and economic policies and against exaggerated reliance upon Soviet economic aid in developing the rest of the Bloc. In fact, Molotov's own inclination, for which his adversaries subsequently denounced him at the July Plenum, was to confine Moscow's future role to the maintenance of the status quo in the Bloc, while drawing upon the resources of the other communist countries, if not through the "Joint" Companies then through other means of control and exploitation. To go beyond that, he indicated, would be to take the offensive prematurely, thus dangerously overstraining the capabilities of the Soviet Union.[52] (In retrospect, this seems to have been a very realistic appraisal.)

Significantly enough, a version of Molotov's speech that was circulated a few days later for distribution abroad toned down several of the points he had made. For instance, while the Foreign Minister had stressed that the various communist countries were all at "different levels of development," it was now merely said that they were "not all in the same stage of development"; whereas he had cautioned that only the "foundations of a socialist society"

---

[51] Ibid.
[52] See footnotes 1, 2, and 7 in this chapter.

had been laid in the USSR, the later version stated that these foundations had "already" been built, in other words, that the USSR presumably was now a stage beyond this level.[53] It may be assumed that whoever had acted to correct Molotov in this fashion had also been responsible, a few days earlier, for the "adjustment" in the Foreign Minister's original text—by adding the orthodox statement that socialism had triumphed in the USSR prior to World War II. (Needless to say, this phrase flatly contradicted the very basis of Molotov's claim that both Russia and the other Bloc countries were still at an early and vulnerable stage, which forced them to proceed with caution.)[54]

Intimately linked with the same question of the present and future character of the Bloc was Molotov's unprecedented and astounding statement that the "socialist camp" was now "headed by the USSR, or, it would be truer to say, by the Soviet Union and the Chinese People's Republic."[55] It was with this phrase that the Soviet Foreign Minister introduced the section of his speech analyzing Bloc affairs and the level of socialist development in individual communist countries. Very possibly, the subsequent pressure on Molotov to recant was due as much to this provocative statement as to his heterodox ideological formulation concerning the precise degree of socialism attained by the USSR. Thus *Kommunist*, in the same editorial that commented upon Molotov's letter of recantation, went out of its way to call for the "close . . . economic . . . cooperation of the socialist countries, *headed by the*

---

[53] The two rival versions may be found in *Pravda*, February 9, 1955, and *New Times*, no. 7, February 12, 1955, pp. 11–30.

[54] Some commentators, leaning heavily upon accusations circulated by Molotov's adversaries after his ouster from the Presidium, have interpreted the dispute over the precise stage of the "building of socialism" in the USSR as being related to the ticklish question of internal relaxation. (If socialism had really "triumphed," class antagonisms would be dying away, and harsh disciplinary measures would no longer be required.) This argument suffers from serious weaknesses. To start with, the statement that socialism was already triumphant had been treated by Stalin as entirely compatible with further cries for "vigilance" and continued terror. There is no particular reason, therefore, why Molotov should have regarded the two concepts as incompatible. Moreover, the context of this phrase in his February 8 address shows clearly that it was connected with quite another problem, namely, political and economic relationships within the Bloc, arising out of the relative stages of development reached by individual Bloc countries. This is borne out by the fact that *Kommunist*, in criticizing Molotov for his "error" on this subject, specifically refers to economic relations between the various communist states and to the question of the leadership of the Bloc. See *Kommunist*, no. 14, September 1955.

[55] *Pravda*, February 9, 1955.

Soviet Union. . . ."[56] This looks suspiciously like a pointed rejoinder to Molotov's suggestion that Peking be accepted as codirector of the Bloc.

The question remains: What precisely did the Soviet Foreign Minister mean to imply by his startling elevation of China's role? It must be recalled that the rest of the passage stressed how very modest the attainments of all the communist countries had been to date, and how large the disparities between them were; the natural corollary was that only cautious and gradual progress could be expected, and that the USSR alone could not conceivably shoulder the burdens of leadership and of assistance to its weaker brethren. (Thus Molotov said specifically that "for all the significance and special role of the USSR," the other communist countries would have to "rely increasingly also on the support they render one another.")[57] Needless to say, the USSR faced the heaviest of these burdens, if it responded to China's urgent requirements and provided the assistance essential for the economic and military modernization of that vast country. Under these circumstances, Molotov's rather oddly phrased offer to share the leadership of the Bloc with Peking was double-edged, to say the least. Read together with the rest of the passage, it implied that Peking should not expect Moscow to assume the role of sole champion and provider for the whole camp. In this context, joint leadership by the USSR and the CPR (Chinese People's Republic) meant simply that Moscow refused to shoulder responsibility for China's defense and development, as the sole head of the Bloc would have been expected to do. It was precisely for this reason (as is now known from revelations concerning the background of the Sino-Soviet dispute), that Peking, prior to 1958, was actually eager to award Moscow the title of leader and guardian of the Bloc. (The Chinese made such an attempt, successfully, during the November 1957 Moscow Conference.) Mao and his associates were quite frank about the fact that they considered Bloc leadership to entail serious duties and responsibilities rather than privileges.[58] Consequently,

[56] *Kommunist,* no. 14, September 1955 (author's emphasis).
[57] *Pravda,* February 9, 1955.
[58] In 1957, the Chinese "emphasized that the socialist camp should have the Soviet Union at its head . . . it does not mean that the CPSU has any right to control other Parties; what it means is that the CPSU carries greater responsibilities and duties on its shoulders." See *The Polemic on the General Line of the International Communist Movement* (Peking: Foreign Languages Press, 1965), p. 335.

it is hardly surprising to find that Chinese May Day slogans, both before and after Molotov's 1955 speech, consistently stressed that the communist bloc was "headed by the Soviet Union," and that, moreover, the Soviet Union was already "building communism" and the East European communist countries were "victoriously building socialism" (in other words, the rest of the camp had reached a stage of development that enabled it to render substantial assistance to China).[59]

There was no reason, therefore, to expect that Peking would be delirious with joy over Molotov's offer to accept China as a co-leader of the Bloc. In fact, the relevant portion of Molotov's speech was ignored in Peking for some time, its unprecedented "compliment" to China notwithstanding.[60] Moreover, on February 11, after the Molotov text had finally been reprinted in the Chinese capital (without comment), Lin Po-ch'u, member of the CCP Central Committee, published an article in the Cominform journal, which, significantly, repeated once again that the "socialist camp" was "headed by the Soviet Union."[61] The only personality in the Chinese capital ever to quote Molotov's surprising words in public was J. M. Lomakin, the Soviet chargé in Peking, a man with a rather sinister past whose political survival, at that stage, was apparently linked to Molotov's fortunes. On February 14, at a ceremonial gathering commemorating the Sino-Soviet Treaty, which was attended by the Chinese leadership, the hapless Lomakin faithfully reiterated his chief's strange proposition that the Bloc was headed "by the USSR, or, it would be truer to say, by the Soviet Union and the Chinese People's Republic."[62] This was the first and last time any Soviet official, in Peking, Moscow, or elsewhere, was to give publicity to this statement. Chou En-lai, who delivered the official Chinese address on this occasion, pointedly refrained from any mention of Molotov's and Lomakin's "compliment"; in order to avoid committing himself on this point, Chou simply did not refer to the "socialist camp" and its leaders and, instead, was content to utter vague sentiments concerning "the peoples of China

---

[59] *Pravda*, April 26, 1954 (TASS dispatch from Peking); Peking Radio, domestic broadcast, at dictation speed, April 26, 1955.

[60] NCNA (New China News Agency), in English, February 9, 1955; Peking Radio, international broadcast, in English, February 9, 1955; first details of the speech appeared on February 10 in NCNA, Peking.

[61] NCNA, in English, February 13, 1955 (the Cominform journal actually appeared on February 11).

[62] Ibid., February 14, 1955.

and the Soviet Union, together with all peace-loving countries. . . ."[63]

The question remains: What exactly prompted Molotov to raise
such a thorny issue at all? It may well be that he really had very
little choice. As has been pointed out,[64] just a few months earlier
Khrushchev had wooed Mao assiduously (and was to continue
doing so throughout 1955); the habit started in 1953 by Malenkov
of treating the Chinese leader as an arbiter in the Moscow power
struggle had become deeply ingrained. (Perhaps it is not too
fanciful to note an ironic reference to this practice in Molotov's
very odd phrase "headed by the USSR, or, *it would be truer to say*,
by the Soviet Union and the Chinese People's Republic" (author's
emphasis). There is no room in the Soviet ideological dictionary
for two operative slogans on the same subject, one of which is
merely "truer" than the other. However, Molotov's words acquire
different overtones if regarded as a slightly sarcastic comment
upon a sad state of affairs. One may then detect some echoes of
the unkind remark that the notoriously matriarchal Doe family
is "headed by [henpecked] Mr. John Doe, or, it would perhaps
be truer to say, by Mr. and Mrs. Doe.")[65] Although Molotov could
not very well ignore his opponents' courtship of Mao, the senior
surviving personality in the international communist arena, he was
unable, and perhaps unwilling, to outbid them by sacrificing
meager Soviet resources and long-established national interests to
an insatiable Peking. Under these circumstances, the mental acrobatics of his February 8 speech appear to constitute a convenient
tactical device for resolving a difficult problem. Molotov hoped,
perhaps, that by paying such far-reaching verbal homage to Mao's
status in the Bloc, that is, by acknowledging Peking as an equal to
Moscow, he would greatly flatter Chinese vanities and thus obscure
the fact that the CPR would gain no practical advantages from
his concessions. (If there was an ironic note in the February 8
address, Molotov would probably expect Mao's inflated self-esteem
to deafen him to such subtleties.)

[63] Ibid.
[64] See "Realignment in the Kremlin" earlier in this chapter.
[65] That Molotov's "compliment" was anything but sincere is indicated by
significant evidence of a general coolness in the relations between him and
Peking. For example, the Soviet Foreign Minister, although in Moscow, did
not attend the Chinese ambassador's ceremonial presentation of credentials to
President Voroshilov. Only junior foreign service representatives were present
(NCNA, in English, February 8, 1955).

The Soviet Foreign Minister cannot have expected to outbid his opponents by such means, but he may well have hoped that his maneuver would suffice to cancel out the advantages they had already secured in Peking and would thus neutralize Mao as a potentially adverse influence in the Kremlin power contest. The fact that the Chinese leaders simply ignored Molotov's overtures probably caused him to instruct Lomakin to bring the February 8 statement prominently to their notice. Chou En-lai's cold disregard of Molotov's and Lomakin's words seemed to imply that Peking was taking sides in the Moscow factional struggle against the Soviet Foreign Minister. The Chinese, no doubt, preferred Khrushchev's material, territorial, and other enticements to Molotov's transparent prestige offer. Peking's attitude, as will be seen, was soon to prove of major importance in determining the outcome of internal disputes between the Russian leaders over such issues as Soviet policy toward the Near East.

It was precisely the Near East that constituted the second major subject of unusual contradictions in Molotov's February 8 address. The words of the Soviet Foreign Minister on this topic were particularly inconsistent, marking an almost unprecedented departure from his traditional norms of preciseness, not to say pedantry. This inconsistency may be appreciated all the more easily by contrasting his treatment of the Near East with his survey of Asian affairs, which, in two separate portions of the speech, immediately preceded the passage dealing with the Near East.

Part I of the Soviet Foreign Minister's review analyzed "Changes in the International Situation"; it noted with satisfaction the transformation of the Asian scene that had resulted from the communist seizure of power in China, North Korea, and North Vietnam and the creation of truly independent states in India, Indonesia, and Burma. Proceeding logically from this analysis, Part III of his address then surveyed Soviet bilateral relations with each of the countries concerned, stressing that friendly ties had now been established not only with the Asian communist regimes but also with the genuinely independent noncommunist governments in that region (namely, India, Indonesia, and Burma).

No such coherency or logic could be found in Molotov's treatment of the Near Eastern situation: as in his Asian analysis, his Near Eastern survey opened with the promising words, "Quite a number of changes have likewise occurred in the Near and Middle East." However, with a notable lack of consistency, he then proceeded to stress that actually there had been no real change in this part of the world, and the Arab countries, now as previously, remained mere dependencies of the West:

We cannot say that the National Liberation Movement in the Arab East, for example, has attained the power and scope which distinguish that movement in a number of Asian countries. The countries in this area, especially those which possess substantial oil deposits, are still painfully dependent on so-called "Western" countries, which have seized control of their oil and other natural resources. It so happens that in these areas governments are formed and deposed only at the will of American and British oil companies and other foreign capitalist concerns.

Molotov could find no relief whatever in this doleful scene, except by making the traditional obeisance to the "National Liberation Movement," which, he said with more pious hope than conviction, was "steadily growing nonetheless."[66]

Although Molotov did not mention a single exception to the rule that Arab countries were mere satellites of the West, with governments that were but fronts for various foreign companies (stressing only that the oil producers were even more enslaved than the rest), he continued, in Part III of his address, to draw conclusions that were diametrically opposed to his premises:

Auspicious facts have lately marked the relations between the Soviet Union and the Arab countries, with the exception of Iraq. . . . It is presumably known in the Arab countries that the people of the USSR entertain friendly feelings for them and that in the Soviet Union they have had, and will have, a reliable support in the defense of their sovereignty and national independence.

If, in truth, the Arab states were "painfully dependent" upon the West, which could depose their governments "at will," how then was it possible that the West had permitted "auspicious facts" to appear in the relationships between the USSR and those same countries? In his review of the Asian situation, Molotov had taken good care, before agreeing that Soviet relations with India, Indonesia, and Burma had, indeed, improved, to note that these were the very states which had "shaken off" colonialism and now enjoyed "genuine national freedom," unlike some other Asian coun-

[66] *Pravda,* February 9, 1955.

tries. Moscow's official doctrine has, of course, always contended that it is a hallmark of genuine independence for an Afro-Asian country to be friendly with the USSR, while dependence upon the "imperialists" can hardly lead to anything better than a one-sided relationship with the West. Why, then, did Molotov's February 8 statement first go out of its way to brand the Arab governments (without exception) as mere Western puppets and then proceed to stress that their relations with the USSR had not only improved but that Moscow would support "the defense of their sovereignty and national independence"? Which Soviet leader has ever believed that governments "formed and deposed only at the will of American and British oil companies and other foreign capitalist concerns" possess any "sovereignty and national independence" for Moscow to defend? Such absurdities have a place neither in Bolshevik philosophy nor in elementary logic, any more than does a paragraph that starts with an assertion that the situation has changed, only to prove that everything has remained as it was.

Almost immediately after the Soviet Foreign Minister delivered his address, several signs indicated that the confusion enveloping his Near Eastern passages had resulted from political infighting rather than from a lack of clear thinking. It will be recalled that, between the second week of February and the early part of March, Khrushchev found it possible to exploit the political constellation to entrench himself more securely and to launch a series of attacks upon Molotov's position and policies.[67] It has already been noted that one of the means employed by the Khrushchev faction to diminish the Soviet Foreign Minister's authority was to "correct" his statements—this being the treatment that was applied, for instance, to Molotov's analysis of the precise stages of development achieved by individual communist countries.[68] Similarly tortuous methods were employed by Molotov's adversaries for the purpose of giving a new slant to his comments on the Near Eastern situation. A closer look at the details of "operation rewrite" provides some indications as to which of the two contradictory paragraphs on the Near East reflected Molotov's own opinions and which represented the views of his opponents.

A version of the February 8 address that was printed a few days later in *New Times*, for distribution abroad, significantly attempted

---

[67] See "Realignment in the Kremlin" earlier in this chapter.
[68] See discussion earlier in this section.

to tone down the passage in which Molotov had made sharply derogatory remarks about the lack of independence demonstrated by the Arab governments. The Soviet Foreign Minister had originally stated, "it so happens that in these areas governments are formed and deposed only at the will of American and British oil companies and other foreign capitalist concerns."[69] Presented in this form, the sentence left no doubt that, basically, *all* Arab governments had to be regarded as Western puppets; in the "revised" version, however, the important little word "only" disappeared, and Molotov's remark was watered down still further by changing "it so happens that in these areas governments are formed and deposed only at the will . . ." to "it also happens in these parts that governments are formed and deposed at the will. . . ." (The latter phrase implied that such self-abasing conduct was the exception rather than the rule, whereas Molotov had made the point that this norm of political behavior prevailed throughout the "Arab East.")[70]

Moreover, the Soviet Foreign Minister's derogatory opinions about the Arab regimes not only suffered emasculation but were completely ignored by the media throughout the Bloc. On the other hand, a considerable amount of publicity was given to the second Near Eastern reference in the February 8 speech, which took a diametrically opposed view of the Arab world. It fully acknowledged the "sovereignty and national independence" of the Arab governments as a serious factor on the world scene and broadly hinted at "auspicious" developments in Soviet-Arab relations, including a Russian offer of "reliable support" (that is, aid) for the "defense" of certain Arab countries. Whoever edited the February 8 statement for publication duly added the word "applause" at the end of this paragraph, as an indication that it was to be regarded as particularly significant. A few days later, *Pravda* and *Izvestia* resorted to the time-honored device of quoting the reports published by leftist newspapers abroad (in this case, Arabic journals), which had "translated" the Molotov speech into terms acceptable to their local public. By reprinting these interpretations without comment, the Soviet press was actually giving Moscow's imprimatur to an entirely new version of the February 8 address. Thus *Pravda* and *Izvestia* approvingly quoted a Lebanese news-

69 *Pravda*, February 9, 1955.
70 *New Times*, no. 7, February 12, 1955.

paper in whose view the Soviet Foreign Minister's statement had promised

that the Arab peoples . . . can look to the Soviet Union for support in defending their sovereignty and independence. This . . . is a *guarantee* of independence . . . for the people of the Arab countries. It is all the more valuable because the Soviet Union is not demanding in return for this guarantee a single iota of territory, intervention in . . . internal affairs or concessions.[71]

In this manner, the Soviet press was extending to the Arab countries a measure of Russian commitment that, in fact, could be read into the February 8 statement only with a great deal of imagination.

It is especially noteworthy that the Czechoslovak media entered the ranks of "interpreters" of the February 8 address at this particular moment (when, as has been noted, their "trade" delegation was on the brink of departure for Cairo to negotiate the grant of Czech credits to Egypt for the purchase of arms). In an editorial paraphrasing Molotov's words, the organ of the Czech party completely reversed the implications of the Foreign Minister's scornful comments on Arab politics by perpetrating the following distortion: "The National Liberation Movement is also gaining strength, despite all the hateful countermeasures of the foreign monopolies, in the countries of the Near and Middle East";[72] one "minor" detail was simply omitted, namely, Molotov's belief that the governments of the Arab countries were mere puppets of the aforementioned Western monopolies. Shortly afterward, the Czechoslovak Radio, in commenting on the policies promulgated during the recent session of the Supreme Soviet, stressed that they would "result in the further raising of the defense capabilities of the Soviet Union" and of Moscow's ability to aid certain "backward countries."[73]

To sum up: immediately after the presentation of Molotov's speech, the Soviet and Czechoslovak media consistently played down and emasculated his contemptuous remarks about the Arab governments, at the same time publicizing and expanding the implications of the opposing passage in the same address, which

[71] *Pravda* and *Izvestia*, February 12, 1955 (quoting a TASS message from Beirut, February 11, 1955); author's emphasis.
[72] *Rudé Právo* (Prague), February 10, 1955.
[73] Commentary by Dusan Ruppelt, Bratislava Radio, in Slovak, February 13, 1955.

offered Russian support to the Arab leaders. There is hardly more than one way of interpreting these data. As the present study has attempted to show, the February 8 statement consisted of passages representing Molotov's views, which his adversaries promptly repudiated, and sections reflecting Khrushchev's opinions, which Molotov, in effect, repudiated during subsequent months. In the period after February 8, the new balance of forces in Moscow left little doubt about whose hands were closest to the reins of power and who, therefore, was best situated to manipulate and reshape the Kremlin's policy. As has been noted, Khrushchev appeared to be achieving increasingly firm control in Moscow between the second week of February and early March, while Molotov suffered a series of major setbacks during the same period.[74] Moreover, there are indications that Khrushchev and his Central Committee Secretariat were coming to regard Soviet relations with Czechoslovakia (and with other Bloc countries) as falling within their exclusive domain,[75] so that the media in that country presumably were beginning to reflect some of the foreign policy views held by the Khrushchev faction. As for the Soviet media, there is considerable evidence that *Pravda*, under Khrushchev's retainer Shepilov, was at that time tending to become the First Secretary's house organ.[76] It seems reasonable, therefore, to conclude that Molotov's cutting remarks about Arab regimes, which were systematically censored in Moscow and Prague after February 8, did, in fact, express the Foreign Minister's personal views, while the contrary passage, advocating a Soviet-Arab entente, which the Bloc media played up in every possible way, actually represented the opinions of the victorious Khrushchev group.

If the analysis outlined earlier in this study is correct, it would

[74] Thus Molotov not only had to sulk in his tent, alone, during the Soviet leadership's "unity" appearance on the evening of February 8, but suffered a dilution in rank on February 28 and was subjected, on March 10, to the humiliation of seeing Tito's personal attack on his policies appear, without comment, in the pages of *Pravda* (see "Realignment in the Kremlin" earlier in this chapter).

[75] Ibid.

[76] This does not mean that *Pravda* could unilaterally alter the Russian text of Molotov's speech, the day after it had been delivered in the heart of Moscow before a large audience (including foreign observers) and fully reported by TASS. It was much simpler to "adjust" this important document by means of a very loose "translation," for distribution abroad, in *New Times*, or by having *Pravda* reprint imaginative Arab newspaper interpretations of key passages in the statement (as has been noted).

seem that the Kremlin's Near Eastern "debate" must have developed along the following lines: the original Molotov draft of the foreign policy statement, prepared during or immediately after the January plenum of the Central Committee, apparently shunned all thought of a Soviet thrust into the Near East. (As the Foreign Minister had indicated with scorn, the governments in the "Arab East" could not be regarded as independent agents; consequently, a Soviet offensive into the region would not be able to rely on the support of trustworthy partners.) It is quite possible, as was pointed out earlier,[77] that Molotov himself, at the time when the statement was first drafted, may have been unaware of the degree of intimacy that had already been achieved in Cairo, Ankara, and elsewhere between representatives of certain branches of the Soviet and Egyptian governments. Khrushchev may well have exploited his control over these particular channels of external communications to keep Molotov in the dark, as part of his premeditated campaign to shunt the Soviet Foreign Minister aside.

In any case, by the end of the first week of February, Molotov could no longer have been ignorant of the true state of affairs, since at that time Moscow must have requested the Czechoslovak government to dispatch its "trade" delegation to Cairo.[78] As the present study has indicated, it was precisely at this moment that the power balance in the Kremlin shifted; resorting to adroit tactical maneuvers, Khrushchev was apparently able to outflank Molotov and have Bulganin endorsed as the prospective candidate for the Soviet premiership.[79] It seems that he followed up on his

[77] See chap. 3, "Indications of Clandestine Contacts," and "Realignment in the Kremlin" earlier in this chapter. It is improbable that Molotov began work on his draft much earlier than the last days of January, when the proposal to demote Malenkov was presented to the Central Committee plenum and it appeared that the Foreign Minister might finally be able to write a new foreign policy platform conforming to his own predilections. By that time, covert Soviet-Egyptian contacts in Cairo (clandestine trade), in Ankara, and in Moscow (Khaled Mohieddin) seem already to have taken place. Since, as this analysis has attempted to establish, Molotov's original text contained nothing but scorn for the Arab governments, it would hardly be reasonable to assume that he knowingly offended personalities with whom Moscow, at that very moment, was establishing delicate, intimate, and most significant relations. Conceivably, therefore, in this as in many other instances, the head of the Foreign Ministry may not have known at the time what the less overt services of his government were doing. In any case, it is fairly obvious that he could not have approved of their actions.
[78] See chap. 3, "Toward a Revised Chronology" and "Early Signs of Soviet-Egyptian Rapport."
[79] See "Realignment in the Kremlin" earlier in this chapter.

success by contesting key passages in Molotov's draft, which were originally prepared at a time when the Foreign Minister's authority still appeared to be undiminished. Thus several issues simultaneously came to a head at this point: Khrushchev was challenging both Molotov's prestige and his policies, while the Soviet Foreign Minister was stubbornly resisting Khrushchev's "private enterprise" in meddling with the Moscow-Peking and Moscow-Belgrade relationships and in arranging a Near Eastern fait accompli behind his (Molotov's) back.

Many signs point to a confrontation between the Soviet Foreign Minister and his opponents, literally hours before Molotov's address to the Supreme Soviet was due to be delivered,[80] with the Khrushchev faction pressing for major changes in the draft of the new government's foreign policy platform, especially its Near Eastern passages. Molotov's adversaries no doubt desired the inclusion of a statement outlining a new Soviet approach toward the Arab world. Molotov's original text, with its Europe-centered concept of international affairs,[81] provided a notably uncongenial atmosphere for such a change of policy, especially in view of the Foreign Minister's obvious skepticism about the feasibility of finding dependable allies among the Arab governments. It seems that, during the last-minute battle over Molotov's draft, Khrushchev and his supporters finally succeeded in introducing some important corrections and additions, including the paragraph that offered Russian support to the states of the "Arab East." However, Molotov's resistance appears to have been particularly stubborn, and it is evident that he was able to protect the greater part of his original text; his natural resentment at Khrushchev's meddling in his bailiwick presumably added to his determination.[82] In any

80 See the opening paragraphs of this section.
81 See footnote 3 in this chapter.
82 The facts seem to show that the final version of the February 8 address, although it appears to have been radically revised, was still considered far from satisfactory by the Khrushchev faction. One of the somewhat formalistic indications of their displeasure can be found in the text of the Supreme Soviet's motion of approval, passed at the end of the foreign affairs "debate." As first reported by TASS, the motion stated, "having heard and discussed the report of . . . V. M. Molotov . . . on . . . the Foreign Policy of the Soviet Government, the Supreme Soviet . . . resolves: to approve *this policy* [author's emphasis] of the Soviet Government" (TASS, in Russian, Hellschreiber to Europe, February 9, 1955). In other words, the Supreme Soviet was asked to approve Soviet Policy as defined in Molotov's speech. Some hours later, however, *Pravda* subtly modified the text of the motion, which was now reported as stating, "having heard and discussed the report of . . . V. M. Molotov . . .

case, according to all the indications, there simply was not sufficient time to permit thorough reediting of the revised foreign
policy document, so that several of the original passages were
retained, which completely contradicted some of the new additions.
With regard to the Near Eastern paragraphs, such mishaps were
quite understandable. Since the pro- and anti-Arab passages appeared in different sections of the document—Parts III and I, respectively—conflicting statements and inconsistencies could well
have been overlooked in the rush.[83] The analyst, however, must
be duly grateful that these clues were not eliminated, since it is
with their help that he can attempt to retrace one of the less
documented developments in Soviet diplomatic history (which
culminated, moreover, in a particularly dramatic dénouement).

The particular value of this background material on the February
8 statement is due to the fact that it tends to confirm the date at
which the Soviet leadership became embroiled in squabbles over
future policy toward the Near East. It is hardly likely to be a mere
coincidence that the Molotov-Khrushchev dispute over Near Eastern (and other) issues can be placed, with some assurance, at a
point midway between the January plenum and the elevation of
Bulganin to the premiership, namely, during the first week of
February 1955; in other words, it predated by only a few days the

---

on . . . the Foreign Policy of the Soviet Government, the Supreme Soviet . . .
resolves: to approve *the foreign policy* [author's emphasis] of the Soviet Government" (*Pravda,* February 10, 1955). The *Pravda* text thus carefully avoided
giving specific endorsement to Molotov's report.

[83] At that particular moment, Molotov cannot have been in an entirely en-
viable position as far as his resistance to Khrushchev's Near Eastern ambitions
was concerned. For what it was worth, the Foreign Minister could feel that
he had every right to be indignant about Khrushchev's underhanded meddling
in this and other areas of international affairs. As will be seen, Molotov undoubtedly continued, then and subsequently, to express the gravest misgivings
with regard to the desirability of any Near Eastern adventure. However, as a
matter of realism, it was not practicable for him to reject the inclusion in the
foreign policy platform of a paragraph that, after all, merely gave verbal recognition to the fait accompli his rivals were already establishing in the Near
East. With the Czechoslovak "trade" delegation about to set out for Cairo, it
was simply too late for Molotov (even had there been a more favorable constellation within the CPSU Presidium) to try and veto Moscow's offer of
"reliable support" to the Arab world. On the other hand, if, under pressure of
time, his opponents failed to observe that Molotov's original anti-Arab paragraph had not been expunged from his text, the Foreign Minister, on his part,
had reason to be gleeful (since his warnings about the true nature of the Arab
regimes had been fortuitously preserved and would thus be voiced from the
rostrum of the Supreme Soviet).

departure of the Czech "trade" delegation for Cairo. Thus it appears to be a reasonable assumption that the Kremlin "debate" was, in fact, triggered by a leakage of information about the clandestine preparations for a Soviet arms deal with Egypt, which had been made during January (presumably at Khrushchev's behest).

Further Corroboration of the Circumstantial Evidence

Fortunately, in this instance (as in the case of the chronology of the Arms Deal itself), it has proved possible to supplement detailed circumstantial evidence with testimony of a less circuitous nature. There is published information supporting the assumption that there were, indeed, disputes in the Kremlin over the political desirability of a Soviet-Egyptian arms deal, that it was mainly Molotov who objected, and that it was Khrushchev who pressed on with the operation, regardless of all opposition.

Some years after the conclusion of the transaction, the Egyptian minister of war, Muhammad Abdul Hakim Amer, while touring Moscow as a guest of the Soviet government, thanked Khrushchev personally because, he asserted, the First Secretary had "done everything for the Soviet government to adopt the historic decision to supply us with arms."[84] Amer's statement indicated quite clearly that Khrushchev had been obliged to apply pressure before the rest of the Soviet leadership would go along with the Arms Deal; in other words, the First Secretary had encountered opposition in the Kremlin. That this had, in fact, been the case was confirmed during Khrushchev's 1964 visit to Egypt, when he chatted for hours, on board the Soviet ship *Armeniya*, with Muhammad Hasanayn Haykal, editor of *al-Ahram*. Khrushchev stressed that

Egypt's resistance to military pacts in 1955 impressed us but we did not imagine that this resistance could display such long endurance . . . *even after* we had agreed to conclude the arms deal, *some* [author's emphasis] thought that this deal was a tactical move on the part of Egypt and that Egypt, once the West was reconciled with it, would soon return to the Western sphere of influence.[85]

The obvious implication of this statement was that certain Soviet

---

[84] Moscow Radio, in Arabic, December 8 and 9, 1960.
[85] *Al-Ahram*, May 15, 1964; MENA, Cairo, in Arabic, May 15, 1964.

leaders had objected to the arms agreement both before and after it was concluded. (In communist parlance, "some," "some people," "certain people" are usually aesopian references to dissident voices within the communist camp.)

As to the precise identity of "some" people in the Kremlin who had suspected Nasser of regarding his agreement with Moscow as a mere "tactical move" to impress the West, Khrushchev informed Haykal in another conversation exactly whom he had in mind. During one of Haykal's trips to Moscow, the First Secretary told him that it had been "*Molotov* [who had] wanted to keep Russia away" from the Near East; however, he, Khrushchev, had "considered this would be catastrophic," because he knew "that a defensive policy was wrong, that attack was the best means of defense, and that flexible diplomacy was needed." The First Secretary, therefore, "decided to support those [in the Near East] who rejected Western domination, in order to ensure that [the region] was not turned into a military base directed against Russia."[86] In a word, Khrushchev had demanded and Molotov had rejected an "offensive foreign policy" in the Near East. One reason for Molotov's attitude was mentioned by Haykal on another occasion, when analyzing the international problems faced by the Nasser regime during its first years. Haykal indicated that, in spite of the parallel interests of the two governments, Soviet-Egyptian relations remained "distant and obscure" for a while, mainly because of one man, "Foreign Minister Molotov [who] only [had] eyes for Western Europe."[87]

Haykal's information seems to have been accurate; as late as February 8, 1955, Molotov insisted that Europe must not "be relegated to the background," however much importance some people might ascribe to Asia.[88] There were, indeed, valid reasons why such a Europe-centered policy could not be compatible with a Soviet thrust into the Near East. As has been noted,[89] communist power in Eastern Europe had, by the 1950s, become increasingly

[86] Reuters, in English, to South Africa, November 24, 1957 (author's emphasis). Haykal revealed the details of his conversation with Khrushchev upon returning from Moscow.

[87] Muhammad Hasanayn Haykal, "Political Enquiry," pt. 2 (Cairo Radio, domestic broadcast, December 21, 1958). Haykal repeated this view several years later, when he stressed that, "influenced by Molotov," Moscow had "devoted most of [its] attention to the European question" in the early 1950s (Cairo Radio, domestic broadcast, March 17, 1967).

[88] *Pravda*, February 9, 1955.

[89] See chap. 1, "Soviet-Egyptian Convergence."

precarious, and it was essential to gain a breathing spell so that
Moscow might have an opportunity to consolidate its position. The
Soviet leader who appears to have been most deeply conscious
of the economic and social weaknesses affecting the USSR and its
East European allies was Molotov, as his February 8 address
illustrated so vividly.[90] The Soviet Foreign Minister left his
audience under no illusions concerning the length of time required to overcome these difficiencies;[91] yet Moscow's problems
could not be tackled unless the West were kept reasonably inactive. For this purpose, it was incumbent upon the USSR to
pursue a policy of great caution and conservatism, in the hope
that the West might rest content, for the time being, to accept the
de facto partition of Europe, so that the communist system east of
the Elbe would have the necessary respite to take root. Since
a Soviet political offensive into the strategically important Near
East could not but provoke the West into counteraction, the shaky
communist regimes of Eastern Europe might provide a tempting
target. This does not mean that Molotov in any sense wished to
appease the West. On the contrary, he clearly believed it would
be possible for Russia to safeguard the status quo by adopting a
convincing deterrent posture and by refraining from exposure of
her obvious weaknesses through futile exercises in summitry[92]
(since any attempt to negotiate an over-all settlement was bound
to produce results that would reflect the real, unfavorable, balance
of power). However, there are significant indications that he was
equally opposed to needless provocation of the West.

It must also be remembered that Molotov had been weaned on
the classical Leninist doctrine of foreign policy, according to which
a relatively weak USSR could operate successfully by exploiting
"radical antagonisms" within the Western camp.[93] In the 1950s,
with the prevention of German rearmament high on Moscow's
agenda, the Leninist approach required that France and Britain
should be persuaded to oppose this and other by-products of U.S.

[90] See "Molotov's February 8 Speech" earlier in this chapter.
[91] He stressed that the way toward the achievement of Moscow's goals
covered "a long historical period of which, so far, we have lived through only
a little more than 37 years" (*Pravda*, February 9, 1955).
[92] "Molotov . . . denied the advisability of establishing personal contacts
between the Soviet leaders and the statesmen of other countries" ("Resolution
of the Central Committee of the CPSU, June 29, 1957," ibid., July 4, 1957).
[93] Lenin's Moscow address of December 6, 1920; see V. I. Lenin, *Collected
Works*, vol. 31 (Moscow: Progress Publishers, 1966), p. 442.

policy in Europe. Needless to say, a Soviet incursion into the Near East, so far from detaching Paris and London from Washington, was likely to have the opposite effect; at that time, British and French imperial interests were, if anything, more vitally affected by the fate of the Near East (and its strategic oil reserves) than was the United States. It was to be expected that, if this sensitive nerve were touched, Western Europe, so far from turning against America, would cling all the more tightly to the Atlantic alliance. These were precisely the considerations that persuaded Molotov to refrain, for some time, from any direct Soviet counterattack against Western defense schemes in the Near East[94] and to concentrate, instead, on a propaganda campaign, which suggested that the Turkish-Iraqi pact and similar developments were merely American devices to oust British influence from the region.[95] However, according to one important source, the Foreign Minister's outlook was not widely shared in Moscow, where "the importance of the [Near East defense] Pact was somewhat exaggerated . . . and its conclusion was seen as a failure of Molotov's policy in the [Near] East. Among the reasons for Molotov's subsequent eclipse was the [Near] Eastern situation."[96]

The Soviet Foreign Minister's caution was no doubt due to his awareness of the fact that Western amphibious striking forces controlled the maritime approaches to Afro-Asia, so that any major Soviet thrust into the Near East was likely to leave the USSR in a particularly vulnerable and exposed position. Moreover, as Molotov saw it, the Russians would eventually find themselves isolated in the Near East, since the local regimes were both unstable and dependent on the West.[97] Thus even radical leaders like Nasser could not be trusted to adopt a long-term policy of unwavering support for the USSR. The Soviet Foreign Minister suspected that Arab politicians would simply exploit a temporary rapprochement with the USSR for the purpose of inducing the West to outbid the Russians.[98] Consequently, the prospect of a spectacular Soviet coup in the Near East did not tempt him; he realized that Russian gains could be made but not consolidated as long as the Soviet presence in the region depended almost entirely on local partners

[94] See Appendix to this chapter, "A Note Concerning Molotov's Position."
[95] See chap. 1, "The Soviet View."
[96] Dallin, *Soviet Foreign Policy*, p. 388.
[97] See "Molotov's February 8 Speech" earlier in this chapter.
[98] See footnotes 85 and 86 in this chapter.

whose reliability was dubious, to say the least. Molotov indicated that he preferred concentrating on the slow and laborious task of building up the "National Liberation Movement," namely, the Afro-Asian communist parties allied to radical elements among the nationalist intellectuals.[99]

In the end, of course, the issue was not decided by the objective validity of the respective arguments advanced by the rival factions. Another factor prevailed: the power constellation that had developed at the end of the first week of February was simply not conducive to success for the Molotov line. As has been noted, sometime between February 5 and 8 Khrushchev was able to make the Presidium endorse Bulganin's candidacy for the premiership and to inflict a number of major setbacks on Molotov.[100] The Foreign Minister had barely delivered his February 8 address, with its pessimistic appraisal of the Arab regimes, when the Czechoslovak "trade" delegation arrived in Cairo and the first major step was taken toward the conclusion of an arms deal with Egypt. However, it soon transpired that Molotov had only lost a battle, not the war. Several developments occurred that, between them, did much to delay and obstruct the natural consummation of the arrangements initiated in January and February.

After February 8

During March and April 1955, events in Moscow, Cairo, and on the international scene seemed to be conspiring to undermine the foundations that had been successfully laid, a few weeks earlier, by the advocates of the Egyptian Arms Deal. The first of these developments concerned the implementation of a proposal that had been advanced ever since the early days of the Malenkov ad-

---

[99] The history of the last decade by no means proves that Khrushchev's exuberant policies of constant overcommitment in the Third World produced more tangible benefits for the Soviet national interest than would have resulted from Molotov's cautious, conservative methods. The Foreign Minister's approach certainly would have cost less—economically, militarily, technically, diplomatically, and in terms of Soviet prestige. Molotov apparently had good cause for believing that the new regimes in the Third World would not be sufficiently dependable, amenable to control, stable, or grateful to compensate Moscow for the dangers and disadvantages of an Afro-Asian entanglement; nor, perhaps, were the returns of Khrushchev's policy commensurate with the ideological price paid by the "World's First Socialist State" in persistently sacrificing Afro-Asian communist parties to the whims of the local dictators.
[100] See "Realignment in the Kremlin" earlier in this chapter.

ministration, namely, a summit meeting of the leaders of the four great powers. At the beginning of the fourth week of March, the summit became, to all intents and purposes, a reality when the USSR accepted the general framework suggested by the Western governments. At that time, as is now known, the Presidium of the CPSU was meeting to discuss key issues in foreign affairs, of which Moscow's relationship with Belgrade was one,[101] and the forthcoming summit meeting at Geneva must obviously have been another. There can be little doubt that Molotov's adversaries at this point found themselves in something of a quandary. According to all the evidence, they were the very people who favored a summit conference with the West;[102] yet, at the same time, they were also the advocates of an arms deal with Egypt. It required no great insight to understand that the Russian leaders could hardly go to Geneva expecting to divide the Western camp with a policy of sudden cordiality if, at that very moment, Western statesmen discovered that a Soviet offensive was thrusting deeply into the heart of their position in the Near East. Presumably, an experienced politician like Molotov would not have been slow to point out the inherent inconsistency shown by his rivals in attempting to pursue both these conflicting lines of approach simultaneously. Under the circumstances, the Presidium could hardly do less than delay the Arms Deal, at least until the conclusion of the Geneva conference.

This obstacle was by no means the only one encountered by Khrushchev during that period. In the Kremlin power struggle, between early February and mid-March, the First Secretary had maintained the momentum of his advance so spectacularly as to arouse dire apprehensions in the bosoms of all his associates, who thought they were beginning to see shades of Stalin. Consequently, a temporary coalition of disparate elements frightened by Khrushchev seems to have gathered in the second half of March, lasting, apparently, until the late spring. Suddenly, the Soviet media carried cryptic warnings about the proper limits of a Party Secretary's powers, quoting jurisdictional definitions attributed to Lenin, while an esoteric battle was joined over the issue of Khrushchev's correct title ("First" or "first" Secretary), accompanied by enigmatic references to Stalin's precise position during the final months

---

[101] See Bialer testimony.
[102] See "Further Corroboration" earlier in this chapter.

of his life.[103] In such an atmosphere, Molotov probably found it much easier than seven weeks previously to gain a hearing for his admonitions regarding the drawbacks and dangers of a Soviet adventure in the Near East; there was now much more opposition to Khrushchev and, for a consummate tactician like the Soviet Foreign Minister, the forthcoming Geneva summit conference provided a convenient excuse to reconsider the Egyptian Arms Deal. He could very well challenge his opponents to make up their minds: if they insisted on a summit conference, they should at least refrain from actions likely to sabotage it.

However, the best argument for a reappraisal in the Kremlin of Khrushchev's activist Near Eastern policy was provided by Cairo itself.

Appendix to Chapter 4:
A Note Concerning Molotov's Position

It is important to understand why, in spite of the serious considerations outlined here, Molotov was unable to prevent the periodic resuscitation, during the years 1951–1955, of the plan for a Soviet-Egyptian arms deal.[104] One should remember, of course, that from 1949 to 1953 Molotov did not head the Foreign Ministry, having been replaced by A. Ya. Vyshinski; moreover, although Molotov was formally a full member of the Politburo (Presidium) and Vyshinski was not, there are strong indications that Molotov was in growing disfavor, while Vyshinski enjoyed direct access to Stalin.[105] Even after Molotov returned to the Foreign Ministry following Stalin's death, he immediately became engulfed in a fierce power struggle and, during the Malenkov period, never gathered sufficient support to rise higher than the No. 3 position in the Kremlin hierarchy. In any case, as has been noted,[106] plans concerning semiclandestine military relationships seem traditionally

---

[103] Conquest, *Power and Policy in the U.S.S.R.*, pp. 263–264, and Rush, *Rise of Khrushchev*, pp. 12–25.

[104] See chap. 1, "Arms Aid"; chap. 2, "Inconsistencies and Misinterpretations"; and the beginning of chap. 3.

[105] See Conquest, *Power and Policy in the U.S.S.R.*, p. 183, and Dallin, *Soviet Foreign Policy*, pp. 3–9.

[106] See chap. 2, "Inconsistencies and Misinterpretations," and chap. 3, "Indications of Clandestine Contacts."

to have emanated from the GRU, where Molotov's influence was apparently very limited. However, he undoubtedly did enjoy sufficient standing in the Presidium to delay, if not to veto altogether, operations in the international sphere of which he disapproved; the fact remains that, prior to 1955, none of the schemes for an Egyptian arms deal reached fruition (although, perhaps, this was also due in some measure to misgivings on Cairo's part). In January–February 1955, an entirely new situation prevailed. As the present study has indicated, the moves to oust Malenkov created a constellation that was initially favorable to Molotov; consequently, after months of enduring Khrushchev's attempts to shunt him aside, the Foreign Minister made a stand on matters he considered to be of significance not only politically but also in his jurisdictional conflict with his rival. GRU operations in the Near East belonged precisely to this category. However, Khrushchev was gradually able to outflank Molotov in the power struggle and, as a result, to force him into concessions on policy issues, although, as will be seen, final and complete victory was by no means yet in Khrushchev's grasp. The First Secretary, on his part, supported a more adventurous policy in the Near East because of a mixture of considerations; as his own statement to Haykal indicated,[107] he was temperamentally disinclined to tolerate for long any policy that could be regarded, however remotely, as passive. Moreover, Molotov's apparent inability to wreck Western defense plans in the Near East obviously provided his adversary with a tempting issue on which to challenge the Foreign Minister's position. In any case, there is no doubt that, in January–February 1955, at least as convincing and powerful a case could be presented in favor of an arms deal with Egypt as against it.[108] Molotov faced a particularly difficult task in contending against Khrushchev's Near Eastern adventure at a time when the First Secretary could support his line with unusually strong and tempting arguments, while the Foreign Minister could counter only with a basically negative proposal for a passive "wait and see" policy.

[107] See "Further Corroboration" earlier in this chapter.
[108] For some of the reasons why, in 1955, a Soviet operation of this nature seemed to provide a tailor-made answer to Moscow's Near Eastern requirements, see chap. 1, "The Soviet View," "Soviet-Egyptian Convergence," and "Arms Aid."

5 Between Moscow, Peking, and Washington

As was noted earlier, Khrushchev has testified that "even after we had agreed to conclude the arms deal, some thought that this deal was a tactical move on the part of Egypt and that Egypt, once the West was reconciled with it, would soon return to the Western sphere of influence."[1] Egyptian evidence confirms that, at this time (late March–early April),

there was a discussion going on in Moscow, but the views and arguments could not be resolved. There were conflicting views and trends at the Soviet Foreign Ministry regarding . . . Gamal Abd an-Nasser's policy. Did he really believe in the policy of nonalignment, which would cost its author a great deal in an area dominated and controlled by Western influence? Or did the dispute between him and the West revolve on matters of detail—a question of the price Abd an-Nasser asked and the price the West offered, so that when agreement was reached on details, the clamor would subside and Gamal Abd an-Nasser would take his position within the West's military plans.[2]

---

[1] See chap. 4, "Further Corroboration."

[2] Muhammad Hasanayn Haykal, "Political Enquiry," pt. 4 (Cairo Radio, domestic broadcast, December 25, 1958). Haykal indicates that these arguments were to be heard in Moscow during the weeks immediately preceding the Nasser–Chou En-lai meeting (which occurred at the time of the Bandung Conference), i.e., in late March–early April 1955.

Cairo Between East and West

The personalities in the Soviet Foreign Ministry who opposed an arms deal with Egypt had good reason to raise such questions just then. It has already been noted that, in late January and early February 1955, Colonel Nasser had begun hinting at Cairo's potential interest in the acquisition of Western weapons; Egyptian sources confirm that this was so.[3] The purpose of the exercise apparently was to raise Western hopes of a possible change of heart in Egypt and thus induce London and Washington to delay the conclusion of the Turkish-Iraqi pact.[4] The move was not crowned with success. However, in the meantime, unobtrusive but growing Soviet-Egyptian cooperation, based on parallel interests, was starting to produce results. In mid-February, as the present study has indicated, negotiations were conducted in Cairo with the Czechoslovak "trade" delegation, and agreement was reached on the provision of Czech credits to Egypt for the purchase of arms.[5] Yet no sooner had this development taken place than the Egyptian leaders turned to Washington, this time in much more direct fashion, and initiated intensive talks on the acquisition of American weapons.[6] It was hardly surprising that such conduct should lead to raised eyebrows in Moscow; the question was bound to be raised just why Cairo, after having received a concrete commitment from the East on the supply of arms, should immediately go and ask the West for military assistance. These Egyptian moves pose problems that require elucidation.

[3] See chap. 2, footnote 13, and "The Course of Arms Negotiations"; also Haykal article in *al-Ahram* (Cairo Radio, domestic broadcast, April 14, 1967). Haykal states that "arguments [about the conditions under which Egypt might take arms from the West] began in January and extended into February 1955."

[4] See chap. 2, "The Course of Arms Negotiations."

[5] See chap. 3, "Toward a Revised Chronology."

[6] See chap. 2, footnote 13 and "The Course of Arms Negotiations." For several months, Colonel Nasser had remained unresponsive to Ambassador Jefferson Caffery's proposal for discussions on the question of U.S. military assistance to Egypt; the flurry of signals from Cairo in late January–early February fell considerably short of serious negotiations. However, toward the end of February, Egypt indicated her interest in full-scale talks. There was a brief interruption, because of the temporary U.S. embargo on military supplies to the Near East imposed in the wake of the Gaza clash; nevertheless, on March 3, Colonel Nasser summoned the new U.S. ambassador, Henry Byroade, and began intensive negotiations on the transfer of American arms to Egypt. See Haykal article in *al-Ahram* (Cairo Radio, domestic broadcast, April 14, 1967).

As was noted previously, in the circumstances prevailing during the first half of 1955, Premier Nasser could not realistically expect to acquire American weapons under conditions compatible with his political aims.[7] In fact, he himself frankly informed Egyptian military leaders, at the very time of his approach to Washington, that "it would be a miracle if we ever obtained arms from this source."[8] What, then, was his purpose in going through these motions? As seen from Moscow, it appeared as if Colonel Nasser intended simply to exploit the Soviet offer and his own overture to Washington for the purpose of initiating a political auction, in which East and West would outbid each other in competition for Egypt's friendship. This is obviously what Molotov and his followers in the Soviet Foreign Ministry suspected when they wondered aloud whether Cairo's "clamor" against the West was not merely "a question of the price Abd an-Nasser asked and the price that the West offered."[9] Moreover, the Kremlin faction opposing the arms deal apparently argued that, by enabling Premier Nasser to hold the threat of an Egyptian-Soviet rapprochement over Washington's head, Russia was, in effect, merely assisting him to effect a reconciliation with the United States on his own terms. For this reason, as Khrushchev subsequently revealed, "some [Soviet leaders] thought that this deal was a tactical move on the part of Egypt and that Egypt, once the West was reconciled with it, would soon return to the Western sphere of influence."[10]

Thus Colonel Nasser's own involved moves during late February and early March apparently helped to stoke the opposition against him in certain Kremlin quarters. However, the charges voiced in Moscow against the Egyptian leader may not have been entirely fair. It is not inconceivable that he was aware, almost from the beginning, that some Soviet leaders were less than overjoyed at the prospect of an arms deal with Egypt; consequently, he may have felt it would do no harm to convince the Kremlin that Egypt had other options available and would exploit them unless Moscow speedily fulfilled its side of the bargain.

However, this thought does not appear to have been Cairo's

[7] See chap. 2, second paragraph, "Inconsistencies and Misinterpretations," "The Course of Arms Negotiations," and "Political Motivations."
[8] Cairo Radio, domestic broadcast, March 31, 1955.
[9] See footnote 2 in this chapter.
[10] See al-Ahram, May 15, 1964; MENA, Cairo, in Arabic, May 15, 1964.

main consideration in asking Washington to open negotiations on military supplies almost as soon as agreement was reached with the Czechs. The real motive seems to have been of an entirely different nature: a mere nine months had passed since another country in a Western-controlled region had attempted to procure Bloc arms by way of Czechoslovakia; the leaders of that country quickly discovered how ill considered and risky their action had been. Their supply of Bloc weapons was interdicted, their state was invaded, and they themselves were forcibly removed from power. The West proved that it regarded such Soviet intrusions into its sphere of influence as utterly intolerable. The country in question was, of course, Guatemala under the Arbenz regime, and the Guatemalan example remained ever present in the thoughts of the Egyptian leaders and was incessantly cited. Colonel Nasser himself makes this point:

About the attempt to break up the arms monopoly . . . I recall . . . how some people reminded me of Guatemala. They told me that Guatemala took arms from the East, but the United States did not leave it alone, that the United States will never leave it alone but will destroy it, and that the United States is bound to destroy us in any way and by any means.[11]

One of the persons who held this view is identified in another account as Ahmad Husayn, Egyptian ambassador to Washington, who, months later, was still reminding and warning Premier Nasser that "they [the United States] besieged Guatemala and invaded it from within because it bought arms from the Soviet Union."[12] According to the same source, "Dr. Ahmad Husayn's conviction . . . was that Egypt was facing the very circumstances which had befallen Guatemala. Guatemala's story was still fresh in people's minds."[13] If this was true as late as the second half of 1955, when Ahmad Husayn was voicing his misgivings, the Guatemalan example must have been all the more "fresh in people's minds" during the period (February–March) in which Cairo initiated negotiations with Washington on the transfer of arms. It appears that the ambassador was brought into the picture only during the

[11] Nasser's speech to the Egyptian National Assembly (Cairo Radio, domestic broadcast, November 25, 1961).
[12] Haykal article in al-Ahram (Cairo Radio, domestic broadcast, April 14, 1967).
[13] Haykal, "Political Enquiry," pt. 4.

final stage, when the Arms Deal was already becoming public knowledge. However, Colonel Nasser, in his account, seems to be referring to the earlier period; the warnings against Cairo's "attempt to break up the arms monopoly" were presumably first voiced when the "attempt" was about to be embodied in an agreement with Czechoslovakia, that is, in February. "Some people" who, at that time, used the Guatemalan example in an effort to deter Colonel Nasser from his "attempt" must have occupied a loftier position than the hapless ambassador. During the initial, highly secret stage, it is hardly likely that anyone other than members of the military junta, a couple of Colonel Nasser's personal assistants, and a handful of technical experts would have been permitted to know what was going on. Of these, only members of the junta could have voiced opposition to a major political decision. Since Colonel Nasser in his account describes these dissident voices as emanating from personalities who were drifting toward "reaction" and who were "afraid,"[14] he is evidently referring to officers who had since been eased out of the junta. In this connection, it is interesting to note that one of the Salem brothers, Gamal, who was removed from power around the time when the Arms Deal was made public, reportedly opposed the enterprise because he feared the probable Western response; moreover, shortly afterward, a journal connected with his brother Salah, who also lost his position in 1955, disturbed the new Soviet-Egyptian idyl by printing remarks about the USSR that were less than enthusiastic.[15] Theirs may have been the offending voices, therefore, that Colonel Nasser had in mind.[16]

Be that as it may, during the period when the acquisition of arms from the USSR was being considered, the Egyptian leader himself had no reason whatever to believe that the Western reac-

[14] Nasser's speech to the Egyptian National Assembly (Cairo Radio, domestic broadcast, November 25, 1961).

[15] *New York Times*, June 11, 1956; *Jewish Observer & Middle East Review*, October 7, 1955.

[16] As was indicated in the Appendix to Chapter 2, Salah Salem is believed to have been rapidly falling out of favor in the first part of 1955 (although, as late as May, he was reported to have participated occasionally in top policy sessions of the junta). Gamal Salem, at any rate, is thought to have been in the inner circle during the crucial period. Neither of them may have known the full operational details of the Arms Deal; however, one or both probably participated in conferences at which the military leadership considered whether such a move was desirable. Consequently, the two brothers may have felt impelled to warn against this step.

tion would be anything but fierce. Significantly, no quotation is attributed to Colonel Nasser personally in which he is portrayed as having ridiculed these fears at the time. All the statements cited earlier merely show that, ex post facto, he contrasted the successful outcome of his enterprise with the needless apprehensions prevailing in Cairo at the moment of decision. He naturally took credit for the former, at least by implication, and disparaged those elements in the Egyptian capital who would not have persisted with the operation. However, this does not necessarily mean that, in the earlier part of 1955, he himself was immune to the fears that gripped others. The fact that, like his entourage, he repeatedly referred to the Guatemalan affair shows how deeply this example remained etched in his mind. After all, he personally shared to the full the popular Afro-Asian belief that the West would naturally and inevitably bring its superior power to bear on recalcitrant smaller states.

His own conversations during that period must, if anything, have reinforced this feeling. As early as March 3, he had started, experimentally, to try and accustom Western representatives to the thought that, as a last resort, Egypt might be forced to secure arms "where it could find them."[17] He continued to speak in this fashion throughout the spring and early summer; the Western reaction was not long in coming, nor could it possibly be misunderstood. Egyptian sources assert that, when he first heard Colonel Nasser broadly hinting at such an eventuality, the U.S. ambassador remarked ominously, "I did not understand this last sentence well." Shortly afterward, the British ambassador is alleged to have commented, "I have completed my service and have reached the age of retirement. If you want my opinion, Sir, I advise you not even to think of such a thing. This is a serious matter, much more than you imagine."[18] The same Egyptian account claims that a special U.S. envoy, who arrived some time thereafter, warned bluntly:

The consequences will be grave. . . . Things may develop to the extent of severing economic relations between the U.S. and Egypt. We might even sever political relations as well. We might even impose a blockade around Egyptian shores to prevent the ships from arriving with the

[17] Haykal article in *al-Ahram* (Cairo Radio, domestic broadcast, April 14, 1967).
[18] Ibid.

arms. . . . When Guatemala bought some arms from the USSR, we reached the stage of war with it, and the Guatemalan government that bought the arms fell.[19]

Whether these reports are entirely accurate or not, they do indicate how grim Cairo's appraisal of the Western attitude was during this period. Consequently, Premier Nasser can have entertained no illusions about the risks that an arms deal with the Bloc entailed; in February 1955, when he had taken the first covert steps toward the acquisition of weapons from the East, the Egyptian leader must have been preoccupied with the search for some adroit tactical move that might help to ward off, or at least blunt, the expected retaliatory measures of the Western powers. Regarded in the light of this requirement, Colonel Nasser's decision, at that moment, to initiate a prolonged dialogue with the United States assumes an altogether more meaningful place in the history of the Arms Deal. Cairo's military talks with Washington, precisely because a successful outcome could not be envisaged, were all the more calculated to cast Egypt in the role of the aggrieved party. It was by no means a matter of indifference, at the time, whether the Western powers were given the impression that the Egyptian leader had turned to Moscow without delay, as an act of deliberate choice, or only as a last resort, after first having attempted in vain to acquire arms elsewhere. Of course, what precluded success in the Washington-Cairo dialogue was not some arbitrary decision or lack of understanding in the U.S. capital but the incompatibility between Egypt's requests, on the one hand, and U.S. public law and diplomatic commitments, on the other.[20] Nevertheless, the very fact that Egypt, after repeated approaches, would emerge empty-handed, could not but leave U.S. diplomats with a vague feeling of regret and even of culpability, which was bound to become more poignant once news of the "Czech" arms agreement was released. Although Egyptian leaders may not have expected that this psychological factor alone would stave off the anticipated Western response to the Arms Deal, they probably hoped that it might substantially weaken the vehemence of the initial emotional reaction, and hence of the Western counterblow. (It is along these lines that an explanation may be sought for the

---

[19] Ibid. The envoy is alleged to have been Kermit Roosevelt.
[20] See chap. 2, second paragraph, "Inconsistencies and Misinterpretations," "The Course of Arms Negotiations," and "Political Motivations."

tendency of Egyptian sources to portray the acquisition of Soviet weapons as a belated reflex action rather than as a deliberate political move.) In the event, Colonel Nasser appears to have calculated correctly.

It is unlikely that the Egyptian leader would have approached Washington at this delicate stage (February–March 1955) without first explaining his motives to Moscow. Cairo's reasons were perfectly sensible and, if believed in the Kremlin, did not have to be regarded as objectionable from the Russian point of view. However, the Soviet leadership tends to be preternaturally suspicious of other people's motives, and Molotov, in this particular instance, was no doubt especially quick to question Colonel Nasser's real intentions. It is true that even the Molotov faction seems to have accepted as genuine Cairo's apprehensions about the anticipated Western response; this is borne out by the reported admission of certain Soviet Foreign Ministry officials that Colonel Nasser's policy of "nonalignment," if sincere, would, indeed, "cost its author a great deal in an area dominated and controlled by Western influence."[21] Precisely because of this consideration, however, the Molotov group seems to have assumed that Egypt's current political actions were merely tactical maneuvers intended to convince Washington that it should narrow the gap between "the price Abd an-Nasser asked and the price the West offered."[22] Thus, in the early spring of 1955, Colonel Nasser appears to have faced something of a dilemma. To proceed from the preparatory steps taken in mid-February to the full and successful implementation of the Arms Deal, he had to go through motions that would help to moderate the strong Western reaction anticipated by Cairo. These same precautionary moves, however, were providing ammunition for opponents of the Egyptian entente in the Kremlin, who naturally hastened to question Colonel Nasser's motives; consequently, there was some danger that the whole arms deal might be jeopardized. As it was, the Russians were apparently beginning to drag their feet because of the forthcoming summit conference and Khrushchev's fluctuating fortunes in the Soviet power struggle. Moscow's Near Eastern project seemed to be going into cold storage, and the Egyptian leadership must have begun to wonder whether Soviet arms would ever be forthcoming. Czech credits

[21] See Haykal, "Political Enquiry," pt. 4.
[22] Ibid.

were of little practical use unless backed by the contents of Russian arsenals. Thus it was incumbent upon Premier Nasser to find ways of strengthening Soviet confidence in his motives and intentions.

The Chinese Factor

This was the situation and, most probably, the mood in which the Egyptian leader set out for the Bandung Conference in mid-April. The Kremlin regarded the conference with mixed feelings. Originally proposed by the Indonesians, it had received its main impetus in 1954 at a meeting between Indian and Chinese representatives. Consequently, China was given the status of a full participant; the USSR, however, was not. Moreover, from the Soviet point of view, it was ominous that several anticommunist delegations had been invited. (The latter, indeed, were to launch repeated attacks upon Russian colonialism in Asia, which even came to be embodied, although obliquely, in the final "Principles" of the conference.) It could not but be noted that, while brickbats were thrown at the Soviet Union, bouquets were reserved for the Chinese People's Republic. To some extent, the "Spirit of Bandung" came to be personified by Chou En-lai's similing face; even previously, the Chinese had been carrying the line of accommodation toward newly independent countries considerably further than Moscow, as yet, appeared willing to do. On the other hand, some Soviet leaders did realize, as the conference approached, that, whatever its disadvantages from Moscow's point of view, it was likely to turn into a basically anti-Western forum; consequently, the Soviet media welcomed the gathering, inner reservations notwithstanding, and devoted increasing space to Afro-Asian developments.

As part of this effort to play upon the contradictions between the West and former colonial countries, the Soviet Foreign Ministry on April 16, the eve of Bandung, published a statement of support for Near Eastern governments resisting Western "pressure." Strangely enough, in spite of a marked proliferation of Soviet-Egyptian contacts, overt and covert, since the beginning of the year (including even the religious field), Egypt rated a mere couple of sentences in the long statement. On the other hand, a sizable passage was devoted to Syria.[23]

23 *Pravda*, April 17, 1955.

Damascus, in the meantime, had acquired a government that, from the Soviet point of view, appeared to hold out considerable promise; its foreign minister and acting defense minister was Khaled el 'Azm, who gave repeated indications of his willingness to reach a basic understanding both with the communist countries and with the local communist party.[24] The change in the Syrian capital had occurred too late to influence Molotov's February 8 address (Khaled el 'Azm having assumed his portfolios only on February 13), but it does seem that, from mid-February onward, the Soviet Foreign Minister placed much more emphasis on relations with Damascus than with Cairo. In part, this attitude may have been induced by Syria's deep hostility toward neighboring Turkey; Molotov apparently regarded Damascus as a useful counterweight to Ankara, on the basis of the old adage "my enemy's enemy is my friend." (After Molotov's ouster from the Presidium, Soviet publications alleged that he personally had been responsible for the sharp deterioration in Soviet-Turkish relations after World War II.) In any case, during the fourth week of March, the Soviet Foreign Minister summoned the Syrian minister in Moscow and offered him "aid in any form whatsoever" against Turkey.[25] Earlier, when Khaled el 'Azm was visiting Cairo, Solod hastened to see him, presumably to make a similar proposition.[26] Thus the Soviet Foreign Ministry statement of April 16 merely confirmed in public the promises that Damascus had already received privately.

On the subject of Moscow's relations with Cairo, however, the Foreign Ministry's release was decidedly terse, saying merely that "considerable [Western] pressure is also being exerted on Egypt." From the Egyptian point of view, the statement actually contained some distinctly negative elements; it singled out for special mention the section of the Supreme Soviet's February 9 declaration that demanded "respect for the territorial integrity of other states."[27] It so happened that, a mere two to three weeks earlier, persistent reports had credited Salah Salem (whose sentiments toward the USSR were reputed to be tepid at best) with a scheme whereby Egypt would acquiesce in Western defense plans for the

[24] Patrick Seale, *The Struggle for Syria: A Study of Postwar Arab Politics, 1945–1958* (New York and London: Oxford University Press, 1965), passim.
[25] Ibid., p. 234; Sharq al-Adna, Cyprus, in Arabic, March 25, 1955; and ANA, Beirut, April 4, 1955.
[26] ANA, Cairo, April 2, 1955.
[27] *Pravda*, April 17, 1955.

region, provided Israel were forced to cede a portion of the Ne-
gev.[28] Moscow's sudden insistence on the "territorial integrity" of
Near Eastern states was therefore a tactically adroit answer to the
proponents of such suspect plans, while simultaneously demonstrating to Colonel Nasser that Cairo's maneuvers had aroused the
Kremlin's distrust and displeasure.

Thus the Egyptian leader, setting out for Bandung, must have
experienced considerable disquiet about the future of his relations
with the Soviet Union, as well as the prospects for a speedy delivery of Czech and Soviet arms. The time had obviously come for
Cairo to act in a manner calculated to assist rather than hamper
those elements in the Kremlin who favored the transfer of weapons
to Egypt and had committed their prestige to the success of the
Soviet offensive in the Near East. It was becoming a matter of
some urgency to recruit further allies in the struggle to convince
the skeptics in Moscow that their suspicions of Colonel Nasser's
motives were unwarranted.[29]

In Rangoon, on his way to the conference, as well as subsequently in Bandung itself, the Egyptian leader found an opportunity for prolonged, intensive discussions with Chou En-lai.[30]
The Chinese, as noted previously, had been striving for some time
to fill the role of intermediaries between the Third World and the
"socialist camp."[31] This tendency was especially evident at Bandung, where Chou En-lai came to be personally identified with
Peking's line of sweet reason toward the newly established regimes
of Afro-Asia. It would seem that Colonel Nasser, intent upon resolving his difficulties with the Kremlin, was very quick to grasp
the potential implications of China's new posture. Peking, after
all, had been gradually assuming the functions of an arbiter in
the Moscow power struggle, although, in most instances, Mao was
merely responding to appeals for support addressed to him by
contending factions in the Russian capital.[32] Chinese interference
in Soviet affairs had ceased being an unthinkable proposition and

---

28 Sharq al-Adna, Cyprus, in Arabic, March 21, 1955.
29 As part of this effort, the Egyptian authorities, in mid-April, finally
filled the vacant position of ambassador to the USSR, choosing Muhammad
Awad al-Qoni (Kony), a diplomat who had previously served both in Moscow
and in Washington (ANA, in Arabic, April 21, 1955).
30 Haykal, "Political Enquiry," pt. 4.
31 See first paragraph of the present section.
32 See chap. 4, "Realignment in the Kremlin" and "Molotov's February 8
Speech."

was rapidly becoming a normal ingredient of Kremlin politics. It appears that Colonel Nasser, during his conversations with Chou, took due advantage of this favorable combination of circumstances to try and influence the Kremlin "debate" on Near Eastern policy by requesting the intervention of a new and friendly element, in the person of the Chinese Premier. Appearing in his role as patron of the Third World, Chou En-lai could obviously help to restore the Egyptian government's progressively declining prestige in Moscow by testifying both to Colonel Nasser's international stature and to his political soundness. For the Chinese to take the initiative in this matter meant, essentially, to back Khrushchev's faction—the advocates of a forward policy in the Near East—against Molotov. Whether the Egyptian leader consciously realized it or not, Peking could act in this fashion without having to change its policy in the least; as noted earlier, the Chinese, since mid-1954, had been increasingly inclined to take Khrushchev's side against Molotov, and their attitude in February 1955 had shown that they saw no possible profit in collaborating with the Soviet Foreign Minister.[33]

It was in this context alone that Chou En-lai could serve as an "intermediary" between Cairo and Moscow; the Chinese Premier was well placed to provide the pro-Egyptian faction in the Kremlin with effective ammunition for use against Molotov in the "debate" on Near Eastern policy. There was every reason for Colonel Nasser to utilize Chou En-lai's assistance in this particular way; hopefully, Chou's intervention could produce a speedy Soviet decision to go ahead with the arms deal at a time when that subject seemed to have become hopelessly entangled in the Kremlin's internecine conflicts. On the other hand, analysis does not bear out the proposition, advanced in some versions of this episode, that Chinese "mediation" between Egypt and Russia should be taken in a much more literal sense: the stories in question suggest that Colonel Nasser needed Chou's help either to let Moscow know of Cairo's interest in Soviet arms (a strangely circuitous channel of communication, considering that Ambassador Solod could be summoned within minutes to Nasser's office) or to provide a conduit for the massive transfer of Bloc weapons to Egypt (although, as has been noted, China in 1955 was technically, politically, and geographically unsuited for this task).[34] Even theoretically, such portrayals of the

33 Ibid.
34 See chap. 2, "Additional Questions."

situation could be valid only if, indeed, by April 1955, Colonel Nasser had yet to make contact with Moscow in his quest for hardware, not to speak of finding a suitable arms conduit. In fact, these two phases of the Arms Deal had been well and truly initiated some three months earlier, and a new stage had been reached in mid-February with the conclusion of a Czech-Egyptian agreement on military credits. However, in failing to take cognizance of these previous developments, the traditional accounts of the Bandung episode may be in excellent company; it is entirely conceivable that Chou himself, at the time, was unaware of what were, after all, operational secrets affecting very sensitive branches of government in Moscow, Prague, and Cairo. Colonel Nasser can hardly have felt at liberty to divulge such confidential details to an outside party, even if the man in question was the Chinese Premier; under the circumstances, he may simply have told Chou that Egypt was seeking an entente with Moscow, including some form of military relationship, but that certain people in the Kremlin seemed to be dragging their feet. It is quite possible that the Egyptian leader's discretion resulted in a misunderstanding: Chou may have thought that he was being asked to broach the subject of an arms deal in Moscow (which, by this time, was a thoroughly redundant move). Colonel Nasser, on the other hand, presumably wanted the Chinese Premier to impress the Kremlin with Egypt's increasing significance on the Afro-Asian scene, so as to overcome Molotov's obstruction.

In the event, Chou appears to have done both. According to a circumstantial Egyptian report, the Chinese Premier sent a long account of his discussions with Nasser to Chairman Mao, who then duly proceeded to forward this dispatch to Moscow. Chou's message is reported to have contained the following five points:

• Gamal Abd an-Nasser represents a new national trend in the Middle East . . . [and] believes in a new role which this . . . force can play in the liberation movements of the Middle East.
• Gamal Abd an-Nasser believes in the policy of nonalignment . . . as a long-term strategy and not as a maneuver by which he seeks to get . . . military, economic, and other aid. Had his differences with the West been a mere tactical measure, he would not have gone so far in his determination.
• [Nasser requires Soviet weapons] in order to overcome the arms monopoly which dominates this part of the world and to be able to

confront the pressure on him. . . . [Chou undertook] to take up the matter with the Soviet leaders. . . .

• [A clash is] inevitable between the new . . . Arab nationalism . . . and imperialism. . . .

• The socialist camp cannot sit on the fence while the inevitable battle takes place in the Middle East . . . our position demands that we should be on the side of the nationalist forces. This is for two reasons: (a) The victory of the nationalist forces will . . . hinder the Western imperialist attempt to encircle the socialist camp with nuclear bases and will make the completion of the rings in the chain of encirclement in the Middle East impossible; (b) . . . the national current will be the new force in the Middle East and so we must have a rapprochement with it. There is a big difference between making this rapprochement now and helping the nationalist force to realize its aims, and between waiting, leaving it to fight the battle alone, and then beginning our rapprochement with it after its triumph. . . .[35]

Significantly, Chou's dispatch made a particular point of defending Premier Nasser against the suspicion that he was executing a mere "maneuver" or "tactical" move rather than a genuine "long-term strategy." As noted earlier, these were precisely the charges that Molotov and his followers in the Foreign Ministry were reported to have brought against the Egyptian leader.[36] Mao's step in forwarding Chou's account to Moscow can thus hardly be regarded otherwise than as an act of direct intervention against Molotov, reinforcing Khrushchev's argument that the situation favored a bold Near Eastern offensive in alliance with local nationalist leaders. In effect, Peking was assisting Khrushchev to overcome his most stubborn adversary. Subsequently, Mao must have had repeated occasions to regret this move.

An additional consideration may, at least temporarily, have brought Peking and Cairo together on the same side. The "outs" normally do not welcome convivial gatherings of the "ins." Governments barred from participation in a summit or other conclave of great powers tend to harbor dark suspicions. In the midst of deli-

[35] Haykal, "Political Enquiry," pt. 4. Haykal claims that he first heard of Chou's report from the Egyptian ambassador to the USSR and, during subsequent visits to Moscow, "had an opportunity to see glimpses of this report" himself.
[36] See chap. 4, "Further Corroboration" and footnote 85; also first paragraph and footnote 2 in this chapter.

cate transactions with Moscow, Cairo may not have rejoiced at the thought that the Soviet leaders would soon meet their Western counterparts at Geneva, to embark upon the practical business of global barter, in which the Near East and other regions would necessarily constitute negotiable items. The fact that it was the Soviets who wished to inscribe the Near East on the summit agenda cannot have been reassuring to the Egyptian Premier.[37] A free and untrammeled discussion at Geneva could hardly be conducive to the speedy implementation of an arms deal that required the cover of obscured political visibility and the sustenance of unbridled East-West rivalry. Moreover, Moscow's attitude provided valid grounds for the surmise that Soviet policy at the summit meeting would be to maneuver the West into accepting the USSR as a full member of the Near Eastern concert of powers. Otherwise, there was little point in pressing for the inclusion of this region among the subjects to be discussed. If the Soviet Union succeeded in its aim, however, and achieved a Near Eastern presence by means of negotiations, it would have no incentive to proceed with an arms deal that was beneficial only to an outside power attempting to force its way into the region; in such an eventuality, the Russians were more likely to pay heed to the dangers than to the dubious advantages of a military agreement with Egypt. (Actually, Moscow was not to prove successful in its efforts to gain Western support for the inscription of this subject on the agenda; but this could not be foreseen in the spring.)

At no time did Cairo feel entirely reassured about Soviet intentions; thus when Soviet leaders visited London a year later, there was immediate concern in the Egyptian capital lest the Kremlin should agree to some form of regional arms limitation in return for British recognition that the USSR was entitled to participate in the Near Eastern concert of powers. Egypt's instinctive countermeasure was to extend diplomatic recognition to the Chinese People's Republic; informed circles explained that, in the eventuality of an embargo enforced by the United Nations, Egypt would be able to obtain weapons through the good offices of her Chinese friends, since they were, in any case, barred from U.N. membership.[38] It is, of course, highly dubious whether this was

---

[37] As late as June, Molotov was still insisting he could not accept Western proposals that excluded the Near East from the summit agenda (Voice of the Arabs, Cairo, June 23, 1955).

[38] See Robert St. John, *The Boss: The Story of Gamal Abdel Nasser*

a practical proposition even in 1956; what seems more likely is that Cairo regarded Peking as a convenient irritant, which could be brought onto the scene whenever Moscow or the West started to take Egypt for granted. In all probability, this was just the spirit in which Colonel Nasser and Chou En-lai came together at Bandung, in April 1955, when both Cairo and Peking were beginning to have cause for uneasiness about Soviet intentions at the forthcoming Geneva conference. Forwarding a report of the Nasser-Chou discussions to the Kremlin may well have been intended as a delicate hint that Peking was now holding a watching brief over relations between Cairo and the Bloc and would make sure that Moscow did not barter away Egyptian interests at Geneva.

Preparing for Implementation

Whatever the precise considerations involved, it seems that China's intervention was quite effective and helped to sway the views of the Soviet leadership in favor of a more "offensive" policy in the Near East.[39] The evidence indicates that, shortly after Colonel Nasser's return from Bandung, Moscow assured Cairo that it would now be possible to proceed with the necessary practical arrangements to prepare for the phase in which the Arms Deal might actually be implemented.[40] Consequently, an unpublicized meeting took place in Cairo between the Soviet military attaché and two important Egyptian representatives, Ali Sabri and M. Hafez Ismail (the officer in charge of the army's procurements), for the purpose of finalizing Cairo's shopping list of hardware to be imported from the USSR and Czechoslovakia.[41]

(Toronto: McGraw-Hill Book Co., 1960), p. 218; also *Akhbar al-Yom* (Cairo), April 21, 1956, and *New York Times*, April 22, 1956.

[39] Thus, in its May issue, *Kommunist* (no. 8, 1955, pp. 74–83) was already giving ideological underpinning to the now victorious Khrushchev line by demanding a change in Moscow's appraisal of the historic role played by certain Afro-Asian nationalist leaders.

[40] Haykal (article in *al-Ahram* [Cairo Radio, domestic broadcast, April 14, 1967] and "Political Enquiry," pt. 4), Salah Salem (Seale, *Struggle for Syria*, pp. 234–236), and several secondary sources agree that, in May, Ambassador Solod conveyed some kind of favorable message about the Arms Deal to the Egyptian government; however, the various accounts differ considerably on the precise details of this occurrence. It would seem that there were, in fact, several meetings in May between Solod and different members of the Egyptian government, including one in the first week of the month, soon after Bandung, and another (as will be seen subsequently) on May 21 with Colonel Nasser.

[41] Haykal, "Political Enquiry," pt. 4.

The period of two and a half months since the Egyptian-Czech military credit agreement of February had evidently not been wasted; the indications are that Major-General Ragab[42] and various experts from both sides spent this time attempting to investigate and correlate the facts concerning the Bloc's armament surpluses and supply capabilities, on the one hand, and Egypt's practical requirements and absorptive capacity, on the other. In the absence of such studies, no realistic, itemized schedule of requests could have been submitted to the Soviet authorities, since, as will be recalled,[43] Egypt and the Bloc lacked any previous mutual experience in the military field on which to base their transactions. It is of some interest that one man, Ali Sabri, was simultaneously dealing with East and West, preparing detailed, but very different, lists for submission to each;[44] this fact is, at any rate, not incompatible with the hypothesis that Cairo regarded its military negotiations with the United States as a tactical component of the Soviet-Egyptian Arms Deal.[45]

These developments, in the wake of the Bandung Conference, seem to have created the impression in Cairo that the deal was fast approaching its consummation and that, therefore, the time had come for certain essential precautionary measures. On May 10, the Egyptian authorities published details of a new regulation, effective retroactively from the end of April, which was ostensibly aimed at encouraging the export of the country's large cotton surplus to Eastern Europe. At first sight, the purpose of the measure was elusive, to say the least. Previously, exporters had collected early payment by having bills of exchange, drawn on East European governments, discounted at Swiss banks. The announcement of May 10 conveyed the impression that, when the bills came to be presented for settlement, the East European authorities, for some reason, could not be relied upon to meet their financial obligations. Consequently, the Egyptian government, against payment of a premium, was compulsorily insuring the cotton exporters; that is, it was taking upon itself the onerous commitment of meeting the bills, if necessary, when they became due. Actually, the new regulation was formulated in such a way that all, or almost all, of the bills seemed destined to end up in the hands of the Na-

[42] David J. Dallin, "D Papers," File E, December 15, 1958, made available to the author by Mrs. Dallin.
[43] See chap. 1, "Logistics."
[44] Haykal, "Political Enquiry," pt. 4.
[45] See "Cairo Between East and West" earlier in this chapter.

tional Bank of Egypt and related institutions, so that the cotton exports would, in fact, be indirectly financed by the Egyptian authorities.[46] No satisfactory explanation was published regarding the precise reason for instituting such cumbersome procedures. The highly unusual, not to say unprecedented, features of this measure immediately aroused surprise and criticism; Egyptian cotton trading circles commented with acerbity:

In no country is there a compulsory guarantee forced on exporters. Normally, exporters should be allowed, if they so wish, to take the risk themselves. Whether this step will [really] promote exports is doubtful.[47]

Under the circumstances, the only logical inference would seem to be that Cairo had good reason not to expect East European payment for its cotton exports; in other words, the cotton shipments themselves were intended to constitute payment for certain commodities that Egypt was receiving, or hoping to receive, from the Bloc. It is equally apparent that the transaction in question had some clandestine aspects; otherwise, there would have been no need to create an elaborate façade merely to cover up the fact that the Egyptian authorities were bartering cotton for East European merchandise (as they had been doing for several years). Under a normal barter arrangement, Egyptian exporters could be paid out of the proceeds of imports from the country with which goods were being traded. In the case of the barter planned in May 1955, however, the commodities to be acquired by Egypt were clearly not intended for commercial sale, so that no proceeds were expected. Thus the purpose of the May 10 regulation apparently was to ensure that bills drawn on East European governments (or at least those bills that in essence constituted mere paper cover for a confidential transaction) should not be discounted at Western banks. Consequently, the measure introduced alternate ways of remunerating Egyptian cotton exporters, which avoided drawing undue Western attention to the fact that commodities were being bartered to Eastern Europe without any visible return. Indeed, instituting compulsory insurance served this purpose admirably by diverting the bills from their normal com-

[46] National Bank of Egypt, *Economic Bulletin*, vol. 8 (1955), no. 2, p. 119; *Egyptian Economic and Political Review*, vol. 1, no. 10 (June 1955), p. 27, and vol. 1, no. 11 (July 1955), pp. 31–33.

[47] *Egyptian Economic and Political Review*, vol. 1, no. 10 (June 1955), p. 27.

mercial channels into the repositories of Egypt's national banking institutions.

With no undue stretch of the imagination, the observer is drawn toward the following conclusion: shortly before May 10, Cairo apparently had reason to believe that the Arms Deal was approaching the point of implementation; thus it became necessary to devise procedures that would permit payment to take place in a discreet manner, at least during the period before the transaction was publicized. Actually, the fact that the new regulation was introduced as early as May, effective for the current cotton season, indicates that Egypt's immediate consideration was to meet her prepayment (or downpayment) rather than repayment obligations toward the Bloc. In over a decade of Soviet military credit agreements with Afro-Asian countries, there were to be repeated instances in which the USSR demanded downpayment of a certain percentage of the total transaction (usually equivalent to one annual installment on the loan in question).[48] It is conceivable that the arrangements made earlier in 1955 between Egypt and the Bloc contained a similar provision, and that this was the reason why the Cairo authorities hastened to promulgate their new export measures on May 10, as soon as the Russians indicated that they were prepared to proceed toward implementation of the Arms Deal. The amount covered by Cairo's compulsory insurance scheme was $28 million, to be apportioned among East European countries in the form of Egyptian "credit."[49] This sum is remarkably close to the level of Egypt's subsequent annual repayments to the Bloc under the Arms Deal, as estimated by competent staff members of the International Monetary Fund.[50]

[48] U.S., Department of State, Bureau of Intelligence and Research, *The Sino-Soviet Economic Offensive Through 1960*, no. 8426 (Washington, D.C., March 21, 1961), p. 12, makes the point that its estimate of Soviet military aid (to Indonesia, Egypt, Iraq, Syria, Afghanistan, Yemen, Morocco, Guinea, and the Sudan) "does not reflect downpayments . . . which are known to exist but for which data are incomplete."

[49] *Egyptian Economic and Political Review*, vol. 2, no. 1 (September 1955), p. 47. It was formally explained that Cairo was, in fact, giving credit to her East European trading partners under various bilateral agreements that contained fairly liberal "swing" provisions. In several cases, the amount of "swing" was increased during 1955; under the circumstances, this meant that, for considerable periods, Egypt would be shipping cotton to Eastern Europe in excess of any visibile returns.

[50] Marcello Caiola, "Balance of Payments of the USSR, 1955–58," International Monetary Fund, *Staff Papers*, vol. IX (1962), pp. 1–36; according to this estimate, Egypt, during the period immediately following the 1955 Arms Deal, was repaying the Bloc to the tune of some $25 million annually.

At any rate, it is noteworthy that, without a compensatory increase of commercial imports from the Bloc, Egyptian barter shipments of cotton to the East doubled during the early part[51] of the
1955 season (compared with the previous, 1953/54, season);
viewed in relation to Egypt's total cotton exports (which were
declining), the Soviet bloc's share expanded even more dramatically during this period, from 8.4 to 21.0 per cent.[52] The
USSR initially absorbed the greater part of this increase, although,
during subsequent months, Czechoslovakia gradually rose to first
place among Bloc importers of Egyptian cotton. Meanwhile, in
Alexandria and Cairo, cotton trading circles, which had met the
new export regulations with open misgivings, were obviously
making the best of the temporary boom. Perhaps this was one of
the phenomena Colonel Nasser had in mind when he commented,
somewhat bitterly, that the same persons who in 1955 had opposed
his various measures to expand Egyptian-Bloc relations were "the
first people to adapt themselves to the new conditions and deal
with the Eastern countries, gaining most of the trade with the
Eastern countries. . . ."[53]

With both the technical and the financial arrangements for the
Arms Deal proceeding apace, the question of how to preempt or
counteract the potential political and, conceivably, military repercussions of the transaction must have confronted Cairo and Moscow
with growing urgency. As has been noted, it was precisely this
problem that caused mounting anxiety in Cairo, where something
of a "Guatemala complex" prevailed,[54] while, in Moscow, Khrushchev's opponents seem to have been equally perturbed by the
dangerous implications of his distinctly adventurous belief that,
in the Near East, "attack was the best means of defense."[55] Since
it appears that most of the responsible personalities in the Egyptian capital and at least several leaders in the Kremlin anticipated
some kind of forceful Western response, the immediate issue would
seem to have been what, if any, Soviet help and protection Egypt
might expect in such an eventuality. Of course, according to all
the indications, Cairo had not entirely abandoned hope that continuing Egyptian-U.S. negotiations, persistent if unavailing, might

[51] That is, the period up to July, well before the existence of the Arms
Deal was officially acknowledged.
[52] *Egyptian Economic and Political Review*, vol. 1, no. 12 (August 1955).
[53] Colonel Nasser's address to the National Assembly (Cairo Radio, domestic broadcast, November 25, 1961).
[54] See "Cairo Between East and West" earlier in this chapter.
[55] Reuters, in English, to South Africa, November 24, 1957.

have the psychological effect of a shock absorber; a show of endeavor to reach agreement with Washington could well impress
Western diplomats with Colonel Nasser's basic goodwill, at least
to the point of dampening the natural flames of Western resentment once intelligence of the Arms Deal was confirmed.[56] Nevertheless, it was clearly imperative to prepare for the (far from
remote) contingency that this attempt might fail. On May 21,
Colonel Nasser held a long meeting with Ambassador Solod;[57] a
few days later, the Premier went into seclusion with certain
selected members of the junta to consider "supreme policy."[58] The
immediate outcome of both conferences would appear to have
been a decision to test Western reactions immediately, so as to
be able to form a better estimate of the West's probable course of
action once the Arms Deal began to be consummated. At any rate,
this is precisely the move that, early in the second week of June,
Premier Nasser proceeded to make; it took the form of a "warning"
to the U.S. and British ambassadors that, unless Cairo's conditions
for a military transaction with the West were accepted, Egypt
would acquire arms "elsewhere," and, in this instance, Colonel
Nasser "was not maneuvering" but meant every word he said.[59] As
was noted previously, the Western response to this ultimatum was
blunt and ominous;[60] it seemed to confirm that the Egyptian leader
would have to face catastrophic repercussions if he proceeded to
implement his threats. Even if the fear-inspiring example of Guatemala was not expressly mentioned by Western diplomats at this
stage, the junta was sufficiently "Guatemala-minded" to spell out
the precise implications for itself. In fact, this is exactly how Cairo
did react.[61] Under these circumstances, Colonel Nasser must have
considered that it was a matter of the utmost importance to obtain
some kind of Soviet guarantee to cover the eventuality of a resort
to force on the part of the West; as Cairo was painfully aware,[62]
the West might attempt to interdict Soviet military shipments, to
institute a total blockade of Egypt, or even to invade that country
and overthrow its regime.

[56] For the probable considerations behind Egypt's moves, see "Cairo Between East and West" earlier in this chapter.
[57] ANA, Cairo, May 21, 1955.
[58] Sharq al-Adna, Cyprus, May 27, 1955.
[59] Haykal article in *al-Ahram* (Cairo Radio, domestic broadcast, April 14,
1967); see also chap. 2, footnote 48.
[60] See "Cairo Between East and West" earlier in this chapter.
[61] See ibid.
[62] Ibid.

Difficulties and Dangers

In June 1955, it was by no means a simple task to persuade Moscow to extend its protection. To start with, Molotov, although considerably weakened, was still very vocal in the CPSU Presidium, as the Egyptians apparently discovered to their cost; it is significant that, toward the end of June, several days after a meeting between the Soviet and Egyptian foreign ministers,[63] a Cairo broadcast found occasion to attack Molotov by name.[64] However, on July 4, the historic July Plenum of the CPSU Central Committee convened, and Molotov was subjected to an onslaught that almost irretrievably undermined his prestige in the eyes of the Soviet elite.[65] From this plenum, the Soviet leaders proceeded to the Geneva summit meeting and, while still assembled there, dispatched Khrushchev's own private "foreign minister," Dimitri Shepilov, to Cairo. Rather unconvincingly, Shepilov's mission appears in some accounts as little more than a courier's trip to carry a message that, normally, would have been conveyed with greater efficiency by cable; he went, supposedly, to inform the Egyptian authorities that Moscow had found Ali Sabri's shopping list to be in order and, consequently, had approved it. This simple task hardly required his personal appearance in Cairo, nor was he a technical expert with whom the remaining details of the Arms Deal could be ironed out. The very fact that his journey was contemporaneous with the Geneva conference[66] would seem to indicate that it could not have been entirely unconnected with the question of how to appraise the intentions of the Western powers and their probable course of action. After all, Khrushchev and Bulganin were sitting face-to-face with the leaders of these same powers, in what had been widely advertised as an attempt to infuse East-West relations with a new spirit; to send Shepilov to Cairo, at such a time, to set in motion an offensive into the very heart of a region regarded as vital by every NATO member, meant, in effect, that the Kremlin had tested its adversaries and found them wanting. As on subsequent occasions, Khrushchev ap-

---

[63] Voice of the Arabs, Cairo, June 23, 1955.
[64] Ibid., June 26, 1955.
[65] See Bialer testimony and Dallin, *Soviet Foreign Policy.*
[66] Shepilov's visit to Cairo was apparently planned before the Geneva conference took place, but he would hardly have been permitted to set in motion the final implementation of the Arms Deal if Khrushchev's impressions at Geneva had given rise to the fear that the West might resort to force.

pears to have been duly impressed with the power commanded by his Western counterparts but to have belittled their determination. Perhaps, like others,[67] he felt that the overenthusiastic reception given to the "spirit of Geneva" in most of the Western media reflected a new public mood, which would seriously hamper any attempt on the part of Western governments to intervene against Moscow's thrust into non-Bloc areas.

To some extent, therefore, Shepilov's mission must have reflected Khrushchev's personal appraisal, nourished by his experience in Geneva, that, if he proceeded with the Arms Deal, the danger of a violent Western counterblow was not prohibitively high. Moscow clearly hoped that in the Near East, within relatively close distance of Soviet territory, the West might consider it risky to take measures of the kind that had been unhesitatingly applied in Central America during the previous year. It was, no doubt, with this deterrent purpose in mind that the Russians, from the spring onward, enunciated a "poor man's Monroe Doctrine," which harped upon the geographic propinquity of the region to the borders of the USSR:

It stands to reason that the Soviet Union cannot remain indifferent to the situation arising in the Near and Middle East since [events there have] . . . a direct bearing on the security of the USSR.[68]

Needless to say, there is no evidence that anyone in Moscow seriously expected to expel the Western powers from the area; the Soviet "doctrine" simply served as an earnest of Russia's determination to permit no undertaking in the Near East from which her participation was barred.

However, even if Khrushchev hoped that the West might be deterred from any forcible reaction to the Arms Deal, his emissary Shepilov's position, when confronted by Egyptian requests for a measure of Soviet protection against such an eventuality, can have been anything but comfortable. It must be recalled that, some months earlier, the concept of a Soviet "guarantee" for certain Arab countries had been bandied about a little too freely in Khrushchevian circles and their organs, including Shepilov's

---

[67] For the belief that the Russians had reason to feel, as a result of Geneva, "that vigilance toward them was relaxed," see Konrad Adenauer, *Erinnerungen, 1953–1955* (Stuttgart: Deutsche Verlags-Anstalt, 1966), p. 477.
[68] *Pravda*, April 17, 1955.

Pravda.[69] The Egyptian leaders could be forgiven for tending to take such terms rather literally—namely, as a Soviet commitment to protect friendly Arab regimes against untoward occurrences. However, a pledge of this kind was simply not on the books; the U.S. Sixth Fleet, then as afterward controlled the air and maritime approaches to the region, and serious Soviet intervention was militarily unfeasible, short of a full-scale invasion across the Caucasus (which, of course, would set off World War III). Under these circumstances, it is hardly conceivable that the Kremlin, for a single moment, seriously considered using force in the Near East. The very fact that Moscow was taking such great care (in this as in the Guatemalan case) to disguise the Arms Deal as a "Czech" transaction, and stoutly refused to abandon this pretense for months afterward, proved Russia's determination not to be drawn into a direct confrontation with the West under any circumstances. As noted in chapter 1,[70] the basic purpose of Soviet Near Eastern policy militated against overt provocations of the West, such as the sudden injection of Russian forces into the region, which could only precipitate a really massive Western counterblow; this was precisely the reason for Moscow's resort to highly complex and circuitous maneuvers. Even a year later, during the Suez-Sinai conflict, when Soviet involvement in the area had become overt and, consequently, Soviet prestige was much more heavily committed, Moscow's immediate "contribution" to Egypt's defense consisted of the movement of Bloc military personnel and newly arrived Soviet planes to places of greater safety.[71] It is quite true that, shortly afterward, Bulganin indulged in "rocket rattling" against London, Paris, and Jerusalem, but, by that time, it had become perfectly clear that the United States was pressuring its British and French allies into submission, so that Moscow risked very little by uttering these threats. There is no sound reason for supposing that, in 1955, the Russians had the slightest intention of acting in a more gallant fashion if the Arms Deal resulted in a second Guatemalan episode.

These considerations inevitably lead to the conclusion that, at the time of Shepilov's Cairo mission, the Kremlin's Near Eastern policy rested upon two fundamental assumptions: (a) the USSR

[69] See chap. 4, "Molotov's February 8 Speech."
[70] See chap. 1, "Soviet-Egyptian Convergence."
[71] See, for instance, the comments on this episode in Asher Lee, *The Soviet Air and Rocket Forces* (New York: Frederick A. Praeger, 1959).

could not undertake to protect Egypt against a Western counterblow; (b) however, such a resort to force on the part of the
Western powers was, perhaps, less likely than Cairo feared. Consequently, the communist countries and Egypt had the option of
ignoring this contingency and proceeding with the Arms Deal on
the supposition that nothing untoward would occur.

If, indeed, this was the brunt of Shepilov's message to Colonel
Nasser, it left the Egyptians to face all the risks; Moscow could
always disengage, more or less elegantly, by insisting that the
transaction concerned only Egypt and Czechoslovakia and that
their governments would have to decide whether they wished to
continue with its implementation.[72] At the most, the Kremlin could
assist Cairo to render the Arms Deal a little less provocative to the
West by reducing its visibility level; thus, during the initial stages,
the employment of Bloc military instructors in Egypt could be
kept to a minimum, Egyptian officers being trained, as far as possible, at Warsaw Pact installations in the Bloc. This procedure,
which came to be adopted,[73] also had the advantage of reassuring
those elements in Egypt that were less than enthusiastic at the
prospect of a massive influx of military experts from the communist countries. Quite clearly, however, mere palliatives could
not help Colonel Nasser solve his basic dilemma—namely, that he
had to take an altogether disproportionate (and unilateral) risk
or abandon the Arms Deal altogether. The evidence indicates that
he felt he had no choice but to go along with Shepilov's suggestions, on the (hopeful) assumption that the West would confine
itself to mere verbal reactions. Thus on July 26, while Shepilov
was still in Cairo, an Egyptian technical delegation took off for
Prague to initiate the implementation of the Arms Deal (by in-
specting the first consignment of MiG-15 jets that were about to
enter the pipeline).[74]

---

[72] The very vagueness of Prague's original arrangements with Cairo (see
chap. 3, footnote 33) lent itself very well to such evasions since, in case of a
Western interdiction of arms supplies, the Bloc could easily find loopholes,
enabling it to renege on the deal without actually breaking a commitment to
Egypt. Under these circumstances, Cairo presumably pressed for the conclusion of more detailed protocols. It is not clear whether Ali Sabri's shopping
list (see "Preparing for Implementation" earlier in this chapter) was intended
to constitute the basis for the draft of such a protocol.

[73] Foreign Aid Program: Compilation of Studies and Surveys Prepared
under the Direction of the Special Committee to Study the Foreign Aid Program, presented to Mr. Green, U.S. Senate, July 1957, Appendix, pp. 712–764.

[74] Seale, Struggle for Syria, pp. 234–237; also chap. 1, footnote 26. Presumably, some of the participants in the Cairo military discussions with Soviet

Although, as one source emphasizes, with this step "arms deliveries had begun,"[75] it seems that the political aspects of the transaction had not been altogether resolved. Shepilov would appear to have returned to Moscow with an Egyptian request for some form of Soviet reassurance. As was noted earlier,[76] Cairo could not rid itself of the suspicion that the Kremlin might be tempted to exploit the Arms Deal as a bargaining counter; both in 1955 and subsequently, the Egyptians feared that Moscow would agree to a regional arms embargo in return for being admitted to the Near Eastern concert of powers. Presumably, therefore, what Premier Nasser wanted was a commitment from the Russians that, if they could not undertake to shield Egypt against a Western counterblow, they would, at least, refrain from treating her interests as negotiable items in an East-West package deal. There are indications that Moscow finally did provide the Egyptian leader with some assurance along these lines. In August 1965, Colonel Nasser reminded his Soviet hosts at a Kremlin banquet (including Mikoyan, who undoubtedly had been privy to the 1955 arrangements) that "exactly 10 years ago . . . we asked you if we could depend on you in breaking the arms monopoly . . . [and] on this very date, and almost on this very day, we received a positive answer from you. . . ."[77] The wording of the question "if we could depend on you in breaking the arms monopoly" does, indeed, suggest that Cairo suspected the Russians might renege on the Arms Deal and agree to a regional embargo, if given sufficient inducements by the West. Moscow's "positive answer" would appear to have been delivered in the second week of August, during a two-hour session between Colonel Nasser and Ambassador Solod in which the Egyptian Premier was also handed an official invitation to visit the USSR.[78]

The Soviet assurance, coming at this time, may have raised the junta's morale somewhat, but, under the circumstances, perhaps

---

representatives two months earlier, such as M. Hafez Ismail (see Haykal, "Political Enquiry," pt. 4), as well as other officials responsible for supplies, had already arrived in Prague to settle the various outstanding details. A military transaction of major proportions, needless to say, required supplementary agreements to cover training, logistics, and other aspects. It undoubtedly took prolonged discussions to make the necessary complex arrangements.

[75] Seale, *Struggle for Syria,* pp. 234–237.
[76] See "The Chinese Factor" earlier in this chapter.
[77] Moscow Radio, in Arabic, August 27, 1965.
[78] *New York Times,* August 10, 1955.

not very much. A few days earlier, Egypt's ambassador to Washington, Ahmad Husayn, had arrived in Cairo for consultations.[79] As has been noted, Egyptian sources claim that his was the voice that, during the following weeks, reminded Colonel Nasser most insistently of the frightening Guatemalan example.[80] Before leaving Washington, he had met with Secretary of State Dulles,[81] who by this time was aware "that a deal to exchange Communist arms for Egyptian cotton was in the making."[82] Presumably, therefore, this meeting provided the ambassador with some indication of the reaction to be expected once it became known in the West that the transaction had actually been implemented. Judging by the warnings he is reported to have uttered during the subsequent period, it would seem that he came away fearing the worst. Added to the serious doubts already harbored by other leading officials in Cairo, this factor probably helped to spread the atmosphere of foreboding that was enveloping the ruling group. Events during the following weeks, as Western reactions intensified with increasingly hard intelligence that an arms deal was under way,[83] appeared to bear out the most pessimistic appraisals. Egyptian accounts claim that, by September, Western emissaries were speaking in terms implying that Premier Nasser and the Russians had miscalculated, and there was going to be a second Guatemala after all.[84] For Moscow this could prove to be a costly error at most, but for the Egyptian leader it was likely to be a fatal mistake. He could entertain no illusion that Russia would protect or succor his country; as has been noted, in its "positive answer" in August, the Kremlin probably undertook to refrain from any deal with the West at Egypt's expense, but it most certainly did not promise to rush into an armed confrontation in order to shield the Cairo government.[85]

[79] Cairo Radio, domestic broadcast, August 1, 1955.
[80] See "Cairo Between East and West" earlier in this chapter.
[81] Cairo Radio, domestic broadcast, August 1, 1955.
[82] See chap. 2, footnote 48.
[83] See ibid., "Additional Questions." Haykal claims that Western "intelligence felt that an inscrutable Egyptian activity was afoot in Prague" when "Egyptian military missions . . . were instructed . . . to . . . proceed to Prague" ("Political Enquiry," pt. 4). As has been noted, this event occurred on July 26.
[84] See "Cairo Between East and West" earlier in this chapter. The statements ascribed to Kermit Roosevelt by Haykal in al-Ahram (Cairo Radio, domestic broadcast, April 14, 1967) are alleged to have been made in September 1955.
[85] See relevant paragraphs earlier in the present section.

Consummation

With arms shipments already arriving, Premier Nasser must have felt that it was too late to retreat; a decision to back down under such humiliating circumstances was likely to mean the end of the regime. He certainly would have lost face irretrievably in the eyes of his officers. Consequently, he went ahead, being able only to hope that, by some miracle, the West might refrain from action. In the event, he was proved right. By late September, the Arms Deal had entered the pages of history.[86]

[86] The present case study is devoted only to the genesis of the 1955 Arms Deal and the light it may help to throw upon Soviet policy processes. Consequently, its scope does not encompass the complex military, technical, and financial details of the transaction itself, nor, for that matter, the wider question of the aftermath and repercussions of this dramatic event. An additional, sizable manuscript might barely do justice to these topics. Suffice it to say, therefore, that, under the original Arms Deal and various supplementary protocols up to the Suez-Sinai conflict, some 200 Soviet and Czech jet fighters, bombers, and transports, well over 300 modern tanks and self-propelled guns, and large quantities of artillery, machine guns, small arms, and military vehicles, as well as a number of naval units, reached Egypt. Altogether, these consignments were quantitatively not far inferior, and qualitatively at least equal, to the total armaments possessed prior to mid-1955 by the five signatories (Egypt, Israel, Syria, Jordan, and Lebanon) of the 1949 armistice agreements. The cost of the 1955/56 Bloc military shipments to the purchaser was estimated at some $200 million (and at a much higher sum in terms of international market value). (For sources, see chap. 2, footnote 28; footnotes 48 and 73 in this chapter; also despatch by Gen. Sir Charles F. Keightley, *Supplement to the London Gazette of 10 Sep. 1957*, no. 41172, September 12, 1957.) There can be little doubt that, by injecting hardware in such massive proportions, the Soviet Union was destroying the delicate military and political balance which the West had maintained so laboriously in this tense region. Unquestionably, the immediate effect was to injure Western interests, but it is highly dubious whether the USSR itself derived any long-term benefits from its military transactions. (This question is discussed in the Epilogue.)

6 Epilogue

Most analysts have regarded the historic Arms Deal as the beginning of a new phase in Soviet foreign policy, during which Khrushchev and his successors penetrated into Afro-Asia, the "soft underbelly" of the noncommunist world, securing major advantages for the USSR. More than a decade after this event, it may be pertinent to wonder whether Moscow's alleged successes in the enterprise have been really pure and unalloyed and whether Khrushchevian ebullience has in any sense "paid off."

In the West, it has long been fashionable to take an apocalyptic view of the Soviet leadership's supposed ability to outscore Western policies throughout the Third World. Near Eastern developments appear to be particularly susceptible to this type of congenital pessimism; every crisis period (1955–1956, 1958, and most recently 1967–1969) seems to have set off renewed waves of despair, with but little cognizance of the fact that each of Moscow's previous "victories" in the region had proved both double-edged and short-lived.

To be sure, the Soviet Union did gain some benefits from the Arms Deal, largely by default, but its achievements were modest when gauged even by the limited expectations of the more skeptical leaders in the Kremlin, while the liabilities incurred proved, within a short while, to be most serious.

The immediate aim of the transaction, as this study suggests, was negative—to prevent, or at least hamstring, plans for a Western defense network in the region. Even this goal was not completely met. The West did, indeed, prove to be unexpectedly

EPILOGUE 159

hesitant and tepid in its reactions, so that much of its earlier momentum in the Near East was lost, with many local leaders beginning to hedge their bets. Nevertheless, the Near Eastern (later Baghdad) security pact proceeded to be implemented, and it was not until three years later that Qasim's revolt in Iraq led to its gradual disintegration (although on paper CENTO still exists to this very day).

Moscow's second aim, acceptance into the Near Eastern concert of powers, was not fulfilled at any time during the subsequent decade and is only approaching realization now. Shepilov tried valiantly, during the Suez-Sinai crisis, to achieve joint U.S.-Soviet hegemony over the region (after Khrushchev had failed earlier in 1956 to tempt Britain and France into a similar arrangement with the USSR), but the Eisenhower administration was not prepared to carry its pique against its West European allies to quite such extremes. The U.S. Sixth Fleet remained (and remains) as visible evidence of the predominance of American power throughout the Mediterranean basin.

Another goal implicit in Moscow's 1955 Afro-Asian offensive was the achievement of a significant measure of leverage over Russia's new associates in the Third World. Throughout the late 1940s and early 1950s, Soviet publications vehemently denounced all forms of Western aid, economic and military, as calculated to give the West control, or at least predominant influence, over the policies of the recipient regimes. It was the unvarying theme of the Soviet media that such control was an inevitable concomitant of the donor-recipient relationship. Although, no doubt, these assertions were meant to serve a propagandistic purpose, the history of Russia's economic and military transactions with her associates in Eastern Europe and East Asia (to take only the Chinese, Yugoslav, and Albanian examples) shows clearly that Moscow herself regarded such relationships as natural channels for the imposition of Soviet control. It seems fair to assume that Khrushchev's offensive southward during the mid-1950s was partly intended to achieve meaningful leverage over the Afro-Asian recipients of new Soviet assistance, especially in the military field.

Indeed, at first sight, such a development appeared unavoidable. The regimes in question were mainly military dictatorships, depending primarily on army support; moreover, because most of them were embroiled in quarrels with neighboring countries, it seemed doubly improbable that they would risk offending the great power on whose goodwill their future supplies of hardware would increasingly depend. After all, most Afro-Asian armies were neither large enough nor sufficiently sophisticated to be able to absorb and integrate disparate weapons from miscellaneous sources. Consequently, any decision to accept Soviet arms seemed likely to constitute a first step toward an eventual Soviet monopoly over military supplies to the countries concerned. Clearly, one could expect the armies in question to adopt Soviet training and Soviet battle doctrine, since it would be self-defeating to use Russian weapons in a military context other than the one for which they had been specifically constructed. In turn, this meant that hardware from non-Soviet sources would become increasingly irrelevant to the needs of any country that had adapted itself to Soviet military standards. Moreover, Soviet and Bloc experts would be required to assemble the newly arrived weapons in the recipient countries and to instruct local military personnel and technicians in their use; senior Afro-Asian officers would have to go to Bloc countries, often for prolonged periods, to be trained at Soviet staff colleges, so that they might be able properly to apply Soviet military doctrine. It seemed probable that these exchanges would open up the military establishment, the most vital and sensitive sector of the power structure in the Third World, to Soviet ideological indoctrination, infiltration, and subversion. What is more, such links with the USSR could hardly be confined to a single transaction. Once the Soviet weapons and training had been accepted, it was assumed that the general staffs in question would naturally wish to go on receiving later models of aircraft, naval vessels, and tanks from the same source in order to deal with the problem of rapid obsolescence. In that case, each subsequent transaction would expose the recipient to renewed Soviet demands and pressure.

Equally important was the consideration that few Afro-Asian states were sufficiently developed to possess facilities for the assembly, maintenance, and repair of sophisticated Soviet hardware or the manufacture of the required ammunition, spare parts, and replacements; nor did the USSR seem likely to prove very liberal in granting production licenses for such purposes. Consequently, allowing for rapid attrition, especially at the hands of inexperienced Afro-Asian personnel, Soviet arms could be expected to become little more than museum pieces unless the USSR were kept in a sufficiently good humor to extend continuous assistance in such areas as maintenance and repair, the supply of ammunition, spare parts, and replacements. This aspect alone seemed bound to ensure ongoing Soviet control over the operative utilization of Russian-produced weapons. The significance of this consideration was underlined by the fact that a number of Afro-Asian leaders had turned to the USSR because they wanted help in recovering their national "irredenta" or in subduing a neighboring rival by threat or use of armed force. U.S. Mutual Security aid and other U.S. military assistance was generally limited to countries promising to employ American arms only for the preservation of internal security or for legitimate defense against aggression; the USSR, on the other hand, persistently boasted that Russian aid was free of such "strings" (which seemed to mean that the recipient had a green light to attack his neighbors). In fact, however, no beneficiary of Soviet military assistance seemed likely to be able to fight a really major battle unless the USSR agreed to dispatch a continuous stream of munitions and spare parts so as to maintain Soviet weapons in battle condition. Thus Russian control over the achievement of the (usually expansionist) "national purpose" of Afro-Asian military aid recipients threatened to prove far more real than the written or verbal strings of the West. Consequently, it seemed reasonable to assume that none of the Afro-Asian leaders concerned would dare to defy Moscow.[1]

[1] This analysis does not attempt to examine in depth another aspect of military assistance (actually barter), which must have seemed of decisive importance to the USSR, namely, the economic consequences.

Admittedly, at first sight, Soviet arms prices appeared attractive, since they seemed to reflect assembly-line costs only, without covering the greater part of research and development expenses. For those items that the Red Army itself was already beginning to replace with newer models, prices were even lower. Superficially, repayment with export goods rather than in cash also seemed to favor the recipients of Soviet arms; after all, most Afro-Asian countries are afflicted with single-crop economies, their one major export commodity usually being buffeted by the fluctuations of an uncertain or glutted world market. Thus Soviet willingness to accept such crops in repayment for hardware constituted a tempting gesture.

On the other hand, this arrangement was fraught with serious dangers. Even if Soviet prices were relatively reasonable, massive arms deals involving increasingly valuable, sophisticated items were likely to prove very costly to marginal economies; crops would have to be mortgaged for years ahead to provide the means whereby to repay Moscow for its arms shipments. As a consequence, it seemed probable that the Afro-Asian nations concerned would eventually jeopardize their traditional markets in the West and that the whole direction of their trade would shift toward the Bloc. This trend was likely to become more marked once the Russians started flooding Western markets with commodities acquired from Afro-Asian recipients of Soviet weapons.

Thus it seemed initially that the USSR was establishing leverage over those Afro-Asian leaders who had permitted their countries

---

Since the USSR's capacity for absorbing tropical and subtropical produce was not very great—most of these commodities belonging to the category of consumer goods—the temptation to dump them at a discount in the West was bound to grow. The recipient states, once their Western outlets were lost, were likely to become increasingly dependent upon Soviet willingness to continue importing their produce, since they might no longer have another major market.

Moreover, such economies seemed fated to become tied to the somewhat dubious system of barter trade, having forfeited their only (i.e., Western) sources of hard currency income. Any healthy inclination to foster a more mixed economy, capable of feeding the local population, was likely to be inhibited by the fact that repayment obligations to the USSR required, if anything, the expansion rather than the contraction of the acreage devoted to the predominant export crop (e.g., cotton, rice, and rubber). Although Moscow persistently blamed "imperialism" for allegedly exploiting the ex-colonial world through the "scissors" effect, whereby world market prices of tropical and subtropical raw materials were persistently depressed while the exports of industrial countries became more expensive, the Russians took good care to become beneficiaries of this phenomenon themselves. In its military and economic trade agreements, the USSR insisted that Afro-Asian commodity repayments should be evaluated in current (depressed) world market prices and, moreover, that there should be annual readjustments, so that Russia might derive full benefit from any further reduction in the value of tropical raw materials. Moreover, Moscow also provided for the contingency that its Afro-Asian trade partners might approach bankruptcy if their main export crops hit rock-bottom prices; the USSR made quite sure that it would receive its pound of flesh, in any case, by insisting that debts which could not be covered in produce at current world market levels should be repaid in fully convertible currency. Thus the recipients of Soviet weapons could expect to find their valuta reserves drained away not only because of the artificial diversion of their trade and the further depression of their export prices but also as a result of direct Soviet calls on their remaining dollar or sterling balances.

For that matter, the actual terms of Soviet "military assistance" were far from generous to the recipients. Only infrequently and to an insignificant extent did the USSR offer its associates military grants rather than commercial sales (in sharp contrast to the original U.S. practice of extending large military grants in aid to friendly countries). Soviet credits for arms purchases usually carried 2 or 2½ per cent interest, repayable over 5, 7, 10, or, at most, 12 years. These terms compared favorably only with *private* Western commercial credits, but not at all with the policy pursued by the United States and other Western governments of subsidizing military sales to friendly countries through additional economic assistance in the form of surplus food (P.L. 480), Development Loan Funds, and other shots in the arm (which were generally repayable either in local currency or at very low interest rates—originally as little as ½ or 1½ per cent over 25 or 30 years, although "harder" terms have recently become usual). In this way, the West often compensated the local economies for the drain caused by military expenditures, whereas Soviet economic aid was usually extended on terms no more generous than military assistance. Moreover, the recipient country had to pay and support Soviet military experts during their period of sojourn there.

to become entangled with the Soviet bloc through arms deals; the consequent dangers in the military, security, political, and economic fields loomed ominously on the horizon. This was certainly the feeling prevailing throughout the West, as a single glance at the statements, articles, and books of that period will show. The Western reaction to the Guatemalan arms deal in 1954 was, of course, predicated precisely upon such assumptions. Nor is there any reason for thinking that the USSR regarded the matter in a basically different light. Indeed, during his Asian visits of 1955 and 1956 and at the Twentieth Congress of the CPSU in 1956, in the first exuberance of the new Soviet "breakthrough," Khrushchev himself spoke in the vein of a man who felt he was within reach of his objectives. His concept of the "zone of peace," a coalition between the communist bloc and the neutrals who were associated with and dependent upon it, was apparently based on the belief that Moscow's newly gained leverage over parts of the Third World would eventually prove to be a decisive factor in the global contest. In their relations with client states inside the communist camp, the Soviet leaders had demonstrated previously, and were to show repeatedly throughout this period, that they would exploit both military and economic "assistance" to apply relentless pressure upon the recipient regimes. For example, the USSR ruthlessly cut off economic and military supplies to Yugoslavia in 1948 and again in 1958, while in 1959/60 the Kremlin abruptly ceased technical, nuclear, and military aid to China, acting in the same manner toward China's friend Albania. There seemed to be every reason for thinking, therefore, that the Soviet Union would attempt to deal in a similar fashion with its new friends in the Third World.

However, there should have been some grounds for doubt whether, indeed, such methods could possibly work when brought to bear upon noncommunist Afro-Asian regimes. After all, even with recalcitrant communist countries the brutal application of Soviet leverage (that is, the interruption of economic and military

---

Altogether, therefore, it appeared very likely during the 1950s that those developing countries which accepted Soviet arms would find their whole economic life mortgaged to the USSR for years to come; if, as could be predicted, the recipients failed to meet some of their debt obligations, they could expect to become entirely dependent upon Soviet willingness to grant moratoria on repayments. A leadership as predisposed to give weight to economic considerations as were the men in the Kremlin could hardly have overlooked these aspects of military "assistance" to Afro-Asian countries.

supplies) had not proved markedly successful in bringing the deviationists to heel; in fact, it only precipitated Moscow's final break with Belgrade, Peking, and Tirana. Once this lesson had been digested, the Russians had to search for entirely different methods of dealing with difficult partners: since leverage had failed to produce the desired results, Moscow was left to confront the bleak choice between outright use of military force (as in Czechoslovakia), or accommodation and compromise (as in its relations with North Korea and North Vietnam). Yet, in theory, communist regimes should have been ideal clients for the application of leverage, since they tend to be intrinsically "rational" (that is, deeply conscious of the cold dictates of self-interest), highly sensible of their vulnerability in the economic and military fields, and thus well aware of their dependency upon a continued supply of Soviet ammunition, spare parts, and army experts. Consequently, it was to be expected that these regimes would feel most reluctant to risk any steps that could conceivably weaken their domestic power base by undermining their military position and depriving them of the force and authority that emanated from their bond with the feared Russians. If, nevertheless, East European and Asian communist governments lacking the ready option of a link with the West (and it must be remembered that Tito was originally more militantly anti-Western than Mao) proved willing and able to defy Soviet leverage, it should have been realized that noncommunist regimes in the Third World would react with even greater recalcitrance when confronted with Russian pressure.

For one, Afro-Asian leaders generally are not as susceptible to the traditional, "rational" considerations of self-interest as Western or communist rulers. A country with a highly developed economy or a sophisticated military structure is, paradoxically, more immediately vulnerable to sanctions in either of these fields than is a relatively retarded area that has remained innocent of complex technical systems which could be immobilized by a stoppage in the flow of vital ingredients. In such an emergency, the less advanced country can more readily revert, without traumatic shocks, to the relatively unsophisticated level of economic and military life from which it is only just emerging. While government in a modern society, accustomed to certain amenities, may find it difficult to survive a major breakdown, rulers in developing regions are far less likely to be judged by purely material criteria, nor are their personal fortunes primarily linked to technical "progress." Their regimes do rely on a measure of force, to be sure, but for that purpose they hardly need modern jets, antiaircraft missiles, or submarines; trucks, machine guns, and rifles are usually quite sufficient for domestic purposes. Sophisticated hardware is required by such rulers only as a status symbol and to extort concessions from their neighbors.

What really counts in most Afro-Asian capitals is the charismatic appeal of the supreme leader; this emotional factor can only be enhanced whenever the chief imparts a feeling of vicarious virility to his followers by proudly defying one of the great powers —in the face of all "rational" considerations. In this context, it should be remembered that lingering resentment against the colonial past often is not necessarily the result of mistreatment suffered; in many cases, it reflects an angry emotion of shame due to the impotent frustration felt for ages by a large indigenous majority obviously incapable of challenging colonial rule by a tiny but securely ensconced European minority. In those instances where the European colonial power granted independence more cr less voluntarily, or where self-government was achieved after a few skirmishes, resentment has been all the stronger because liberty was not wrested from the adversary in victorious battle, and past humiliation, therefore, has not been blotted out. The pride, sensitivity, and touchiness, the tendency of Afro-Asian leaders to overreact to any demands advanced by a great power, are all part of this syndrome: quarrels with mighty states are actually welcomed, because they enable the local charismatic leader to assert his own and his followers' self-esteem, to win verbal "battles," and thus to "fight" anew for independence. Material considerations are usually of secondary importance when compared to this emotion; hence the repeated instances when Afro-Asians have gone out of their way to tell a great power "to hell with your aid." Consequently, it is unrealistic for the donor to hope that his assistance will result in immediate or obvious political benefits; it is particularly counterproductive to expect gratitude, since many Afro-Asians regard it as humiliating to be in a relationship of obligation to the donor. They also believe that aid is not a favor bestowed upon the beneficiary but, rather, a just tribute paid to newly acquired independence, a fair recompense for past wrongs, or, in the case of the USSR, a moral obligation owed by a "fraternal, socialist country" to its Afro-Asian comrades. Thus there is relatively little inclination to reward the donor; if anything, there is a tendency to ask "what have you done for me *lately*"? Moreover, the Third World has become wedded to the slogan of "unconditional assistance" and regards any indication of strings as an unpardonable breach of faith. In the last resort, "nonaligned" leaders, consciously playing off East against West, have always had the simple option of going over to the other side—or threatening to do so—when faced with unacceptable conditions or requests.

Above all, the Third World discovered some time ago (first in its relations with the West and subsequently in its dealings with the communist countries) that all great powers will initially attempt to exert some form of leverage but, when angrily defied, will usually end up by appeasing their irate Afro-Asian clients. The reason for this strange phenomenon is not far to seek. Even a state like the USSR, which feels relatively few inhibitions in applying naked power, cannot do very much with its nuclear might or with its vast conventional forces unless it is prepared, if necessary, actually to invade and annihilate any and every small country that defies or displeases it. This would hardly be a safe or realistic modus operandi in the era of the thermonuclear stalemate, especially in a "border zone" such as Afro-Asia. After all, the USSR must always consider the reactions of the other superpower. Actually, Moscow is particularly handicapped in the Third World, because Soviet military operations there are likely to precipitate prompt Western counteraction, and it so happens that Western striking forces, such as the U.S. Sixth and Seventh Fleets, are still maintaining regional military supremacy over the naval and air approaches to the Southern Hemisphere. Thus a great power like the Soviet Union can occasionally threaten its Afro-Asian associates, but if such warnings are ignored or defied a very nasty dilemma is bound to arise: since overt violence is out of the question, Moscow's choice of possibilities is really quite limited. The donor country can, in theory, proceed to implement its threats and cut off military and economic aid; in reality, however, such a step can be as damaging to the stronger as it is to the weaker partner. After all, the donor has presumably made his material, diplomatic, and psychological investments for the purpose of building up goodwill and leverage in the recipient country and is likely to lose all these investments the moment he actually attempts to pull the lever. He is unlikely, therefore, to be at all eager to turn off the faucet of assistance, especially once it has become evident that the recipient will probably not be cowed by such measures, rating "loss of face" far more highly than mere material benefits. More-over, if the recipient's defiance continues after sanctions are ap-plied, the donor's unsuccessful attempt to implement his threat will only prove its hollowness to the world at large. On the other hand, a weak surrender by a superpower like the USSR, permitting Afro-Asian aid recipients to ignore Moscow's interests and desires while the latter meekly continues to deliver the goods, is hardly going to prove less disastrous in terms of global prestige. Moreover, in that case, some of the more skeptical minds in the Kremlin are bound to ask the General Secretary what useful, practical purpose the whole Soviet offensive into Afro-Asia has really served.

Both unsophisticated tribal leaders and radical, semi-educated urban demagogues in the Third World have proved remarkably adept in grasping the fundamentals of this situation. Consequently, they have contemptuously rejected requests and warnings issued by the great powers, frequently threatening the latter in return, feeling reassured that nothing very terrible was likely to happen as a result of such defiance. They have realized that he who sends them assistance, with the aim of building up leverage, dare never pull the lever for fear that it might break off in his hand. If these considerations apply to Afro-Asian relations with the superpowers in general, they are doubly relevant to dealings with the USSR; after all, Moscow has always claimed that its aid is "uncondi-tional," that it attaches no "strings," and that, unlike the West, it allegedly puts forward no requests and does not interfere in the internal affairs of the recipient country. (So far, many Afro-Asian leaders have failed to draw the proper inferences from the Soviet invasions of Hungary and Czechoslovakia, believing that their own regions are exempt from the fate meted out to countries within the Soviet sphere.) Consequently, it is especially embarrassing for Moscow to be caught applying pressure to "nonaligned" recipients or to see them publicly rejecting Soviet demands.

The combined weight of the aforementioned factors has made Afro-Asian recipients of Russian weapons particularly unsuitable clients for the application of Soviet leverage. If, however, they are not easily amenable to Russian pressure, this fact carries with it not merely disadvantages but actual dangers from Moscow's point of view.

As the author has pointed out elsewhere:

Military relations between the Soviet Union and certain developing countries constitute a particularly significant example of the complexity and the potential dangers of Moscow's policy. The USSR had originally extended arms credit to newly independent or revolutionary regimes as a bait, to secure entry into regions such as the Near East, Africa, and the S.E. Asian archipelago, where the West enjoyed conventional military predominance. Unable to confront a stronger opponent, the USSR had resorted to outflanking tactics. The regimes enticed by Soviet weapons were generally embroiled with their neighbours, their national purpose usually enshrining the recovery of some irredenta. The West, whose protective aegis extended over these regions, pursued a policy of even-handed friendship towards local powers, regarding the maintenance of a balance between them as the best guarantee of stability. A local arms race or the growth of military imbalance, tempting some ruler in the area to surprise his neighbour, could therefore not be welcome to the West. The Soviet Union, on the other hand, an outsider without share of responsibility for regional tranquillity, considered it advantageous to pour arms, exacerbating local conflicts. The West was bound to be embarrassed since, in areas under its own aegis, it could hardly compete with the USSR in creating turbulence.

Such Soviet calculations were sound only so long as Afro-Asian arms recipients utilised Russian weapons for *political* purposes—e.g. to gain prestige and extort concessions from weaker neighbours, or to equip militant insurgent elements in other states. [Once, however, a Soviet arms recipient, tempted by an abundance of hardware, drifted into *armed conflict* with a pro-Western country, the USSR was bound to face a dilemma. Soviet leaders naturally assumed that the West might interpose itself in case of such dangerous confrontation, in order to halt the conflict.] Since the West had maintained military predominance over the approaches to Afro-Asia, the USSR would then be obliged either to resort to a nuclear strike or to abandon its local arms recipient, with the consequent loss of prestige, influence, and investments. Neither alternative being palatable, the Soviet national interest clearly required measures to prevent full-scale local wars of this type. Nor, for that matter, could the USSR welcome the embarrassing possibility of conflict between its arms recipients and other Afro-Asian beneficiaries of Soviet favour. The problem was how to steer emotional and erratic regimes away from such dangerous paths.[2]

This problem may, in fact, be almost insoluble if, as the present analysis suggests, Moscow's leverage over Afro-Asian recipients is actually extremely limited and if, moreover, the recipients to some extent exert leverage over the donor country, which, psycho-

---

[2] Uri Ra'anan, "Tactics in the Third World: Contradictions and Dangers," *Survey*, no. 57 (October 1965), pp. 30–31.

logically unwilling to abandon its military, economic, and diplomatic investments, is tempted time and again, after each debacle, to throw good money after bad.

What is likely to occur, under such circumstances, is a repetition of what has already taken place on several occasions, namely, the tail wagging the dog or, to be precise, the Soviets being pulled along in the wake of their more militant and less "responsible" associates.[3] The first such instance was Suez-Sinai, when Colonel Nasser, emboldened by the original Arms Deal and his consequent close ties with Moscow, embarked on a collision course with the West, ending in the bloody confrontation of October–November 1956. The second case was the June 1967 Near Eastern war, when President Nasser went beyond his original understanding with Moscow (namely, to "rescue" the Syrian Ba'ath government and create a "second front" against Israel by mobilizing his troops in the Sinai Peninsula) and permitted himself to be tempted into reimposing the blockade of the port of Eilat, fully aware, as he has since then stated, that this meant war.

It is perfectly true that Moscow on both occasions was able to avoid being itself drawn into the armed conflict. However, in each instance the Kremlin was brought perilously close to the "moment of truth" at which a decision had to be made between two unpalatable alternatives, one of them fraught with the most dangerous implications. At Suez-Sinai, the USSR could either stand by helplessly, watching its investments going down the drain, a Russian-trained army being destroyed, and Russian weapons being captured intact—with consequent devastating loss of Soviet prestige—or stage a (nuclear) confrontation with two NATO members. Moscow's immediate choice, needless to say, was to regard

---

[3] The term "responsible" as applied in Moscow, the capital of a thermonuclear superpower, is not necessarily identical with the definition acceptable to Afro-Asian leaders. A well-publicized case in point is the Russian reply purported to have been given to an Algerian delegation that, in 1967, requested more direct Soviet action to "liquidate the consequences" of the June war: "And what do you think of atomic war?" Moscow's Near Eastern associates do not automatically share the premises of this posture and, by their own lights, their views of what the national interest requires are entirely "responsible." If the term is defined simply to mean "circumspect," then it would seem to have been applicable to different personalities at different times: the Egyptian leader, for instance, certainly appears to have been motivated by calculation rather than passion in his adroit handling of the 1955 Arms Deal, as the present study indicates; how some of his subsequent actions, in 1956 and 1967, should be judged is an entirely different question.

discretion as the better part of valor and quietly to evacuate the most valuable items of Soviet military equipment and the majority of the Russian experts. In the event, the Kremlin was spared an agonizing dilemma, since it speedily became evident that the USSR had been joined by an unexpected ally, namely, the United States, and that American pressure was causing London and Paris to falter midway in "Operation Musketeer"; at that point, of course, it became safe for Moscow to start rattling its rockets and to proclaim loudly that Russian "warnings" to Britain, France, and Israel had rescued Egypt.

In the case of the June 1967 war, a Soviet-manufactured scenario —according to which Egyptian forces were to create a diversion, "saving" the Syrian Ba'ath regime from an allegedly imminent assault—stampeded Cairo into mobilizing suddenly, deploying its army in Sinai and Gaza, expelling the United Nations Emergency Force, and then succumbing to the lure of a renewed blockade of Eilat, thus precipitating the outbreak of hostilities. The immediate result, once again, was the annihilation of Soviet-equipped and trained armies, the capture of sophisticated Soviet weapons, and a resounding setback for Soviet prestige. Moreover, this time, unlike in 1956, Moscow was not rescued from its dilemma by sudden American aid and protection for Russia's Near Eastern clients; consequently, the USSR could only make menacing but impotent gestures while the recipients of Soviet arms went down to shattering defeat. There remained the theoretical alternative of direct Soviet military intervention in the Mediterranean, with the probable result of a full confrontation with the U.S. Sixth Fleet; however, there is singularly little evidence for believing that serious advocates of such a move were to be found among the Soviet leaders, the Kremlin's almost immediate recourse to the "Hotline" pointing in the opposite direction.

The repeated assertions of certain Western commentators that the aftermath of the June 1967 war has, nevertheless, produced "major Russian gains" in the Near East must be regarded as very unconvincing, at least when viewed from the Soviet angle. It is surely not a good recipe for the preparation of the "dish called success" to "start by losing one war." The truth is that Moscow has been left uncomfortably face-to-face with its bitterly disappointed clients, who know perfectly well the difference between meaningful aid in war and vituperative speeches at the United Nations and who are only too conscious that Soviet "sympathy" has not helped them to regain one square inch of territory. Russia does *not* derive unalloyed joy from the so-called polarization of the Near East, which saddles her with sponsorship of the embittered, unpredictable losers, while the United States is regarded as a co-beneficiary of the victors. Moscow has little taste for shouldering the burdens of another Cuba, at a daily cost of over $1 million, and is believed to have let Cairo know repeatedly that it is unrealistic to cut all ties with the West, since economic succor, in the last resort, must come from the United States. Similarly, when importuned to help recover the Sinai Peninsula, the USSR has insistently intimated that Washington is the proper capital to pressure on this question. The Kremlin is regretfully aware that nothing but embarrassment awaits a donor state like Russia whose clients constantly challenge it to "put up or shut up" at a time when the physical presence in the Mediterranean of the rival superpower precludes direct Soviet military action. It is thus unlikely that the USSR could score any real or lasting gains in the region *unless* the West were to disengage unilaterally, that is, to withdraw, so that it would become safe for the Russians to intervene forcibly on behalf of their local associates.

To sum up, it would seem that the USSR has precious little to show for its involvement in escapades that the late Joseph Stalin would have regarded as unacceptably adventurous (not to speak of the squandering of Soviet equipment and hardware worth billions of dollars, some of it ultramodern and sophisticated, which is in fairly short supply even among Warsaw Pact members). Refueling privileges for Soviet naval vessels—which, in fact, the USSR had already gained prior to the June 1967 war—can hardly compensate Moscow for the perpetual danger that Russian entanglements in the Near East might lead to a confrontation with the United States. (In any case, the Soviet strategic blueprint provides for a navy that will eventually reach self-sufficiency, with its own fuel and depot vessels, so that shore facilities will become largely irrelevant.) Russia's lack of real leverage over her Near Eastern associates is undoubtedly a matter of deep concern to the Kremlin, where there are vivid memories both of the bitter quarrels and of the dangerous outbreaks that have occurred because the USSR was unable to exercise full control over the recipients of Soviet arms. Moscow cannot entirely forget Nasser's 1959–1961 anti-Soviet press and radio campaign and the Iraqi Ba'ath regime's rupture of relations with the USSR in 1963 (after using Russian arms to kill Kurds and massacre Baghdadi communists); nor can the Politburo remain altogether tranquil when recalling the rapid escalation of perilous moves and countermoves in May–June 1967 that could well have dragged the Soviet Union into incalculable adventures. The debacles suffered in 1956 and 1967 might have been expected to produce a Soviet decision to disengage; however, the USSR's military, economic, diplomatic, and, above all, psychological investments in the region have become so considerable as to preclude such a move for the time being. Consequently, while trying its best to assert increasing control and to limit the dangers involved, the Kremlin has felt compelled to make still further commitments so that twelve years of feverish Soviet activity in the Arab world would not have to be written off as a total loss; the Russian leaders, therefore, have actually enlarged their stakes in the area—with reluctance, to be sure—replenishing the depleted arsenals of their Near Eastern clients to the tune of several billion dollars (for the second time in just over a decade). In retrospect, it would seem that the reservations and misgivings voiced by Molotov and other opponents of Khrushchev during the 1955 "debate" on the implementation of the Arms Deal with Egypt were extremely well founded.

PART II
RELATIONS BETWEEN
RECIPIENTS AND DONORS:
INDONESIA, 1956–1960

7 The General Background

In the summer of 1956, Indonesia's military leadership intensified its efforts to obtain modern arms abroad. Such a development would have been natural enough under normal circumstances, because some four fifths of the country's military equipment was of World War II or earlier vintage.[1] In Indonesia, however, any step toward modernization of the services had profound political implications.

The Indonesian Scene

Since 1950, a section of the army, headed by its (then) chief of staff, Abdul Haris Nasution, had attempted to demobilize part of the amorphous mass of regulars, revolutionary fighters, guerrillas, and gang leaders of various ideological shadings and to replace it by a disciplined, mobile, highly trained, and well-equipped force. By the fall of 1952, this policy had produced a major crisis, leading to Nasution's temporary removal. The proposed changes had encountered the vested interests both of paramilitary elements unwilling to face civilian life and of extremist political parties backing various armed bands, such as the left-wing "Bambu Runtjing." The Indonesian Communist Party (PKI), in particular, was resisting the creation of a smaller, more modern, professional army; in September 1948 and in August 1951, the PKI's hopes had

[1] *New York Times,* August 15, 1956.

been quashed by firm military action, and the party clearly desired the dilution rather than the perfection of an army it had come to fear.[2]

Opponents and supporters of the proposed reforms assumed, in the mid-fifties, that the acquisition of modern weapons and the concomitant intensive training of select cadres in Indonesia and abroad would automatically produce a cohesive, streamlined military unit, impervious to political penetration. It was not easy then to foresee that sharp personal competition within the military leadership and bitter rivalry between the services would neutralize many of the benefits of modernization and that President Sukarno's policies of politico-military "confrontation" with Indonesia's neighbors would eventually increase rather than diminish the number of superfluous, half-armed, and semitrained "troops."

It seems that Sukarno himself did not share the army's technical aspirations; he had been partly responsible for the defeat of Nasution's reform plans in the fall of 1952. It is true, of course, that Sukarno required an impressive military force as a political trump card in the implementation of his foreign policy. He had shown his overriding preoccupation with territorial questions, especially West New Guinea (West Irian), as early as January 1951; later on, he came to make the most of such issues on his long path to personal power. His actions in later years indicated, however, that he never envisaged the realization of his external ambitions by purely military means but, rather, by political and paramilitary pressure. Thus he needed a large army and showy weapons that could be brandished as an earnest of Indonesia's intentions instead of a shipshape, tough little fighting force, possessing modern but not necessarily top-heavy equipment. Moreover, Sukarno had learned to distrust and fear the Bonapartist tendencies of his officers, which in 1952 and later he could overcome only by personal intrigue within the services rather than by an open showdown. He had little incentive, therefore, to work for cohesion in the armed forces, since he had discovered it was the army's disunity that enabled him to survive.

In any case, during the mid-fifties, President Sukarno was engaged in a precarious tightrope act that did not allow him to lean heavily in any one direction or to make decisive commitments. He

[2] Justus M. van der Kroef, "Communism and Islam in Indonesia: A Western View," *India Quarterly*, October–December 1954.

had revolted against the attempts of a series of prime ministers to reduce him to the status of a reigning rather than ruling monarch, a role for which he was temperamentally unsuited. He wished to concentrate power in the presidential palace, but he could do so only by removing both Indonesia's parliamentary government and the moderate, democratic parties upon which it rested —parties that probably enjoyed the support of the majority of Indonesians. Therefore, he needed an alliance with whatever forces were amenable to his offers or opposed to the status quo. Apart from some opportunist elements within the orthodox Moslem leadership, which he could win over, and certain nationalists, who were attracted by his foreign policy, Sukarno had to rely primarily upon two allies: a section of the military elite and the PKI. Since these were diametrically opposed forces, Sukarno was obliged to proceed with great subtlety.

The PKI, under D. N. Aidit's highly competent "rightist" leadership, was already well on the way to becoming the largest communist party outside the communist bloc. Overcoming the bloody setback of 1948 in a few years, it had made the most of its opportunities through complicated maneuvers with certain sections of the national bourgeoisie. The PKI's massive success with the Javanese peasantry, however, and its large poll in Indonesia's 1955 elections had alarmed important parliamentary groups, and there were signs of an incipient anticommunist coalition under the moral leadership of Sukarno's great adversary, Vice-President Hatta. The PKI realized that it could not mobilize the masses to overawe its parliamentary opponents without risking a fatal clash with the army. Under these conditions, the PKI leaders and Sukarno needed each other; he could help them by undermining the anticommunist coalition, while they could assist him to bypass parliamentary government as such.[3]

As for the army, the most reformist elements within the officer corps had become thoroughly disillusioned with democratic processes in 1952, when the modernization of the forces was sabotaged by a temporary coalition of disparate parliamentary groups; the officers, therefore, were not opposed in principle to a presidential seizure of power, provided Sukarno showed more consideration for military interests. There was, of course, deep army hostility toward

[3] Arnold C. Brackman, *Indonesian Communism: A History* (New York: Frederick A. Praeger, 1963), passim.

the PKI, which had opposed the demobilization of the armed bands and which later was to raise the slogan of "arming the masses." Sukarno's temperamental affinity for "permanent revolution" rendered him receptive to the concept of a citizenry in arms, but he undoubtedly realized that the military leadership would uncompromisingly resist such a development.

Under these circumstances, any clear-cut decision on the precise character and status of the armed forces was out of the question in the mid-fifties. To retain the goodwill of the officers, Sukarno had to assist in the search for modern equipment, without, however, committing himself to any drastic reform of the size and nature of the services. (The air force formed an exception, since its very functions ensured professionalism.) This compromise fitted well into Sukarno's general scheme of foreign policy. He was determined to escalate the struggle for West Irian, both for genuine emotional reasons and because such a development was admirably suited to create a wave of national solidarity around his person. The acquisition of arms would serve to prove that Indonesia must be taken seriously, while the maintenance of large forces and, in later years, the procession of parading civilian "volunteers" would both intimidate the enemy and keep up the requisite pitch of patriotism and unity at home. The smaller professional army envisaged by the general staff would not have served such political purposes at all.

The International Constellation

To realize his external aspirations, what Sukarno needed above all was maneuverability in his relations with the great powers— what he called "an active, independent policy." He had to find a way of pressuring the outside world into acquiescence with his aims.

It is true that the West had shown some sympathy for the Indonesian army's modernization plans, which, indeed, had originally been drafted in collaboration with the Dutch military mission. The United States had provided light arms to equip the Mobile Brigade, the most highly disciplined unit in Indonesia, had aided the air force, and had offered arms under section 511(A) of the Mutual Security Act—a well-meant suggestion that was torpedoed by Djakarta's internal politics. Britain was showing willingness to help Indonesia enter the jet age. However, all these steps were clearly intended to further the maintenance of internal security, not to abet Indonesia in any external adventures. The United States had gone as far as seemed advisable in adopting a policy of neutrality and abstention in the dispute between its NATO ally, the Netherlands, and Indonesia over West Irian.

As Sukarno undoubtedly realized after his meetings with Dulles and Eisenhower in the spring of 1956, it was unlikely at that stage that the Western powers would voluntarily go beyond this line to back Djakarta or that they would consent to provide large quantities of really heavy armaments if Indonesia proceeded toward confrontation with the Dutch. Moreover, the increasingly friendly relations between Sukarno and the PKI were bound to—and indeed did—disturb the West to the point of repeated reappraisals of policy toward Indonesia.

These being the cold realities of the mid-fifties, it seemed that Indonesia had to acquire further leverage if it wished to budge the West from its position. A possible way of achieving this aim was through an entente with the Soviet Union and the Chinese People's Republic (CPR), including collaboration in the economic, cultural, scientific, and, perhaps, military fields. Such a development could possibly impel Western statesmen to make further concessions in the hope of preventing a close alliance between Indonesia and the East. These concessions could take various forms: the West might compete with the Soviets in economic and military aid to Indonesia, or it might even decide to pressure the Dutch into abandoning West Irian.

It was only in 1954 that maneuvers of this kind became feasible policy for Asian leaders; during the previous decade, the cold war had made for extreme polarization, so that East and West alike tended to regard neutralists with impatience and distrust. Even two years later, it still behooved Third World leaders to pursue their maneuvers with great caution, lest they overstep the mark. Egypt, in the fall of 1956, and Indonesia, during the rebellions of 1957/58, were to find that some of the Western powers could still be provoked into massive reprisals—overt or covert. Thus any form of collusion with the Soviet Union, especially in the sensitive field of weapons, had to be managed most circumspectly and, in its initial stages, secretly until the world could be faced with a fait accompli. After all, the West had proved as recently as 1954, in Guatemala, what a dim view it took of arms deals with the Soviet bloc.

The Soviet Union itself did not become fully "available" to neutralists until 1954, although Stalin had shown some signs of gradual change toward the Third World during the last years of his life.[4] The great Soviet offensive into Afro-Asia, however, started on its way only with the Geneva conference of April 1954 and gathered additional steam after the Bandung Conference of April 1955, the July 1955 Plenum of the Central Committee of the CPSU (Communist Party of the Soviet Union), and, finally, the Twentieth Congress of the CPSU in February 1956. By that time, East and West alike acknowledged and paid homage to the importance of neutral leaders, wooing particularly India's Nehru and Sukarno, the host of the Bandung Conference.

Ideologically, Moscow's new approach was buttressed by a "rightist" line in Afro-Asia, including a radical revision of all previous harsh judgments about national bourgeois leaders and a call for collaboration between such leaders and the local communist parties. To some extent, Moscow was only limping after Peking in adopting a more realistic appraisal of conditions in the area; however, at no time were the ideological nuances of Soviet and Chinese policies toward the region absolutely identical. As far as the PKI was concerned, the new general line of world communism amounted to no more than a final ratification of a course the party had been following successfully ever since 1951/52. Only one element of change was brought in: whereas, previously, the CPSU had acquiesced in PKI policies as an exceptional case, valid merely for *internal* Indonesian affairs, now intimacy became possible between the Soviet and Indonesian governments. The establishment of full diplomatic relations between the two countries in 1954 constituted a first step in this direction.

Soviet Considerations

Moscow's new approach was of great practical value in furthering Soviet national interests. Whereas in Europe the Russians had essentially reached the position of a status quo power by 1955, with a great deal to lose and comparatively little to gain, this was hardly true of the Soviet position in the developing regions, which —except in the Far East—was still insignificant. The West had retained important economic, political, and military assets even in newly independent countries and, moreover, kept naval and air

[4] See chap. 2, "Inconsistencies and Misinterpretations."

supremacy over the approaches to these areas. However, the Western position in the region was highly vulnerable from within, which was not the case in Western Europe. Afro-Asia abounded in artificial frontiers and in unappeased territorial, ethnic, and personal appetites. As "custodian" of the area, the West was bound to strict neutrality in local disputes; it naturally wished to avoid involvement in such squabbles and the consequent resentment of one side or another, since it had dealings with all of them. These conflicts were particularly undesirable because they weakened regional stability and, therefore, undermined the position of the status quo powers.

The Soviet Union, as an outsider, had nothing to lose from such local friction, at least as long as it could avoid being drawn into a direct clash with the West. Therefore, Moscow's interests demanded discrete encouragement and assistance for Afro-Asian opponents of the status quo, in support of their political claims against small pro-Western countries; in this way, the West could be confronted with maximal local hostility, neutralizing its influence in strategic areas. As an outsider, the Soviet Union did not have to maintain equally good relations with all Afro-Asian states, was therefore not bound to neutrality, and could prefer one side over another. Thus it could always outbid the West in gaining the favor of a particular government or leader. On the other hand, the USSR had to make sure that it maintained sufficient leverage over newly acquired friends to restrain them from rushing into full-scale wars, with the consequent danger of great-power involvement. Apparently, Moscow soon came to regard military assistance as an eminently practical way of administering a suitable mixture of control and encouragement to new associates in ex-colonial areas. The Egyptian example was to prove that this method, too, was not without its perils, but the Soviet Union learned, during the Suez crisis, how to spirit away some of its equipment and most of its personnel from danger zones.

The new Soviet approach toward Afro-Asia seemed precisely attuned to the long-term requirements of Sukarno's foreign policy. Of course, subsequent events were to show that Moscow had not the slightest intention of risking direct, armed confrontation with the Western powers, not even with a small NATO power like the Netherlands, over a side issue like West Irian. It could be expected, however, that the USSR might lend its moral and practical support to a policy of demonstrative acts intended to intimidate the West, and it might perhaps help deter the West from retaliatory acts against Indonesia. Sukarno and his associates calculated, rightly as events proved, that under such circumstances the Dutch would eventually be isolated, since the United States and Britain would do their utmost to prove to the Indonesians that they did not have to rely entirely on Soviet support. Alone, the Netherlands would be unwilling and unable to sustain prolonged confrontation with an Indonesia assisted by Moscow and Peking.

From the Soviet point of view, it could well seem worthwhile to permit the USSR to be "used" in this way for Indonesia's purposes, in the hope that growing intimacy between the foreign ministries and armed forces of the two countries and prolonged tension with the West would finally eliminate Western influence in this strategic sector of Southeast Asia. The establishment of such a relationship with Djakarta, however, was not devoid of serious problems. Sukarno was by no means sole ruler of Indonesia; fiercely anticommunist elements were still strongly entrenched and were to demonstrate their power during the following two years. The "progressive national bourgeoisie" was split, and one could not calculate precisely who would emerge on top. Indonesia had demonstrated in its past relations with other countries, as well as with the USSR, that arrangements made by Indonesian emissaries were frequently repudiated in the capital. As for confidences, Djakarta was not particularly famous for its discretion.

A second Soviet problem concerned the CPR; although the Sino-Soviet conflict still lay in the future, Peking had shown considerable touchiness about its great-power status in 1950 and again in 1954. China had enjoyed something of a communist monopoly in its relations with most of Southeast Asia and, indeed, had established full diplomatic relations with Djakarta four years earlier than the Soviet Union. On the other hand, the PKI leadership had previously tended to take guidance from Moscow, although some PKI elements were deeply enmeshed with sections of the Overseas Chinese community in Indonesia. While there is conflicting evidence whether a formal division of Asian spheres of influence ever existed between Moscow and Peking, it does, at any rate, seem clear that Indonesia was excluded from any such arrangement.[5] Djakarta thus was open hunting ground for both

---

[5] Testimony of Aleksander Yurievich Kaznacheyev, U.S., Congress, Senate, Committee on the Judiciary, *Hearing before the Subcommittee to Investigate*

Russians and Chinese and, as such, was certain to cause friction between them.

Perhaps the most complex question facing the USSR in any relationship with Indonesia concerned the PKI. There were quantitative and qualitative differences between allowing the PKI to "assist" the national bourgeoisie "as the rope supports the hanged man" and permitting the Soviet government to give real sustenance to the instruments of bourgeois power in Indonesia, especially the army. In its relations with other developing countries, Moscow did not encounter this problem to anything like the same extent. Either local communists were insignificant and could be ignored, as in many parts of the Middle East, or they were firmly contained by a vigorous ruling stratum, as in India; in the latter case, the USSR was obviously justified in doing business with a power group that appeared to be invincibly established. In Indonesia, however, Moscow had to deal with the largest, strongest, most competently led communist party by far, facing a feeble, deeply divided petty bourgeoisie, sections of which had been infiltrated. Prospects for communism seemed unusually hopeful. It was at least questionable whether Soviet economic, military, and diplomatic aid, given of necessity on a government-to-government basis, would be at all helpful to the PKI.

Some persons in Moscow and in the PKI leadership may conceivably have thought that intimate contact between the two countries would open many channels for Soviet influence, pressure, and, perhaps, even indoctrination and subversion. On the whole, however, it seems doubtful that this was a majority view. Indonesia was by no means the first developing country to enter into a close relationship with the USSR; it had already become quite clear in other countries that crude Soviet operations were out of the question, that neutral leaders were hypersensitive and proud and had to be tackled with subtlety and forbearing. Moscow's returns, if any, would be painfully slow in coming. The fact remains that, over a decade of Soviet relations with the Third World, there were to be relatively few attempts at crass interference in the existing power structure of noncommunist recipients of Russian aid. (The USSR was infinitely cruder in its actions toward communist states.) It seems most unlikely that the Russian behavior

the Administration of the Internal Security Act and Other Internal Security Laws, 86th Congress (Washington, D.C., 1959).

pattern would have revealed such restraint had the Soviet leaders entertained sanguine expectations of success or had they really believed that high-handed methods could be employed with impunity.

If these assumptions are correct, it must have been painfully apparent from the outset that Soviet assistance to Indonesia might serve to prop up the existing shaky power structure in Djakarta and, therefore, impede rather than further the aspirations of the PKI. Thus, for instance, Soviet political support might well enable Indonesia to realize its territorial aspirations, but such an achievement would primarily redound to the advantage of Sukarno's government, even if the USSR and the PKI were to be allowed some credit for it. Russian economic aid would probably stimulate intense East-West competition to see which side could pour more goods into Djakarta; the end result, however, might be to enable Indonesia to implement industrialization without revolution. Above all, Soviet military assistance would primarily strengthen the Indonesian army, which, like the Egyptian army before it, would no doubt try to ensure that Russian training was unaccompanied by indoctrination. The creation of a modernized and highly professional army, moreover, had been opposed by the PKI for many years and for the very best of reasons.

No powers of prophecy were required in 1956 to envisage these pitfalls. With such considerations in mind, it seems less than likely that the PKI was wildly enthusiastic about the prospect of Soviet aid to Indonesia. The fact remains that during a decade of Moscow-Djakarta collaboration in many fields, the PKI was to give credit to Soviet largesse only in the most mealymouthed and perfunctory fashion. For long periods, the PKI "discreetly" ignored the subject, in spite of its apparent propaganda value; in later years, the PKI leaders were even to discover ways of casting aspersions on Moscow's assistance, but that, of course, was after the Sino-Soviet dispute had come into the open.

It may, perhaps, be a legitimate inference that these complex considerations constituted the main reason for the prolonged sojourn of D. N. Aidit in the communist countries during the spring of 1956, following his attendance at the Twentieth CPSU Congress. The bewildering interplay of the conflicting interests of some eight or nine separate elements (the USSR, CPR, PKI, Sukarno, the Indonesian army, various Indonesian parties, the United States, the United Kingdom, and the Dutch) presumably could not be sorted out without prolonged analysis and deliberation; in any case, Aidit spent many weeks in discussions with leaders of the CPSU and the CCP (Chinese Communist Party). It was only after these problems had been thrashed out, although not necessarily agreed upon, that the Soviet Union, in April 1956, extended an invitation to Sukarno to visit Moscow.

8   The Covert Arrangements, 1956–1958

A search for the roots of the Indonesian-Soviet entanglement is likely to miss significant clues unless sufficient attention is given to the 1956–1957 period. Of course, one widely accepted version of history maintains that Indonesia's military relationship with the Soviet bloc was initiated only in 1958, after Djakarta had waited many months in vain for a U.S. agreement to sell arms; according to this interpretation, the threatening dimensions of a revolt against Sukarno in the Outer Islands, allegedly abetted by the West, compelled the Indonesian government to strengthen its forces immediately. However, it is apparent that this portrayal of events, which was naturally favored by Sukarno, contains a notable amount of special pleading. While not entirely incorrect with regard to the bare facts, it omits enough important information to be misleading. Closer analysis would seem to indicate that the origins of the relationship should, in fact, be sought in Sukarno's Moscow and Peking visits during the fall of 1956 and in the involved developments of the subsequent months.

Soviet Credits for Indonesia

As has already been noted, the Indonesian army had for some time been eagerly shopping for modern weapons, and, in 1956, primarily for political reasons, Sukarno was inclined to support these attempts. The subject was raised in most capitals visited by Indonesian leaders prior to Sukarno's Moscow trip and, as we now know from his own account,[1] the question came up during his discussions with Mao Tse-tung immediately following the Moscow talks. It would hardly seem likely that Moscow was the one place where tight-lipped silence was maintained on this matter. In fact, pointers are not entirely lacking that the Indonesian-Soviet conversations of August–September 1956 really did touch upon military problems. Marshal Konev and, to a lesser extent, Marshals Malinovsky, Sokolovsky, and Zhukov were present at important occasions, and Sukarno had General M. I. Kazakov (later commander of the Warsaw Pact forces) seconded to him throughout the visit, in addition to being accompanied by the CPSU leader from Uzbekistan, S. R. Rashidov. Whatever the precise significance of these facts, there are more concrete indications that Sukarno's Russian journey had a bearing upon his military requirements. At Moscow, final agreement was reached on the grant of sizable Soviet credits to Indonesia; later developments provide important clues that these sums may have been partly intended to ease Indonesia's burdens, should she purchase Russian-made military equipment somewhere in the Soviet bloc.

In mid-August 1956, a Soviet-Indonesian trade agreement was signed. Some weeks later, the two foreign ministers summed up Sukarno's Moscow visit in a communiqué that called for the conclusion of a second agreement, on economic and technical cooperation, including Russian long-term credits to Indonesia. A few days afterward, in mid-September 1956, such a document was, in fact, signed in Djakarta. It provided for a $100 million Soviet loan to Indonesia, repayable over twelve years at $2\frac{1}{2}$ per cent interest in goods, sterling, or other freely convertible currency. Compared to other Soviet aid and credit agreements of the 1955–1958 period, which normally covered specific and detailed projects in definite geographic locations, the Djakarta text was unusually vague and general, except for a reference to the training of Indonesian specialists in the peaceful uses of atomic energy.[2] All of two and a half years passed before a more detailed protocol for the utilization of the loan was signed, in January 1959, while supplementary protocols were being worked out as late as July, August, and

---

[1] Sukarno's speech at Bandjarmasin, July 20, 1957 (AFP, in English, July 20, 1957).

[2] *Pravda*, September 18, 1956; *New York Times*, September 16, 1956.

October 1959, expanding the Soviet credit to $117.5 million.[3] Not until this time were the initial surveys and studies taking place, preparatory to construction of the projects themselves.

Thus when Khrushchev arrived in Djakarta a few months later (February 1960), only a small proportion of the $117.5 million could conceivably have been expended on any activities covered by the protocols. One observer estimated that, at most, one third of the Soviet credit could have been allocated by the time Khrushchev arrived.[4] (As will be shown, even this amount must have been made up primarily of expenditures other than those stipulated in the 1956 technical aid agreement.) Yet, during his 1960 visit, Khrushchev quickly granted Indonesia another loan, of $250 million, as if the previous credit had already been used up or was about to be exhausted; what strengthens the impression that part of this money was being utilized for other purposes is the fact that the new Russian loan covered projects that could hardly be regarded as serious so long as related programs under the 1956 credit had barely been initiated yet. For instance, according to the January 1959 protocol, the original Soviet credit was to have helped Indonesia construct two steel mills in Java, each producing 50,000 tons annually. Time passed without any real work being done and, by the time of Khrushchev's 1960 Djakarta visit, Soviet commentators were no longer referring to the plan for building two steel mills, mentioning instead the possibility of a single mill of larger capacity.[5] A few months later it was, indeed, admitted that the projected two mills had been "consolidated" into a program for the construction of only one mill in Java, with a capacity of 100,000 tons.[6] (Incidentally, even this project of some $36 million remains uncompleted a decade later.) In spite of the obvious lack of progress registered by the steel production program—although it was located in relatively advanced and accessible Java—Khrushchev's new $250 million loan in 1960 blithely allocated a much larger sum (some $110 million) for the construction of a huge steel complex, with a capacity of 250,000 tons, somewhere in the remote wilderness of Kalimantan.

3 *Pravda*, July 29, 1959; *Izvestia*, August 15, 1959; and *Vneshnyaya Torgovlya Soyuz SSR*, 1960, no. 2, p. 56.

4 *Christian Science Monitor*, February 29, 1960.

5 S. Skachkov commentary, *Pravda*, February 10, 1960; see also *Soviet News* (Soviet Embassy, London, Press Dept.), February 29, 1960, and *Pravda*, February 29, 1960.

6 *Pravda*, July 2, 1960.

Needless to say, to this very day the latter project has never even passed through the preparatory stage.[7]

It seems difficult to avoid the conclusion that Khrushchev's additional bounty was required not so much for the implementation of a clearly impracticable scheme as for the purpose of constituting a financial reserve from which Indonesia might draw funds to cover the fact that portions of the 1956 loan had been devoted to purposes other than those which had been officially stipulated. The latter supposition would appear to be a little more than a mere hypothesis, in view of events that occurred in the months immediately following Sukarno's 1956 Moscow trip; on at least two occasions during this period, the USSR gave Indonesia equipment related to her defense requirements, and in both instances credit arrangements had to be provided to cover the purchases. In one case, there was at least a link between the credit extended and the $100 million loan obtained by Sukarno in Moscow; in the other, the money came directly out of the $100 million. Moreover, these two transactions apparently led straight into the 1958 Indonesian-Soviet-Czech arms deal, which, therefore, may originally have been financed at least partly from the same source. It is necessary to pursue these developments in some detail, since they provide significant indications that Indonesia's military relationship with the USSR may have originated in the fall of 1956 rather than in the spring of 1958.[8]

To start with, it must be understood why the Soviet leaders did not simply conclude a clandestine military credit agreement with Sukarno in September 1956, apparently preferring more cumbersome and tentative arrangements for future Indonesian purchases of defense equipment. One explanation could be that Sukarno was not in a position at that time to carry through a full-blown arms deal with Moscow and may, therefore, have been content to accept the offer of an option that could be taken up when convenient and utilized gradually. This was the period of Ali Sastroamidjojo's second coalition cabinet in Djakarta, which, contrary to Sukarno's wishes, had excluded the PKI but included the democratic, anti-

---

[7] The evidence for the present state of Soviet aid projects is contained in a study conducted in Indonesia by Mr. Robert C. Horn of the Fletcher School, whose work on the subject is in progress.

[8] Thus U.S. delays, during 1957/58, in responding to Djakarta's arms request can hardly have constituted the sole root cause of an Indonesian policy trend that had already been initiated in 1956 and that, moreover, continued unabated even after the United States reversed itself in 1958 and gave arms to Indonesia.

communist Masjumi. Moreover, Sukarno's rival, Vice-President Hatta, had not yet carried out his threat to resign and still had to be taken into account. The army itself was riven by a struggle between Premier Ali, who also held the defense portfolio and was supported by Nasution, and the antiparliamentarian Colonel Lubis. Under such conditions, it would have been quite impossible for Sukarno to implement a major military transaction with the USSR, a feat that undoubtedly required tough and autocratic handling by a unanimously anti-Western leadership capable of preserving secrecy at least temporarily. Only much later, and by very gradual methods, was Sukarno able to achieve such a state of "guided democracy" and to subdue the opposition. In 1956, some of Sukarno's colleagues and most of his rivals regarded the Soviet Union with suspicion; one group of officers apparently wished to confine arms purchases entirely to Western countries, since the prevailing standards, training, and military doctrine of the Indonesian army were completely Western and the injection of weapons from another source could cause confusion and impair efficiency. Sukarno himself no doubt regarded the problem in a political rather than military light: a cautious and flexible arrangement with Moscow would give Djakarta a certain freedom of maneuver, so that East and West might eventually be played off against each other and concessions extorted from both. Precisely because of such considerations, it was necessary to shun precipitate, overt actions that could cause a breach with the West and leave Djakarta alone with Moscow.

If Sukarno, therefore, felt uneasy about possible Western reaction to a major arms deal with the USSR, so apparently did the Russians, who persisted until 1959 with the attempt to present their military transactions as "Czech" or "Polish" arms sales, which could be disavowed more easily. For all these reasons, both sides may have felt in 1956 that the practical solution was to sign a seemingly innocuous economic and technical cooperation agreement, including a long-term loan. These credit facilities could then be utilized by Indonesia for occasional purchases of defense equipment in the communist bloc, escalating gradually from semi-military to heavier items. In this way, an arms relationship could eventually be established without grave repercussions in Indonesia or elsewhere.

If these were, indeed, the calculations that prevailed in September 1956, developments of the following weeks must have interfered with such plans and expectations. The economic and technical co-operation agreement with the USSR immediately encountered deep suspicion and hostility in Indonesia, and it proved impossible to obtain ratification for almost eighteen months. Some forces inside the cabinet delayed submission of the agreement to parliament, where, in any case, the democratic parties still wielded enough strength to hamper approval of such a bill.[9]

Official proposals for cooperation with Moscow found the Djakarta atmosphere particularly uncongenial just then because of general resentment at the joint communiqué signed in Moscow at the end of Sukarno's September 1956 visit. Indonesians sharply attacked the foreign minister of that period, R. Abdulgani, who, in the Moscow statement, had unilaterally underwritten the Soviet point of view on global affairs without ensuring that the Russians should at least return the compliment by permitting inclusion of a reference to Indonesia's West Irian claim.[10] To compound the injury, this step had apparently been taken with Sukarno's consent, but without bothering to obtain the approval of the cabinet in Djakarta.[11] This act reinforced the prevalent suspicion that there was more to the Moscow meeting than met the eye. Significantly, a mere two weeks after Sukarno's departure, the Soviet slogans for the anniversary of the October Revolution included a prominent and unprecedented paragraph on friendship with Indonesia.[12]

More direct evidence was to show that uneasiness in Djakarta about the real nature of the Moscow talks had been warranted. Thus high Indonesian officers who had enjoyed full access to confidential information in 1956, revealed after their rebellion against Sukarno that the $100 million loan arranged in Moscow had, indeed, been intended to help in covering military purchases.[13] Later, this statement was confirmed in an address to Congress in Manila by Philippine Foreign Minister Serrano.[14] He derived his information from a personal consultation with his well-informed ambassador in Djakarta, Fuentabella, who stated publicly that Indonesia's acquisition of defense equipment from Russia well

[9] *Pravda*, April 3, 1957.
[10] TASS, in English, to Europe, September 11, 1956; Associated Press, September 17, 1956.
[11] *New York Times*, September 20, 1956.
[12] *Pravda*, October 25, 1956.
[13] Menado, Minahassa regional broadcasting service, in Indonesian, August 10, 1957.
[14] Reported in the Philippine press and on radio, April 29 and 30, 1958.

antedated the year 1958.[15] Since it was not until the spring of 1958 that Sukarno's assistants were able to push through parliamentary ratification of the $100 million Soviet loan,[16] one may presume that Moscow and Djakarta must, in the meantime, have reached some substitute credit arrangements to cover interim purchases. Analysis of various transactions during 1957 and 1958, in fact, reveals traces of at least two deals of this kind.

Soviet Military Vehicles for Indonesia

Part of Russia's $100 million had been intended to provide credit for the importation to Djakarta of various goods enumerated in the August 1956 Soviet-Indonesian trade agreement, including motor vehicles.[17] Early in 1957, it became known that the Indonesian government was already purchasing items within that category, but that the vehicles in quesion were actually 4,000 Soviet half-ton military scout cars. The Indonesian armed forces had been conducting tests with these Russian jeeps and they were intended to replace lighter Western vehicles; the purchase was taking place under a Soviet five-year credit agreement, and the Ministry of Defense subsequently stressed that, in future, modern military equipment would be bought "from *any* country prepared to sell on a long-term credit basis."[18] First Minister Djuanda later explained that this was an "advance purchase prior to the settlement of the $100 million Soviet loan"; in other words, the new Soviet credit had been temporarily and discreetly extended to cover the period until the $100 million agreement could finally be ratified by the Indonesian parliament.[19] Presumably, the loan for the vehicles was to be consolidated afterward with the $100 million credit. The Soviet interim loan for the jeeps, to the tune of $6¾ million, was granted by the Russians in February 1957, only a short while after Sukarno returned from Moscow and almost as soon as it became clear that the $100 million credit was encountering difficulties in Djakarta.[20] The need for separate legislative approval for the transaction was

15 AFP, in English, April 10, 1958.
16 The exchange of instruments of ratification took place in April 1958.
17 *Pravda*, August 14, 1956.
18 Antara (Djakarta), in English, July 17, 1957 (author's emphasis).
19 PIA, in English, January 11, 1958.
20 *Vneshnyaya Torgovlya*, 1959, no. 6, p. 17. Actually, Indonesia was not to derive much benefit from the Soviet jeeps; it became known later that their

simply sidestepped by the Indonesian government, apparently on the specious grounds that this was a relatively short-term financial obligation.

These developments naturally gave rise to further suspicions concerning the real character of Sukarno's relations with the USSR; the Djakarta press reported that Hatta was attacking the new transaction and, in this connection, was also casting aspersions upon the nature of the $100 million loan. Observers felt that the government's lack of frankness on this matter was aiding the opposition.

On the Soviet side, there were additional motivations for discretion, which prevailed at least until the late spring of 1957. During Sukarno's 1956 Moscow visit, the Russians had refused to respond to his many public hints and to range themselves openly behind Indonesia over the West Irian issue. When Sukarno went to Prague at that time, the Czechs were even blunter in rejecting any suggestion that they should publish a statement of support concerning West Irian.[21] One reason for the attitude of the communist bloc was probably the desire to weaken the United States by means of a rapprochement with Western Europe, a concept that dominated Moscow's policies throughout 1955/56. Although Paris and London were the main objects of this flirtation, the Russians felt they should also avoid gratuitous offense to any of the smaller West European states, including the Netherlands. It was only after the 1956 Suez and Hungarian crises that Moscow began to consider a policy of dealing directly with the United States rather than with the smaller NATO countries. Moreover, until April 1957, it remained uncertain whether Sukarno would be able to impose his concept of government upon Djakarta and whether, therefore, Indonesia would be a dependable partner worthy of a public Soviet commitment. However, by May 1957, when Voroshilov arrived in Djakarta, reciprocating Sukarno's 1956 Moscow visit, these difficulties had been overcome. The USSR had become disenchanted with Western Europe, Sukarno had successfully installed a cabinet submissive to presidential power, and Hatta had resigned (although opposition to Sukarno still remained vociferous). Therefore, Moscow now authorized Voroshilov to state, "we fully support your

---

steering was faulty and their windshields buckled in the Indonesian climate, to mention only a few shortcomings.

[21] As was revealed at a later date by the Indonesian press (Djakarta Radio, in English, to Australia, February 1, 1958, quoting *Merdeka*).

just demand for the reunion of West Irian with your country—
Great Indonesia."²²

Soviet Vessels for Indonesia

The Soviet jeeps did not actually arrive in Indonesia until the
late fall of 1957. By that time, Russian support had encouraged
Sukarno to take a major step toward "confrontation" with the
Netherlands over West Irian. Having failed in the last of several
attempts to apply pressure on the Dutch through the United
Nations, Djakarta now took steps against Dutch economic interests
in the East Indies, especially in the field of sea and air communications. The immediate result was that coastal shipping activities
almost ceased in Indonesia; this was a catastrophic development
for a country consisting of thousands of islands, especially since
military elements in the Outer Islands had effectively disregarded
Djakarta's authority for many months and were soon to declare
themselves in open revolt, for the second time within a year. The
supply of ships to Indonesia thus came to be a subject with military
implications, since the restoration of control over the islands beyond
Java was inconceivable without some degree of sea power. Nor
could there be a really impressive "confrontation" over West Irian
without a previous reassertion of Sukarno's authority over East
Indonesia.

By November 1957, the Soviet press had initiated a strong pro-
Djakarta campaign on the West Irian issue, and Khrushchev went
out of his way to give special and favorable mention to Indonesia's
foreign policy.²³ In mid-December, Moscow threatened the Netherlands that "it is not far from a small to a great disaster," that "it
is easy to start a war, but not to stop it," and that "Indonesia will
not remain alone in the face of economic threats by colonizers."²⁴
Since there was actually no serious possibility whatever of an
armed clash between Indonesia and the Dutch at that time, the
Soviet campaign was apparently intended to provide a verbal

²² Djakarta Radio, in English, to Australia, May 15, 1957; L. Dadiani,
"West Irian Belongs to Indonesia," *International Affairs*, 1959, no. 4. (Throughout this work, *International Affairs* refers to the Moscow publication of that
name. See chap. 3, footnote 19.)

²³ In his interview with Henry Shapiro, *Pravda*, November 19, 1957; see
also *Pravda*, November 15 and December 7, 1957, and *Izvestia*, December 4
and 17, 1957.

²⁴ *Red Star* (Leontyev article) and *Pravda*, December 15 and 16, 1957.

cover for growing Russian involvement in Indonesian affairs. A bare forty-eight hours after the Soviet warnings were issued, it became known that Moscow was providing Indonesia with credit to charter or buy Soviet ships.[25] A few weeks later, this step was supplemented by a Polish offer of freighters for Indonesia's requirements, a gesture that eventually led to a long-term Polish shipbuilding program on Indonesia's behalf.[26]

The USSR was soon involved in detailed negotiations with Djakarta, and it was generally suspected that the size of the participating Soviet delegation signified that much more was involved in these talks than the handing over of a few vessels. It became known immediately that there was not, in fact, to be any new Soviet credit, but that the ships were to be purchased under the $100 million loan of 1956, although none of the previously published details of that agreement provided for such a deal.[27] It turned out that ten transport ships of 23,000 tons, barely four years old, and two tankers were included, at a total estimated cost of 12\frac{1}{4}$ million.[28] There could be little doubt that this step had been carefully planned for months, since some of the vessels actually arrived in Indonesian harbors, ready for action in tropical waters, less than a week after the arrangement was formally concluded in March 1958. The opposition Socialist organ *Pedoman* drew attention to this remarkable fact and publicly wondered if these ships were really "empty," as official sources had hastened to claim.[29] The rebels in Sumatra, including officers who had until recently been trusted members of the Indonesian establishment, stated that one task of the Soviet vessels had, in fact, been to transport Russian arms to Djakarta and that the rebel forces would therefore now purchase Western weapons.[30] By this time, the Indonesian government was no longer denying its eagerness to acquire military equipment in Eastern Europe, although it did not yet fully admit that this step had already been taken. It is interest-

---

[25] Reuters, in English, December 18, 1957.

[26] AFP, in English, January 17, 1958.

[27] Antara, in English, March 11, 1958; V. Rymalov, in *International Affairs*, 1959, no. 9, p. 27.

[28] Djakarta Radio, in English, to Australia, March 18, 1958; Antara, in English, March 20, 1958; Willard A. Hanna, "Bung Karno's Indonesia," pt. 23, "The Russians Are Willing," American Universities Field Staff Reports (New York), December 14, 1959.

[29] Antara, in English, March 19, 1958.

[30] Reuters, Singapore, in English, March 20, 1958.

ing that, whereas Soviet organs vehemently denied the presence of Russian military pilots in Indonesia, which had been reported when the ships arrived, there was no Soviet reaction to rumors that arms were unloaded from these vessels. Moreover, no one would reveal what cargo they did carry or why they should have been sent empty over such a distance.[31]

Shortly after the arrival of the ships, the presence of Soviet bloc weapons in Indonesia became obvious and undeniable. In any case, the vessels themselves and a major part of their Soviet crews, including captains, navigators, engineers, and radio operators, went into action immediately, the Russian personnel remaining in Indonesian waters for almost a year. Their presence played a fairly significant part in helping keep the sea-lanes open to those regions in which Indonesian forces were combatting the rebels; one of the Soviet captains later published an article on his own and his colleagues' experiences (incidentally, full of unconcealed contempt for the alleged backwardness and superstition of Indonesian seamen), in which he left little doubt that the vessels were plying the very waters where the armed forces were campaigning: "Working conditions were extremely difficult . . . fighting was still going on."[32] In April 1958, at least one of the Soviet ships was strafed by rebel planes.

Thus there is little room for doubt that the 1956 Soviet loan was utilized, and apparently was meant to be utilized, for the acquisition by Indonesia of items of military significance, although this was, of course, at odds with the published terms of the 1956 trade agreement. These transactions were initiated, respectively, in February 1957 and in the late fall of 1957, that is, well before the Indonesian government's admission, on the eve of 1958, that it was seeking to purchase military equipment from Eastern Europe.

Talks on Chinese Arms for Indonesia

There are other significant indications that the search for suitable armaments from the communist countries started as soon as Sukarno left Moscow in September 1956. On his way home, Sukarno

---

[31] AFP, March 17, 1958, quoting *Red Star;* George Matveyev, "In Indonesian Waters," *New Times,* 1959, no. 20 (May).
[32] Matveyev, "In Indonesian Waters."

visited Peking, where, on October 1, 1956, he reviewed a military parade together with Mao Tse-tung. As Sukarno revealed later, Mao told him that all the military equipment shown, including guns, rifles, trucks, and jeeps, had been manufactured in China, adding "just inform me in case you need such materials."[33] Indeed, by this time, the Chinese, having persuaded the Russians in 1954/55 to aid them in constructing a rudimentary defense industry, had made considerable progress in producing their own small arms and artillery and even light piston aircraft, some tanks, submarines, and small patrol craft. They had also made a beginning in the partial construction and assembly of jet fighters and, only a couple of weeks before Sukarno's arrival, had flown the first "Chinese" jets.[34]

Sukarno apparently took Mao at his word; no sooner had he strengthened his authority in Djakarta, through the establishment of the Djuanda cabinet, than he sent an important military mission, led by the army's Deputy Chief of Staff Colonel Subroto, to Peking in May 1957.[35] (The Indonesian delegation just missed Marshal Voroshilov, who had passed through Peking a few days earlier on his way to Djakarta.) Upon its arrival, the mission received a strange welcome: Defense Minister Marshal P'eng Teh-huai uttered some formalistic phrases concerning closer comradeship in arms in the common struggle for Formosa and West Irian. Then, however, he apologetically stated that the Chinese People's Liberation Army (PLA) "still has its shortcomings," and that he would "welcome our friends pointing out our shortcomings and helping us in achieving definite progress." Subroto, clearly nonplused, since he was apparently sent to choose equipment in fulfillment of Mao's promise, replied shortly, "The purpose of my visit to China is to learn *from you*."[36] Although the delegation was received by Mao, was shown Chinese military schools, and was briefed on Chinese military training and demobilization—a subject of considerable interest to Indonesian military reformers wishing to speed

[33] Sukarno's speech at Bandjarmasin, July 20, 1957.
[34] Raymond L. Garthoff, "Sino-Soviet Military Relations," *Annals of the American Academy of Political and Social Science*, September 1963, and Colonel Robert Rigg, "Red Army in Retreat," *Current History*, vol. 32, no. 185, p. 5.
[35] Antara, in English, April 13, 1957.
[36] Peking Radio, domestic broadcast, in Mandarin, May 11, 1957 (author's emphasis).

up the integration of veterans in civilian life—it obviously did not acquire anything in the way of equipment.[37] At the ceremonial farewell dinner, Subroto played down the importance of the visit, describing its objective as merely "the promotion of understanding between Indonesia and China," thus contradicting his own statement upon arrival in China.[38] Marshal P'eng drew attention to the fact that the mission was leaving ahead of schedule, although the tour had actually lasted over a month and had been cut short by only a few days; he again claimed that the Indonesians had "offered us a number of valuable suggestions," a statement Subroto brushed off by saying that the Chinese PLA had already "reached the highest international military levels."[39] It is hard to avoid the impression that this exchange of oriental pleasantries was simply meant to underline the Chinese army's refusal and/or inability to help Indonesia with equipment, in spite of Mao's earlier promise. It is surely no accident that Sukarno, for the first time, publicly revealed the contents of Mao's offer a few weeks after the mission's return from China, thus clearly indicating his disappointment at Peking's unreliability.[40]

This curious episode is of some interest, since it shows Djakarta in the role of supplicant for communist military aid as early as April and May 1957, and because it may be related to Sino-Soviet competition for influence in Indonesia at that early date. It is true that Indonesian rebel officers claimed that the $100 million Soviet loan had been intended in part for the purchase of Soviet arms through China, namely, that there was collusion between Moscow and Peking.[41] This allegation may well rest upon a misunderstanding, however. It is quite possible that the Moscow discussion in September 1956 had touched upon the possibility of purchasing equipment elsewhere in the Soviet bloc with the aid of the Russian credit. If so, the Indonesians no doubt took it for granted that Mao's offer, which came immediately afterward, was related to the arrangement made in Moscow. In that case they may have been mistaken, for there was actually very little coordination then or later between Moscow and Peking in the politico-military

---

[37] NCNA, Peking, in English, to Southeast Asia, May 18, 1957.
[38] NCNA, Peking, June 11, 1957.
[39] Peking Radio, international broadcast, in Indonesian, June 12, 1957.
[40] Sukarno's speech at Bandjarmasin, July 20, 1957.
[41] Menado, Minahassa regional broadcasting service, in Indonesian, August 10, 1957.

field.[42] This is clearly borne out by the fact that Mao was offering Sukarno jeeps at a time when the Soviets themselves had such a deal in mind, and there was apparently a similar case of duplication later on, between China and Czechoslovakia, involving jet fighters. In all its triangular military arrangements during that period (for example, with Guatemala, Egypt, and Syria), the USSR used advanced industrial countries like Czechoslovakia and, occasionally, Poland as plausible forwarding agents of communist weapons. The USSR, at that time, felt that efficient defense industries in Czechoslovakia and Poland could be useful adjuncts to its own war machine and, therefore, gradually permitted these countries to step up the quality and quantity of their military products to the point where they could dispose of some surplus items that might be useful to developing countries. From Moscow's point of view, it would have been unreasonable to include the CPR in the same category of potential arms suppliers as Czechoslovakia, since the Chinese were decades behind and were only beginning laboriously, and at Russia's expense, to establish themselves in the armaments field.

From Indonesia's point of view, however, the situation may have looked somewhat different. It should be recalled that China in 1956/57 appeared to have rather more to offer a developing country, as far as weapons were concerned, than was the case four or five years later. In 1957, China had the MiG-15 and some MiG-17s, while most Afro-Asian states were still training their very first jet pilots. By the early 1960s, however, Egypt and Indonesia were about to put the MiG-21 into operation, while the Chinese had long since ceased receiving Soviet military aid and had difficulty maintaining a few MiG-19s.

It is, at best, possible to hazard a guess why the Chinese should have executed a volte-face toward Sukarno in 1957. Mao, in this as in other instances, may not have been overly concerned with the technological importance of China's progress in armaments production. He probably regarded such successes primarily as political and propaganda counters, as was shown by the fanfare accompanying the maiden flight of the first jets produced in China, just before Sukarno's arrival.[43] To Mao it may well have seemed a useful gambit to attract Indonesia into Peking's orbit by showing that the

[42] Garthoff, "Sino-Soviet Military Relations," and Rigg, "Red Army in Retreat."
[43] Ibid.

CPR now had something to offer, independently of the rest of the Bloc. It is likely that the note of Asian self-reliance was stressed even at that date. Those leaders of the Chinese armed forces, however, especially (then) Chief of Staff Su Yü and Marshal Yeh Chien-ying, who desired the construction of an independent nuclear deterrent, badly needed interim Soviet assistance in order to reach their goal, whereas the more traditionalist pro-Soviet elements, like the defense minister of that period, Marshal P'eng Teh-huai, probably were resigned to long-term dependence upon Soviet conventional military aid, buttressed by the Russian nuclear shield. It is unlikely that either of these competing military groups laid quite as much store by masses of ill-equipped human flesh as did Mao; nor could either faction have regarded with indifference any act that might irritate the Soviet Union at that particular moment. Kuo Mo-jo, president of the Chinese Academy of Sciences, who seems to have played a central part in negotiating the 1957 Sino-Soviet nuclear assistance agreement, revealed later[44] that Premier Chou En-lai had sent a message to Bulganin in May 1957, precisely when the Indonesian mission arrived in Peking. Judging by Kuo's testimony, this note contained a detailed blueprint for future Chinese nuclear development and an urgent request for Soviet participation. This moment would hardly have seemed propitious for Chinese actions that were uncoordinated, to say the least, with Soviet plans in Southeast Asia. It is by no means inconceivable, therefore, that the Chinese military leaders persuaded Mao to avoid any untimely entanglement with the Indonesians, and it was, perhaps, no accident that Defense Minister P'eng should have been the man who gave the Indonesians a polite hint to forget Mao's promises. Moreover, it is entirely possible that Voroshilov's entourage, stopping in Peking on its way to Djakarta, gave indications of displeasure at Mao's undertaking to give Chinese equipment to the Indonesian military mission and that this development caused the Chinese marshals to intercede with Mao.

In any case, Colonel Subroto may well have convinced himself during his tour that the Chinese were really not an ideal partner for long-term sophisticated military aid, since their facilities were very limited. There are also some indications that the Chinese leaders, especially Premier Chou En-lai, were beginning to feel

<hr>

[44] In his interview at the end of 1957 with *New Times* (see Alice Langley Hsieh, "Sino-Soviet Nuclear Dialogue," *Journal of Conflict Resolution*, June 1964).

unhappy with Sukarno's 1957 cabinet and with his new foreign minister and former ambassador to Moscow, Dr. Subandrio, whom the Chinese minority in Indonesia regarded as racially prejudiced. At any rate, Chou refused Sukarno's invitation to visit Indonesia after Voroshilov's tour.[45]

During the summer of 1957, Sino-Indonesian relations were subjected to irritations: the two parties, for different reasons, obstructed implementation of the two-year-old Indonesian-Chinese Dual Citizenship Agreement, and the Indonesian army kept closing the schools of the Chinese minority in the Lesser Sunda Islands. Frantic appeals issued by the local Chinese consul were able to achieve only slight alleviation for these Overseas Chinese.[46]

At this time, Peking found an elegant way of demonstrating its displeasure with the Indonesian authorities: Mohammad Hatta, the former vice-president and Sukarno's most important opponent, was officially invited in August 1957 to visit the CPR.[47] This occurred less than two weeks after Hatta had sharply attacked Sukarno and the USSR over the Indonesian-Soviet jeep agreement. Peking blithely disregarded such details, and Hatta, when he arrived seven weeks later, was welcomed by Premier Chou as "an outstanding statesman" and warmly praised for his fight against colonialism.[48] As far as Chou was concerned, Hatta was the man who had recognized the Chinese People's Republic seven years earlier, and his anti-Soviet sentiments were apparently regarded as irrelevant. Hatta, accompanied by Lieutenant Colonels Suwido and Sujatmo, was received by Mao and by Chief of Staff Su Yü, and the two Indonesian officers afterward held discussions with Chinese military representatives.[49] At a banquet for Hatta, Chou delivered a much more unequivocal statement, to please his guest, than either Peking or Moscow had previously been prepared to issue on Sukarno's behalf. Chou declared, "We firmly support your just struggle for the recovery of West Irian and are convinced that you will certainly win complete victory."[50] (It should be recalled that this statement was made in October 1957, six weeks before the Soviet press started its campaign of support for Indonesia.)

[45] Reported in the Indonesian press, May 24, 1957.
[46] Antara, in English, August 6, 1957.
[47] AFP, in English, August 1, 1957.
[48] NCNA, in English, September 21 and 22, 1957.
[49] Djakarta Radio, domestic broadcast, October 1, 1957; NCNA, in English, to Southeast Asia, September 24, 1957.
[50] NCNA, Peking, in English, to Southeast Asia, October 2, 1957.

In his reply, Hatta gave a strong indication of the precise subject of the Peking military discussions. He revealed that he had been taken to see

the jet plane plant. In the manufacture of jet planes, China has surpassed certain Western countries which have hitherto been regarded as advanced in this field. What surprises me is that these plants have been built in so short a period of time. At the start of China's construction, it was really assisted by Soviet technicians and other forms of aid, but within a short time China has produced its own experts and administrative staffs.[51]

Not long after Hatta's return, the Indonesian press revealed that Chou had offered Hatta assistance "partly . . . in equipment" and that this Chinese gesture was probably related to the West Irian campaign, namely, that the "equipment" mentioned was military. There was also reference to a Chinese promise of a loan for the purchase of textile machinery.[52] In view of Hatta's remarks in Peking, there would seem to be little doubt that the Chinese offer of "equipment" to help Indonesia acquire West Irian actually consisted of jet planes.

In this connection, it is of some significance that almost at the precise moment when Hatta viewed the Chinese jet assembly plant, Dr. Prajudi of the Indonesian Ministry of Industries returned from a visit to Prague and revealed that the Czechs had repeatedly invited Indonesia to accept "credit . . . in the form of airplanes. . . ."[53] The fact that the Czechs offered planes to Sukarno's representative at the same time as the Chinese offered jets to Sukarno's rival would seem to indicate that Peking and the Soviet bloc were competing rather than collaborating, just as they had eleven months earlier, when both sides simultaneously promised Indonesia jeeps.

Whatever the case, it seems clear that the Chinese had once more reversed their stand and were now prepared to offer Hatta what they had a few weeks earlier refused to give to Colonel Subroto's delegation. In this context, it may be significant that, shortly before receiving Hatta, the Chinese chief of staff, Su Yü, had reason to believe that he was at long last achieving his main

---

[51] Ibid.
[52] *Suluh Indonesia,* December 21, 1957; also ibid., November 9–14, 1957.
[53] Antara, in English, to Asia, September 27, 1957.

ambition and that the Russians were now prepared, in principle, to aid China in her nuclear program. While Hatta was in Peking, no fewer than 640 Soviet scientists were already working with their Chinese counterparts to draft a twelve-year joint scientific program. Although the agreement was formally signed only three weeks later,[54] it was clearly "in the bag." In view of this development, the Peking faction favoring nuclear development may have become a little less nervous about the possible effect upon Moscow of minor irritations resulting from China's Indonesian policy. The Russians were hardly likely at that late stage to cause a major clash with Peking by withdrawing from the scientific aid program because of relatively petty annoyances. Such considerations, as well as their temporary displeasure with Sukarno's cabinet, may have impelled the Chinese to reopen for Hatta the arms offer that had originally been made to Sukarno. It is not clear whether Peking believed that Hatta might stage a comeback in Indonesia. In any case, he failed to do so, and Sukarno had apparently already made his decision to go ahead with a Soviet-Czech arms deal and did not respond to the new Chinese offer, which had probably irritated him because of its very manner. On the other hand, he seems to have taken the lessons of the Hatta-Chou flirtation to heart and started to tone down the anti-Chinese campaign. A few days after Hatta's return, Peking gave publicity to a new promise given by Sukarno to the Chinese minority, according to which there would be no more distinctions between the "original and nonoriginal" inhabitants of Indonesia.[55]

From Covert to Overt Links

As the year 1957 approached its end, the Indonesian government could look back upon some fifteen months of highly complex and tangled politico-military relations with various parts of the communist world. At least two deals of a semimilitary nature had been made with Moscow and covered by Russian credit arrangements; these Soviet funds could apparently be stretched also to finance arms purchases from other East European sources, and contact had already been established with the Czechs on the subject of airplanes; Peking had twice offered arms to Indonesia and had met with some response on one occasion.

[54] See Hsieh, "Sino-Soviet Nuclear Dialogue."
[55] NCNA, Peking, in English, to Southeast Asia, October 21, 1957.

Thus, clearly, a wide and covert basis had been created for further intimacy between Indonesia and the communist countries in the sensitive security field. Djakarta could now go on to acquire large quantities of heavy and sophisticated weapons from the East without need for any radical departure from policy, but as a simple and natural development of established procedures.

At this precise point, however, the PKI leader, D. N. Aidit, delivered himself of a very frank analysis of the situation, which reemphasized how little interest the Indonesian communists had in a purely military buildup and how much they were concerned with the political exploitation of the situation, short of a resort to the armed forces. In a statement to the new West Irian command on November 4, 1957, Aidit said that the people would back "action of a more advanced stage" against the Dutch; but then he immediately showed that he meant economic action, explaining that the Dutch would depend on their military strength only as long as they could defray its costs. Thus, if Dutch economic interests in Indonesia were injured, through "spontaneous" expropriation by the masses, West Irian would inevitably fall into Indonesia's hands. The armed forces should not be involved unless "the time is ripe"; Aidit merely advocated concentration of these forces, clearly as a political move to intimidate the Dutch. Only if that were not enough should further measures be taken. He then said that contemporary Asia would not permit the imperialists to trample upon Indonesia. It is interesting that he should have referred to the deterrent power of Indonesia's fellow Asians, rather than of the communist world, as a shield for Indonesia's actions. In its implications, his statements certainly could not be taken as enthusiastic support for the reequipment of Indonesia's armed forces by the communist countries or anyone else.

From Sukarno's point of view, however, it was obviously very important to acquire large quantities of heavy equipment, which he could eventually brandish to prove that he was the leader of a truly great power and that his aspirations must be taken seriously and satisfied. Neither the military leaders nor, perhaps, Sukarno himself had much faith in economic actions against the Dutch, realizing only too well that such measures would damage Indonesia itself. Of course, the President and the army were as little inclined to fight an open war in New Guinea as were the communists; yet the officers probably felt that the armed services rather than the "masses" would eventually reap the glory of gaining West Irian, by becoming so imposing a military force that the Dutch would give in without a fight.

By December 1957, the Indonesian government was preparing the stage for the first overt transactions that would gradually legitimize the existing furtive liaison between Djakarta and the East in the eyes of the world. Sukarno was grappling with a serious dilemma: if an arms deal with the Bloc was prematurely publicized, there might be massive Western retaliation. (Western support for the anti-Sukarno rebels in 1958 was to show that such fear was not entirely unfounded.) However, as long as such transactions remained entirely undercover, they were failing to fulfill one of their purposes, which was to shock the West into making major concessions so as to "rescue" Indonesia from the East. What was required, therefore, was a gradual leakage of information, after the arms deal was a fait accompli and after an adequate and convincing alibi had been set up.

This may have been one reason why Indonesia, in December 1957, went through the motions of receiving a U.S. emissary, Gordon Mein,[56] for discussions on possible U.S. sales of arms to Indonesia, although the United States had clearly stated its stipulations and safeguards and Djakarta had previously shown its disinterest in buying on these terms. There was always a chance that Washington might offer concessions so as to meet Indonesia's demands halfway; what was more likely, however, after such talks, Djakarta could claim that it had shown plenty of goodwill, had awaited a positive U.S. reply for months, and must now look elsewhere. The fact that Indonesia had not precisely been "waiting" but had already established important links with (and received significant, if minor, aid from) the military establishments of the East was known to very few people.

[56] John Gordon Mein, Director, Office of Southwest Pacific Affairs, U.S. Department of State.

9   The First Overt Transactions, 1958–1960

On December 26, 1957, as the talks with Mein were barely ending, an official Indonesian military source revealed that an armed forces mission was leaving for Czechoslovakia, Poland, and Yugoslavia and might place orders there for as much as $200 million worth of military equipment. It was also stated that a list of equipment for sixty infantry battalions, for the navy, and for the air force, valued at $150 million, had been submitted to the United States, that no favorable response had been elicited, but that this list would not be withdrawn.[1] At this point, a stream of mutually contradictory statements issued from Djakarta. Foreign Minister Subandrio backtracked and told a press conference that it was merely a possibility that an arms mission would be going to East Europe, and only if the United States continued to evade Indonesia's requests. Moreover, he claimed that it was untrue that equipment for the navy and air force would be purchased.[2] Shortly afterward, however, Premier Djuanda stated that arms would be requested from *both* the United States and Eastern Europe. At the same time, the real reason for Subandrio's equivocations was spelled out when the information minister expressed the hope that the United States would continue, in spite of everything, to maintain neutrality between its Dutch ally and Indonesia.[3] A few days later, the Foreign Ministry's secretary-general, Kusomowi-

---

[1] *New York Times*, December 27, 1957.
[2] AFP, in English, December 28, 1957.
[3] Djakarta Radio, domestic broadcast, December 29, 1957.

dagdo, publicly contradicted his own chief, Subandrio. He proclaimed that it was "completely wrong to say that the sending of the mission was motivated by the question of whether or not the U.S. was prepared to sell arms to Indonesia." He frankly admitted that the purchase of arms from Eastern Europe "had been planned long ago," but added that West European countries were approached as well.[4] Finally, the Indonesian army's spokesman, Harsono, definitely stated that countries in Eastern Europe had been approached prior to the dispatch of the mission; however, he would not say whether an agreement had already been concluded and if the Soviet Union itself was involved. "A reliable government source" added that Indonesia could probably utilize the $100 million credit from the USSR but, in reply to a further question, refused to commit himself as to whether this money was actually intended for arms.[5] At that date the Indonesian parliament had still not ratified the loan agreement. "Government officials" were quoted as saying that they must "take into account Western reactions if Indonesia closed a big arms deal with either Russia or China."[6] The nationalist newspaper *Suluh Indonesia* warned on January 2, 1958 that the Western reaction would be strong but could be anticipated, and that care should be taken to avoid political or military "strings" from the East.

These statements leave little doubt that the arms deal had, in fact, been carefully prepared over some considerable time and was probably about to be implemented, that cautious circumlocutions and alibis were being used for fear of Western reaction, and that, for the same reason, the smaller East European countries were being substituted for the Soviet Union itself. What had been a shrewd plan of procedure, however, was botched at the moment of implementation by poor coordination, as the many public contradictions showed.

Training and Spare Parts

As the Indonesian military missions were setting out on their way, another problem made its appearance, causing concern in the technical no less than in the military field. It was obvious that any major acquisition of Soviet bloc military equipment would

[4] AFP, in English, December 31, 1957.
[5] Reuters, in English, January 2, 1958.
[6] Ibid.

necessitate the retraining of Indonesian servicemen by communist experts in Indonesia or in the Bloc. It was equally clear that significant Russian aid in the economic field would require the presence of Bloc technicians, and this ticklish question was raised during the parliamentary debate on the $100 million Soviet loan. Finance Minister Slamet felt impelled at the time to assure parliament that the government "will see to it that the presence of Soviet technical workers in Indonesia does not jeopardize the interests of our own state."[7] An undertaking was given that Russian technicians would come to Indonesia only during the earliest phase, and that the cabinet would make arrangements to send Indonesians to the Soviet Union for technical training to replace Soviet experts in Indonesia.[8] If it was considered necessary to extend such assurances in the relatively innocuous field of economic aid, it may well be imagined how much trepidation must have been caused by the thought that Bloc officers would shortly be making their appearance in Djakarta. A last-minute attempt was made to defuse this explosive issue by diverting the venue to neutral ground.

It was noted at the time that some of the members of Indonesia's various military missions were departing together on their way to Cairo, where they later split up and proceeded on their separate journeys to Eastern and Western Europe.[9] Sukarno and Subandrio, on the first leg of an extended international tour, also made their way to Cairo early in the new year. On January 16, 1958, Subandrio told a Cairo news conference that the possibility of an arms agreement with Egypt was being explored, adding that Soviet weapons were better and cheaper than Western equipment. On the following day, the *Times of Indonesia* analyzed "the recent arms deal between Indonesia and Egypt and Yugoslavia," saying that "since these two countries themselves obtained their weapons from other powers, what Indonesia got from them would not be enough to make any force . . . effective."[10] Shortly afterward, Subandrio explained that Indonesia was still studying the quality and price terms of the Egyptian offer.[11]

The arguments put forward by the *Times of Indonesia* were, of course, very much to the point. Egypt could not conceivably equip

---

[7] Djakarta Radio, domestic broadcast, January 14, 1958.
[8] AFP, in English, January 15, 1958.
[9] *New York Times*, December 31, 1957.
[10] Antara, in English, January 17, 1958.
[11] Djakarta Radio, domestic broadcast, January 22, 1958.

a major Indonesian force from its own stock of communist bloc weapons; the Egyptian army itself was still being reequipped by the Soviet Union, following the losses in tanks and planes suffered at Sinai and Suez. Moreover, Egypt in 1958 was not producing any parts, spares, or ammunition for Russian-made arms. Although Cairo was receiving the first MiG-17s, it was not yet in a position to phase out its MiG-15 fighters. Therefore, as the Indonesians knew perfectly well, an arms deal between Indonesia and Egypt could not possibly mean more than the transshipment of some unopened crates of Soviet weapons via the Suez Canal, with Cairo requiring immediate compensation from the USSR for each item passed on to Djakarta. This would have been a very transparent device with no apparent political advantage, since by that time Indonesia had admitted that it was buying arms from Eastern Europe. The only possible purpose of such an exercise would have been to take advantage of a few crates that perhaps were more immediately available in Alexandria than in Vladivostok. It is quite obvious that this could hardly have been the reason for the serious discussions between Egypt and Indonesia, especially since, in January 1958, before the second flareup of the anti-Sukarno rebellion, there was not yet a desperate need to rush weapons to Djakarta within days. No information is available whether any such transfers from Egypt to Indonesia ever occurred, but they are unlikely to have been of major proportions.

It can, however, be shown that the Cairo talks *did* produce an agreement on an entirely different aspect of Indonesia's decision to purchase Soviet arms. Some seven weeks after Subandrio's trip to the Nile, a high rebel officer informed Western correspondents that "at least 30 Indonesian pilots were now in Egypt being trained by Soviet jet pilots and . . . on their return they would man the Russian jets." He claimed that "Egypt was the go-between for the communist countries and Indonesia in the supply of arms and other assistance."[12] Shortly afterward, diplomatic sources in Djakarta (apparently British or American) were quoted as saying that "four Indonesian pilots were believed to be training in Egypt." The Indonesian Foreign Ministry did not deny this report.[13] In the following year, the substantial accuracy of these reports was confirmed by a highly authoritative official Indonesian source, the

---

[12] Melbourne Radio, domestic broadcast, March 9, 1958.
[13] Reuters, in English, April 4, 1958.

deputy chief of staff of the air force, Colonel Siswady, who stated in Sydney that "Egypt trained three of our pilots and a group of ground staff in handling MiG and Ilyushin aircraft and those returned and trained the rest of our crew." He claimed that it took only a short training period to teach the pilots of Vampires to handle the new Soviet jets.[14] It is a matter of some historical irony that the young pilot who, in March 1960, tried to assassinate Sukarno by strafing the palace from a MiG-17 was reportedly a member of the group whose flight training in Egypt had been negotiated by Sukarno two years earlier.[15]

One fact stands out: Djakarta would not have negotiated an agreement with Cairo, early in January 1958, to train Indonesian pilots to fly Soviet jets unless Indonesia already was certain that it was about to receive those jets. The observer is thus left with no alternative but to conclude that Djakarta had reached an airplane agreement with Moscow and Prague before the Indonesian arms delegation ever departed for East Europe—which, of course, it did only at the time of the Cairo talks. It is equally clear that, two weeks previously, when Subandrio was talking to Gordon Mein and threatening the United States with a communist arms deal unless Washington responded quickly, the Indonesian government knew very well that it was buying Soviet jets in any case. Thus the arms mission must have been sent to follow up on details —the choice and inspection of weapons, discussions on finances, and delivery schedules—and not to negotiate an agreement in principle, a step that had already been well and truly taken.

The advantages of training air force crews in Egypt seemed obvious. In view of the misgivings previously aroused by the very prospect of Soviet economic technicians operating in Indonesia, it seemed wise to cushion the further impact of an arms deal by avoiding, as far as possible, the presence of large numbers of Bloc military experts. Since Soviet instructors were in Egypt in any case, it appeared an ideal place in which to train Indonesians, obviating the need for bringing large numbers of Soviet officers to Indonesia and sending Indonesian officers to Bloc countries. Developments in February 1958, however, rendered this plan inadequate. With the rebellion in the Outer Islands and the urgent need for air superiority to reestablish Djakarta's authority, it be-

---

[14] *Times* (London), February 11, 1959.
[15] See Arnold C. Brackman, *Indonesian Communism: A History* (New York: Frederick A. Praeger, 1963), p. 273. The pilot was Lt. Daniel Maukar.

came obvious that training would have to proceed on a much faster and wider scale than was possible in Egypt alone. Moreover, there were maintenance problems that, it turned out, could only be solved on the spot, in Indonesia, and with the aid of Bloc experts. Therefore, as was later reported, Djakarta in its final arms protocol with the East included a specific provision for the dispatch to Indonesia in 1958 of Czech instructors to train pilots in the use of Soviet jets.[16]

It would appear that the tasks of these instructors were interpreted rather broadly; soon after the first Soviet planes arrived in Indonesia in the spring of 1958, a rebel source identified seven Czech air force officers by name and passport number and stated that, although brought over officially to serve as "clerks" in the Hotel Transaera in Djakarta, they had actually flown two strafing missions for the Djakarta government.[17] A little later, rebel sources stated that three or four Indonesian air force officers who had just been trained in Egypt were engaged mainly in assembling Soviet jets from newly arrived crates and that they were working under the supervision of three Soviet instructors at Surabaja. Another fifty-three Indonesian air force technicians who had received a preliminary course in Egypt had proceeded to Czechoslovakia for advanced training.[18]

The precise dates on which the various stages of Indonesia's "Czech" arms deal unfolded are still a matter for speculation. Presumably, the agreement in principle to purchase Czechoslovak jets was finalized sometime between the appearance of the news concerning repeated Czech offers, late in September 1957,[19] and the leakage of the report, in the second half of December 1957, that an arms mission was actually setting out for Prague.[20] Moreover, as noted previously, the subject apparently had already come up for discussion with the Russians and the Czechs during the fall of 1956 and later, at least as far as the provision of Soviet credit for military equipment was concerned. The technical protocol on delivery schedules, spare parts, ammunition, repairs, and maintenance was probably drafted when the Indonesian military

[16] *New York Times*, June 17, 1958.
[17] At Padang on April 17 and at Bukittinggi on April 22 (Central Sumatra Station YHZ9, in English, April 24, 1958).
[18] Melbourne Radio, overseas program, May 1, 1958; Menado, Permesta Radio, in English, May 16, 1958.
[19] Antara, in English, to Asia, September 27, 1957.
[20] *New York Times*, December 27, 1957.

delegation arrived in Prague on January 15, 1958. That such a spare parts agreement was part of subsequent Indonesian arms deals with the Bloc has been reported by reliable sources;[21] moreover, it is known that the parallel arrangement concerning the Soviet jeeps, which was made only some months earlier, also included provisions for spare parts and repair facilities. (In January 1958, two Soviet vessels arrived in Indonesia with 282 jeeps, 25 mobile repair shops, and 1,063 cases of spare parts.)[22] The general stipulations concerning the future behavior of the Czech personnel due to serve in Indonesia and, probably, also some additional details concerning the dispatch of Indonesian goods to Czechoslovakia seem to have been settled with Czechoslovak Premier Siroký and his entourage, who arrived in Djakarta on January 24, 1958. Siroký promised the Indonesian parliament that Czech aid policy would be based on equality and respect for the rights and interests of the recipient nation; surely this was no coincidence, coming, as it did, a mere two weeks after parliament had voiced anxiety over the prospect of Bloc experts operating in Indonesia.[23] A few hours later, Siroký stated that the current international situation favored Indonesia's efforts to realize her demand for West Irian; Czechoslovakia was ready, insofar as Indonesia desired it, to supply scientific and technical experience, within the scope of her possibilities, and to offer actual aid to Indonesia.[24] The Indonesian press commented favorably on Czechoslovakia's new willingness to change from tacit approval of Djakarta's claim to West Irian, as in 1956, to full public support in 1958.[25]

As for the over-all credit cover for the arms deal, there is little doubt that it was settled with Moscow rather than Prague.[26] Nasution, in fact, later referred to it as the 1958 military agreement with the USSR.[27] For reasons already outlined, it might perhaps have been more accurate to call it the 1956 or 1957 arms arrangement. It was hardly accidental that parliamentary ratification of the Russian $100 million loan of 1956 was rammed through only

[21] *Indonesian Observer,* January 17, 1961.
[22] Djakarta Radio, overseas broadcast, in English, February 1, 1958.
[23] Antara, in English, January 29, 1958; also Djakarta Radio, domestic broadcast, January 14, 1958, and AFP, in English, January 15, 1958.
[24] Antara, in English, January 30, 1958.
[25] Djakarta Radio, in English, to Australia, February 1, 1958, quoting *Merdeka.*
[26] *New York Times,* April 8, 1958.
[27] *Indonesian Observer,* January 3, 1961.

six days after Siroký's visit and only one day after the Indonesian government announced that it was definitely receiving ten Soviet vessels, which, as noted before, seem to have constituted the means of transportation, directly from the USSR, of at least part of the "Czech" arms consignment. These ships were, of course, paid for from the $100 million credit.

The Weapons Arrive

At this point, the rebellion in the Outer Islands flared up, and the Djakarta regime's position for a brief period appeared quite precarious, especially since there were increasing signs of Western sympathy and even some unofficial Western assistance for Sukarno's opponents. One result was that the rebels were able to keep their few obsolescent planes in the air rather more efficiently than the government forces, a serious matter since Djakarta needed to transport its troops from island to island across exposed waters. This development injected a note of immediacy into the contacts with the Bloc. Urgent consultations were held with the Soviet ambassador to Djakarta, Zhukov, accompanied by an unusually large staff; within days, Soviet vessels were docking in Indonesian harbors, soon followed by a swelling flood of reports concerning the arrival and assembly of Soviet-made planes at Surabaja and elsewhere.

The Soviet leaders, in public statements and in a major press campaign, covered their increasingly direct involvement in the Indonesian situation with a barrage of invective and threats against alleged Western intervention on behalf of the rebels. *International Affairs* said that "the sympathies of the whole of progressive mankind" were with Sukarno.[28] *Izvestia* condemned "the colonialist war" against Indonesia and praised Djakarta's foreign policy.[29] A TASS statement excoriated "SEATO machinations" against Indonesia.[30] On March 14, 1958, Khrushchev told a preelection meeting in Moscow's Kalinin district:

The Soviet people cannot be indifferent to the imperialist machinations in Indonesia. Why are the imperialists trying to interfere in the internal

28 L. Dadiani, in *International Affairs*, 1958, no. 1.
29 *Izvestia*, February 22, 1958.
30 *Pravda*, March 9, 1958.

affairs of that country and organizing plots there? This cannot be allowed.[31]

Ideological justification came in another *International Affairs* article, which supported "guided democracy" in Indonesia as helpful
to the PKI, at the same time denouncing the Masjumi and the
rebels;[32] a subsequent piece in the same organ played up the
continued withholding of West Irian from Indonesia and revealed
that the USSR regarded the Moscow talks of September 1956 as
a turning point in relations with Indonesia, that attempts were
made in Djakarta in 1956 and 1957 to reverse this trend, but that
Sukarno, since March 1957, had been regarded by Moscow as the
final victor.[33] The same issue of *International Affairs* claimed that
"the imperialists took steps to supply the rebels with arms" and
concluded by quoting from a resolution of the World Peace Council, which said that "foreign interference . . . imperils world peace."
The Soviet slogans prepared for May Day extended "fraternal
greetings to the people of Indonesia, who are defending their freedom and independence in the struggle against foreign imperialists
and their lackeys."[34] On May 14, 1958, the campaign reached its
climax with an official Soviet government statement denouncing
intervention in Indonesia as a "threat to peace" in Southeast Asia.
Indonesia was praised for taking the road of "independent national
development and economic regeneration," and the West was said
to be supplying the rebels with arms, ammunition, and equipment
from Singapore, the Philippines, Taiwan, and even from the United
States, to be training rebel forces, and to be trading with them.
Moscow drew attention to the "grievous consequences" that might
ensue: "Entire responsibility for the dangerous consequences" must
be placed upon the West.[35] The following day, a joint communiqué summing up Nasser's visit to Moscow, which had coincided
with these events, devoted a separate paragraph to the "threat to
peace" arising from foreign interference in Indonesia.[36] No doubt
this rather unusual step reflected contemporary Soviet-Egyptian
collaboration over Indonesia, which had found expression in the

[31] Ibid., March 15, 1958.
[32] A. Lavrentyev, in *International Affairs*, 1958, no. 3.
[33] V. Perov, in ibid., 1958, no. 5.
[34] *Pravda*, April 13, 1958.
[35] TASS, May 14, 1958.
[36] *Pravda*, May 16, 1958.

training of Indonesian air force crews by Soviet instructors in Egypt.[37]

Some twenty-four hours after the May 14 Soviet government declaration, which had drawn repeated attention to the alleged involvement of Chiang Kai-shek in Indonesia, Peking issued a statement of its own, attacking U.S. actions in Southeast Asia. It recalled that the Chinese People's Republic had already supplied Djakarta with cotton and rice on credit and "is prepared to give further assistance within its ability, as may be required by the Indonesian government."[38] In this statement, there could be detected traces of the dubious experiences Peking and Djakarta had had with each other in 1957. The operative words were "within its ability," that is, Peking was extending no blank check, while the whole offer was made conditional upon a clear request from Djakarta, perhaps because in October 1957 Sukarno had left Chou's extended hand hanging in midair.[39] For that matter, it is less than certain that the Moscow and Peking statements of support for Indonesia were the result of Sino-Soviet coordination, although Dr. Subandrio chose to treat them as such, thanking the two governments jointly.[40] Only a few weeks previously, a curious episode had occurred: while the Russians were still vehemently denying reports of the involvement of Soviet military personnel or matériel in Indonesia,[41] and Djakarta kept repudiating any admissions concerning the arrival of Bloc weapons, Peking's official organ attacked the United States, alleging that it was trying to frighten Indonesia out of its arms deal with the Bloc.[42] By inference, this Chinese statement was the very reverse of a denial and amounted practically to an admission that there *was* an arms deal; thus Peking was really contradicting Moscow's and Djakarta's protestations, showing, at the very least, that Sino-Russian coordination was not functioning.

Actually, it took a full five months from the departure of the Indonesian arms mission to East Europe before Djakarta finally and fully admitted that a military transaction had taken place and that

[37] *Times* (London), February 11, 1959.
[38] NCNA, in English, to East Asia, May 15, 1958.
[39] See chap. 8, "Talks on Chinese Arms for Indonesia."
[40] Djakarta Radio, domestic broadcast, May 16, 1958.
[41] *Red Star*, March 17, 1958.
[42] *People's Daily* (Peking), April 8, 1958; NCNA, in English, April 8, 1958.

Bloc weapons had arrived. As reports from rebel and diplomatic sources became more circumstantial, Djakarta's reactions became more evasive. By March 1958, the Indonesian authorities admitted the conclusion of a light arms procurement agreement with Yugoslavia, but they denied that it included Soviet MiGs.[43] (No serious report had ever claimed that it did.) Even at that late date, months after the arms deal was well and truly concluded, the authorities persisted in their attempt to portray Indonesia as still uncommitted on this issue. Thus, at the end of March, Western-type arms captured from the rebels, including recoilless antitank weapons, were displayed in Djakarta, and the Indonesian press criticized the continued U.S. refusal to let the government troops have U.S. weapons while the civil war was continuing.[44] Both the newspapers and Foreign Minister Subandrio, as late as April, were still warning the West that, although Indonesian forces were "standardized in the Western pattern" and Indonesian officers had been trained in the United States, this "may have to change"; Bloc weapons might have to be purchased, *unless* the West would agree to give arms[45] (as if, at that hour, there was still any choice open). In fact, crates of MiGs were almost certainly being unpacked at that precise time.

While Subandrio was still maintaining this pose, diplomatic sources in Djakarta quoted Indonesian military authorities to the effect that "60 MiG jet fighters, 32 Ilyushin jet bombers and 11 Ilyushin jet transports" had been ordered from the Bloc.[46] Djakarta hastened to deny the report, although, within weeks, this information was proved by events to have been both authentic and reasonably accurate. By this time, the whole affair had become so transparent that the *Times of Indonesia* asked somewhat testily why the government should deem it necessary to go on with these denials; Indonesia had the right to buy such weapons if it wished to do so.[47] Nevertheless, a few days later, Subandrio called U.S. Ambassador Howard P. Jones on the carpet because the Washington spokesman of the State Department had intimated that Indonesia was purchasing arms from the East.[48] In the middle of April

---

43 Djakarta Radio, domestic broadcast, March 13, 1958.
44 Antara, in English, March 27, 1958, quoting *Suluh Indonesia*.
45 Subandrio's United Press interview, April 4, 1958.
46 Reuters, in English, April 4, 1958.
47 Antara, in English, April 3, 1958.
48 Ibid., April 8, 1958.

1958, Subandrio contradicted his own representative at The Hague, who had admitted and justified the arms deal.[49] On April 21, Indonesian planes strafing the rebel base at Bukittinggi were identified as Soviet-made[50] and, at the same time, Subandrio, who was passing through South Vietnam, finally confirmed that Indonesia had bought arms in the Bloc.[51] Five weeks later, the Indonesian radio was already describing practice flights in Java of two Czech MiG-15s and of a number of Czech AVIA-14 cargo planes ordered at $250,000 apiece. They were said to be flown by Indonesian pilots, although it was made clear that only a handful of these pilots were trained to fly the new planes, and that some more weeks would pass before even as many as twelve fliers would be ready.[52] Thus there would seem to be little doubt that the rebels had been right in charging that the Soviet-made planes, which had attacked them over a month earlier, had been piloted by officers from the Soviet bloc.[53]

The Politics of Nonalignment

On May 22, 1958, the United States reversed its position and announced that licenses would be given to Djakarta for the sale of aircraft parts and of some $500,000 worth of light arms, the beginning of a new policy that soon led to much larger American sales to Indonesia. Earlier, Washington had studied measures to prevent further involvement of U.S. citizens in Indonesia's internecine conflicts; at that time, the capture of an American citizen, Allan Lawrence Pope, piloting a B-26 for the rebels, had provided fresh fuel for propaganda attacks from the communist countries. After the change in Washington's arms policy toward Indonesia had taken place, Subandrio accidentally provided some convincing evidence to prove that the military deal with the Bloc had not been caused merely by the prolonged U.S. delay in acceding to Indonesia's request. In reply to a question, he now admitted very frankly that the improvement in the U.S. attitude would not make him suspend "other purchases"; Indonesia would buy weapons

[49] Reuters, in English, April 14, 1958; Djakarta Radio, overseas broadcast, in English, April 17, 1958.
[50] Menado, Permesta Radio, in Indonesian, April 21, 1958.
[51] Viet Hoa Van Bao, Cholon, in Chinese, April 20, 1958.
[52] Djakarta Radio, domestic broadcast, May 28, 1958.
[53] Central Sumatra Station YHZ9, in English, April 24, 1958.

from both East and West.[54] Thus he contradicted his own earlier
protestations that the approach to the East was conditioned entirely by Washington's silence and showed that his subordinate,
Kusomowidagdo, had been right in stating that Indonesia would,
in any case, conclude an arms deal with the Soviet bloc.[55] In fact,
it had been Djakarta's policy since 1956 to create maximal maneuverability by precisely such transactions with both blocs.

In spite of Indonesia's growing military involvement with the
communist countries, the full extent of which was to become apparent only after a year or two, the PKI could by no means consider itself a beneficiary. The Soviet-made jets, apparently flown
with the aid of some Bloc personnel, had helped "to break the
initial air supremacy of the rebels."[56] This factor played no small
part in ensuring a comparatively painless victory for the government forces,[57] a development that rescued the army from the exposed position in which it had found itself when so many of its
leading cadres had fought on the opposing side. Striving for
reconciliation with the defeated officers, the army by the summer
of 1958 was taking stringent measures against the PKI, which, at
the sixth plenum of its Central Committee, had issued dire warnings against any tacit understanding with the rebels. While, in the
early spring of 1958, it had seemed as if the Indonesian civil war
might become the front line of an East-West confrontation, with
the government finding itself handcuffed to the Soviets, by August
1958 the announcement of the arrival of new U.S. arms shipments
in Djakarta symbolized the fact that Indonesia would now be able
with safety to take weapons and aid from both sides. Within six
months, twenty battalions of infantry were reequipped by the
United States, although the bulk of heavy air and naval equipment continued to stream in from the Bloc.

The successful initiation of this policy, which might, perhaps,
more accurately be termed "multiple alignment" rather than "nonalignment," was accompanied by a deepening of relations with the
country that stood for precisely the same principle—Yugoslavia.
Early in March 1958, a light arms procurement agreement was
signed in Belgrade.[58] Soon a Yugoslav fact-finding mission arrived

[54] Antara, in English, May 27, 1958.
[55] AFP, in English, December 31, 1957.
[56] Speech by Djuanda (Antara, in English, August 14, 1958).
[57] Although some opposition smoldered on for a long time.
[58] Djakarta Radio, domestic broadcast, March 13, 1958.

THE POLITICS OF NONALIGNMENT 219

in Djakarta, and early in April a preliminary agreement was reached for the provision of Yugoslav credit—on somewhat "hard" terms—to cover the Indonesian acquisition of Yugoslav ships, the dispatch of Yugoslav experts to Indonesia, and the utilization of the Yugoslav port of Rijeka (Fiume) as the primary channel for Indonesian goods sent to any part of East Europe.[59] In October 1958, Premier Djuanda

confirmed that Indonesia has purchased arms and military equipment from Yugoslavia and that a part of the purchase has already arrived. He emphasized that, for the time being, the government would not make any more arms deals with Yugoslavia in view of the Indonesian financial situation.[60]

Djuanda then visited Belgrade and, soon thereafter, Marshal Tito himself arrived in Djakarta. His trip, according to the Indonesian press, was partly devoted to assisting Indonesia in her acquisition of military equipment. Tito was prominently accompanied by naval officers who met with their Indonesian counterparts. The communiqué summing up the visit contained hints that there were "realistic possibilities" of expanding the flow of Yugoslav aid to Indonesia, namely, that ways had been found to cope with Indonesia's financial plight.[61] The statement also stressed the common interests of the "nonaligned." Djuanda's and Tito's trips apparently settled the monetary and training arrangements connected with the military transaction between the two countries; in November–December 1958, the most important delivery had already arrived, consisting of six Yugoslav submarine chasers of the Kraljevica class (225 tons each with a speed of some 19 knots) and three Yugoslav landing craft.[62] Soon afterward, a meeting of a joint Indonesian-Yugoslav technical commission revealed that Belgrade had in the end agreed to transfer its ships on much "softer" credit terms, as requested by Djakarta.[63]

On his way home from Belgrade, Djuanda visited Cairo, the capital of another prominent nonaligned state. Before setting out from Djakarta, he had spoken of the need for creating the basis of

[59] Antara, in English, April 15, 1958.
[60] Ibid., October 10, 1958.
[61] TANYUG (Belgrade), in English, December 30, 1958.
[62] Antara, in English, April 30, 1959; see also *Jane's Fighting Ships*, 1964, and Djakarta Radio, overseas broadcast, in English, March 18, 1959.
[63] Djakarta Radio, domestic broadcast, March 25, 1959.

an Indonesian arms industry by setting up assembly plants and factories manufacturing spare parts.[64] In Egypt, he inspected newly established arms factories producing light automatic weapons and ammunition. At the same time, in December 1958, Indonesia extended an agreement with India, the third of the important nonaligned states, for cooperation between the two navies.[65] During the second half of 1958, naval orders were given to West German shipyards, and attempts were made to tighten naval relations with Britain.

These steps, intended to free Indonesia from dependence on any one bloc and to build a closely knit Third Force with prominent Indonesian participation, created increasing friction with the communist countries and with the PKI. In the Moscow Declaration of November 1957, the majority of communist parties had already given vent to their increasing suspicion of Titoism, an emotion that fed upon the events of the previous year in Eastern Europe. In April 1958, Njoto, the second deputy secretary-general of the PKI, had attended the controversial Seventh Congress of the Yugoslav League of Communists and had then proceeded to Peking. On June 23, *Harian Rakjat,* the organ of the PKI, published a sharp attack upon the Yugoslav line but, in view of the Djakarta-Belgrade friendship, was still cautious enough to include a proviso to the effect that interparty friction need not necessarily disturb good intergovernmental relations. On July 10, 1958, however, Moscow announced that it was "deferring" its credits to Yugoslavia, allegedly because of the pressure of domestic economic requirements. It transpired later that the Russians had suspended military as well as economic assistance to Yugoslavia. *Komunist* of Belgrade retorted that this was a unilateral decision, ruling out any further negotiations. By the time Marshal Tito arrived in Djakarta in December 1958, the PKI's *Bintang Timur* was prepared to go so far as to accuse Tito of having come as a representative of U.S. interests in Southeast Asia. During the same period, the Chinese were launching vitriolic attacks upon Yugoslavia, because the "revisionists" were not backing Peking sufficiently over the Quemoy struggle. Since Chou En-lai soon saw fit also to accuse Tito of sabotaging the Bloc's relations with certain African and Asian governments, sections of the Indonesian press close to Sukarno began to retort that Peking's statements were really insulting to Afro-

---

[64] Antara, in English, October 10, 1958.
[65] Djakarta Radio, overseas broadcast, December 3, 1958.

Asians, especially to Indonesians, no less than to Yugoslavia.[66] By that time, Indonesia had been forced to shelve the plan of using the Yugoslav port of Rijeka for transshipments to other communist countries, since the Bloc was boycotting Yugoslavia.[67] Similarly, the growth of intimacy between Djakarta and Cairo in the later part of 1958 began to run counter to the temporary trend of divergence between Egypt and the communist bloc. Earlier in the year, Aidit had warned Sukarno and the army not to repeat "the lessons of Egypt," that is, not to dissolve political parties.[68] The sudden absorption into Egypt of leftist Syria had given the Russians cause for misgivings, and, after the summer of 1958, the views of Cairo and Moscow concerning the future of revolutionary Iraq clearly were in conflict. By January 1959, Aidit was sharply attacking the Egyptian leadership, eleven days before the Russians finally ventured to do so, and at a time when the Cairo and Djakarta governments were collaborating in important areas.[69]

These general differences in approach and policy toward the nonaligned countries could be expected to leave their traces upon the bilateral relationship between Moscow and Djakarta and, even more, between Peking and Djakarta. After prolonged friction over the temporary suppression of the printing of Chinese-language newspapers in Indonesia, Peking again complained to Djakarta in June 1958 over the alleged activities of a Chiang Kai-shek emissary in Indonesia. In return, the Indonesian nationalist press soon drew angry attention to Chinese limitations upon the movement of Indonesian diplomats in Peking.[70] A few weeks later, the Chinese expressed the "hope" that there would be "wise" Indonesian arrangements for the Fourth Asian Games, since the CPR simply would not attend if Formosa were permitted to participate. At that time, *International Affairs* prominently reprinted, without comment, an earlier warning from the Chinese press against the activities of a Taiwan representative in Indonesia, containing a veiled warning that Djakarta should so something about this situation in order to prevent harm to Indonesian-Chinese relations.[71]

In September 1958, a nasty little conflict developed between

[66] E.g., *Indonesian Observer*, April 22, 1959.
[67] Reuters, February 20, 1959.
[68] PKI, *Documents of the Sixth Plenum of the Central Committee of the PKI* (Djakarta, 1958), pp. 47–49.
[69] PIA, in English, January 9, 1959.
[70] *Times of Indonesia*, July 7, 1958.
[71] "Indonesia: A New Plot," *International Affairs*, 1958, no. 8.

Djakarta and Moscow over Russia's massive dumping of tin on the world market, causing Indonesian tin prices to take a steep dive. Kuznetsov, the Soviet chargé d'affaires in Djakarta, blandly insisted that "the Soviet Union, being a tin-producing country, is exporting," that is, Russia had a perfect right to continue this practice.[72] In fact, the USSR at the time was importing some 20,000 tons of tin annually[73] and, as later transpired, had been hoarding large quantities of tin (some 180,000 tons) sent by the CPR in repayment for Soviet aid.[74] It was with a portion of this Chinese tin that Moscow was flooding the world market, injuring both China's and Indonesia's export possibilities. The Moslem Workers' Union prodded the Djakarta authorities into firm action,[75] but it was only in January 1959 that Moscow finally agreed to an arrangement whereby Soviet tin exports would not exceed two thirds of Indonesia's quota. Some more unpleasantness between Indonesia and the USSR occurred in the field of bilateral trade. The CPR in October 1958 sold additional rice to Indonesia at fairly reasonable prices. Some weeks later, the Indonesian parliament considered passing a resolution against a similar agreement with the USSR, since it turned out that Moscow insisted on charging far more and delivering less speedily than Peking.[76] Within one week, the Russians lost their battle in this little price war and, to prevent being outbid by the Chinese, succumbed and brought the cost of their rice down to Peking's level.[77]

All these developments, however, gave rise to relatively minor friction in comparison to the reverberations caused by Indonesia's attitude toward the delicate subject of Soviet participation in Afro-Asian meetings. Already in December 1958, there were sharp repercussions in Djakarta when it became known that the Indonesian delegation to the Cairo Afro-Asian Economic Conference had protested against Soviet participation. In February 1959, the PKI's *Harian Rakjat* deplored the decision not to send an Indonesian delegation to the Cairo Afro-Asian Youth Conference and

---

[72] PIA, in English, September 23, 1958.
[73] *Studies on the Soviet Union* (Munich), vol. 1 (1962), no. 4, p. 105.
[74] "Letter of the Central Committee of the CPC of February 29, 1964 to the Central Committee of the CPSU," *Peking Review*, vol. VII, no. 19 (May 8, 1964), pp. 12–18.
[75] Antara, in English, October 10, 1958.
[76] Ibid., November 4, 1958.
[77] Ibid., November 11, 1958.

added bluntly that this was due to the fact that some circles in
Djakarta did not approve of the participation of the Soviet Union
at the conference. In what may now be read as a particularly
poignant piece of historical irony, the PKI paper proceeded to
castigate those who did not wish to acknowledge that the greater
part of the Soviet Union belongs to the Asian continent.[78] A mere
five years later, the PKI was to be second only to Peking in ridi-
culing all Soviet assertions that some six million square miles of
Asian territory entitled Moscow's "modern revisionists" to a seat at
Afro-Asian gatherings.[79] It is interesting to note that the Indonesian national bourgeoisie had thus anticipated the views of
Messrs. Aidit and Chou En-lai by several years.

Seen both from Moscow and from Peking, although for different
reasons, Indonesia's behavior from the summer of 1958 onward
could be considered somewhat provocative. As has been noted, in
the case of communist countries such as Yugoslavia, tensions of
this kind could and did suffice to cause Moscow to turn off the flow
of aid. (In a purely ideological context, Belgrade's "offense," of
course, was much graver than Djakarta's, but the Yugoslav government's *actions* were actually very restrained.) Yet there appears
to be little doubt that, in the case of Indonesia, the Russians were
hesitant to resort to their assistance program as a means of leverage upon the Djakarta authorities. On the contrary, in the economic field, there was actually competition between Moscow and
Peking—as over the sale of rice—to show who could give Indonesia more and who could present better terms. Thus, in the fall
of 1958, Chou En-lai made an offer to an Indonesian parliamentary
delegation: this provided for Chinese capital and technicians,
"without strings," to build a steel mill. He added that, as soon as
Indonesian workers could take over the plant, the whole Chinese
staff would return home.[80] Chou's offer came a full six months
after Indonesia and the USSR had exchanged instruments of ratification over the September 1956 agreement, providing Russian
credit for the construction of two steel mills in Indonesia. There
was, at that stage, no serious possibility whatever of establishing
additional steel plants; on the contrary, Djakarta and Moscow
themselves soon decided that they had to consolidate the two

[78] PIA, in English, February 3, 1959.
[79] See chap. 10, "Aftermath."
[80] *Merdeka,* November 1, 1958.

projected mills into one.[81] Thus it must be assumed that Chou was really suggesting that the CPR, rather than the USSR, should build a steel mill in Indonesia.

By that time, the Chinese had invented their own, elegant way of intimating that Soviet and East European aid to Indonesia was neither usable nor bona fide. Thus Peking's NCNA, slyly blaming "U.S. sabotage," found it necessary to draw attention to the fact that the engines of the Soviet ships sent to Indonesia were found upon arrival to be damaged, and so was machinery from East Germany,[82] Hungary, and Czechoslovakia. As for the Russian captains of the vessels, one of them had allegedly refused to follow Indonesian instructions with regard to the cargoes to be loaded— although this, too, was brought out in the context of "U.S. slanders."[83] There is thus every reason for concluding that, in spite of differences with the Djakarta authorities, Moscow and Peking not only continued economic aid in 1958 and 1959 but sharply competed for the honor of doing so.

There was no appreciable decline in Bloc military shipments to Indonesia during this period of friction, any more than in economic assistance. The flow of hardware continued unabated in 1958 and 1959. Moscow's comparatively favorable treatment of Indonesia during this time, and during the much tenser period of 1964 and 1965 when Djakarta supported Peking's anti-Russian campaign, stands in significant contrast to the punishment meted out to Yugoslavia in 1958 and, even more strikingly, to the retribution in the economic and military sectors wreaked upon Yugoslavia in 1948, upon China in 1959/60, and upon Albania. As in the Indonesian case, so also the USSR was most hesitant to penalize the UAR, during periods of sharp conflict, by turning off the tap of economic and military aid, although the Russians gently reminded Egypt not to "cut down the tree that gives the shade." Clearly, therefore, the Soviet leaders were painfully aware that noncommunist countries had realistic options open to them if crudely pressured by Russia, whereas it was apparently assumed that communist leaders were more seriously circumscribed in their

---

[81] S. Skachkov commentary, *Pravda*, February 10, 1960; also *Pravda*, July 2, 1960.

[82] The "sabotaged machinery" from East Germany was presumably an ill-fated sugar mill that broke down upon installation and was persistently rumored to have been a beet-sugar plant erroneously sent to cane-sugar producing Indonesia.

[83] NCNA, in English, August 3, 1958.

actions and would therefore find themselves in a grave predicament if they antagonized the USSR. History proved, however, that even Yugoslavia, China, and Albania could survive Moscow's wrath, and the Soviet leaders took this lesson to heart later, when it came to tackling Rumanian recalcitrance.

The Buildup in the Air

During 1958–1960, Indonesia's military buildup by the Bloc continued steadily and without major interruptions. The first two MiG-15s had made their public appearance in Djakarta at the end of May 1958.[84] Actually, it might have been more accurate to refer to these planes as CS-102s, Czech-built MiG-15s with Soviet engines, or CS-103s, similar jets with Soviet-designed engines constructed in Czechoslovakia.[85] It was only three months later, however, that eight of the Czech jets became officially operative, being transferred from a maintenance unit to Indonesia's new jet squadron. Interestingly enough, Premier Djuanda utilized the opportunity, in the presence of members of the Czech embassy, to thank those who had earlier "joined in the operations against the insurgents" and had helped "to break the initial air supremacy of the rebels."[86] The implication would seem to be that those who had flown against the insurgents in April and May must have been Czechs rather than Indonesians, since presumably the official transfer of the jets from the (Czech) maintenance unit to the Indonesian squadron had been delayed until August because it took that long to train a sufficient number of Indonesian pilots. A few days after the transfer, the MiG-15s flew in formation over Indonesia's Independence Day parade.[87] In the beginning of October, it was reliably reported that eight new Soviet Ilyushin-28 light jet bombers had arrived, joining a few IL-28s received a little earlier from Czechoslovakia.[88] Since the Czechs had only started producing their own IL-28s many months after they had begun to

---

[84] Djakarta Radio, domestic broadcast, May 28, 1958.
[85] Basic details on the planes produced in the Bloc are to be found in the 1962 edition of Asher Lee's standard work, *The Soviet Air Force*, rev. ed. (New York: John Day, 1962).
[86] Speech by Djuanda (Antara, in English, August 14, 1958). Even in the fall, the rebels still were reported to have seven B-26s, six P-51 Mustang fighters, and three B-29 bombers (PIA, in English, October 1, 1958).
[87] Djakarta Radio, overseas broadcast, in English, August 24, 1958.
[88] Hilversum (Netherlands) Radio, domestic broadcast, October 2, 1958.

turn out MiG-15s and, moreover, had sent some to the Middle East, it is likely that they did not have enough of these bombers to fill all of Indonesia's needs; a number, therefore, may have had to be bought directly from the USSR.[89] On October 5, 1958, Indonesian Armed Forces Day, six IL-28s, nine MiG-15s, and six AVIA transports, as well as five Western planes (three Vampire jet fighters and two Mustang fighters), swept past, maneuvered, fired rockets, bombs, and machine guns, and dropped paratroopers. A Russian observer was quoted as having praised the ability of the Indonesian pilots and as having stated that Soviet flyers, who in May 1957 had brought an IL-14 passenger plane as a present for Sukarno, had admired the "bravery and agility" of the Indonesian pilots.[90] It is not quite clear how they could have witnessed "bravery" in May 1957, when there was no fighting and when the Russians could hardly have seen the Indonesians in action. However, the Indonesian crew of that particular Ilyushin had been trained in Russia,[91] and it is known that in the summer of 1957 a Soviet crew came to fetch the plane back "for an overhaul";[92] they were accompanied on the trip by a number of Indonesian air force officers who then stayed in the USSR for some time.[93] It is at least possible that, as early as August 1957, these officers were already being trained in Russia to fly Ilyushin-28s, as well as watching the Ilyushin-14 being repaired, and it was their behavior under tough flying conditions that aroused the admiration of their Russian colleagues.

Altogether, as the amount of Bloc hardware in Indonesia accumulated, it became obvious that efficient operation and maintenance alike would require increasing numbers of qualified officers and technicians and that a considerable proportion of them would have to be trained in communist countries, since Indonesia was reluctant to have too many Bloc instructors on her soil. Before the fall of 1958, the only definite reports concerning Indonesian military personnel in communist countries referred to fifty-three air force technicians, sent on from Egypt to Czechoslovakia for advanced training,[94] and the original air force crew of Sukarno's

[89] See Lee, *The Soviet Air Force.*
[90] Antara, in English, October 5, 1958.
[91] *New York Herald Tribune,* September 12, 1956.
[92] Djakarta Radio, overseas broadcast, in English, June 29, 1957.
[93] Ibid., August 5, 1957.
[94] Melbourne Radio, overseas program, May 1, 1958; Menado, Permesta Radio, in English, May 16, 1958.

IL-14, trained in Russia. In December 1958, however, a Czech mission headed by František Maček, chief of the general technical management department of the Ministry of Foreign Trade, signed an agreement in Djakarta covering "matters relating to the training of Indonesians in the use of technical instruments coming from Czechoslovakia."[95] The Indonesian Defense Ministry, however, bluntly stated that this agreement "provides for the giving of specialist training to Indonesians in the use of military equipment purchased from Czechoslovakia."[96] Since the functions of Czech instructors in Indonesia had already been covered in an earlier agreement,[97] it is to be presumed that the December 1958 protocol concerned the dispatch of further Indonesian officers and men to Czechoslovakia and, perhaps, elsewhere in the Bloc. Why such further training was needed became apparent two months later, when Indonesia escalated to a more advanced type of Soviet jet fighter; in February 1959, eight MiG-17s were transferred from a maintenance unit to the air force's jet squadron.[98]

While the air force was being built up by the Bloc and the infantry by the United States, the navy was receiving equipment from all parts of the world, including four Italian frigates as well as Gannet naval planes from Britain. The general modernization of the Indonesian armed services and their weapons appeared to be a major step in implementing the program for the creation of a trim, shipshape, professional force as desired by Indonesia's military reformers. During the second half of 1958, spokesmen for the Indonesian army explained that it was now being planned to cut down on the manpower of the permanent standing army, perhaps by as much as one half, that is, to shunt aside older men and nonprofessional elements. A bill presented to parliament provided for conscription, with a selective call-up, to compensate for this reduction in manpower by building up a new, young reserve force that would be competently trained to use Indonesia's modern equipment. The remodeled army would be mobile, handpicked, and well able to take care of internal security.[99]

There are no signs whatever that the PKI greeted this prospect with enthusiasm, nor could it have been expected to do so. The

95 Djakarta Radio, overseas broadcast, in English, December 1, 1958.
96 PIA, in English, December 2, 1958.
97 New York Times, June 17, 1958.
98 Djakarta Radio, domestic broadcast, February 9, 1959.
99 Reuters, in English, August 22 and October 15, 1958.

seventh plenum of the PKI Central Committee, in November 1958, devoted time to the demand that foreign economic aid for Indonesia be kept free of "strings,"[100] and Aidit, around the same time, complained that Indonesia's exports to the communist countries were still a mere 4 per cent of total exports.[101] While these PKI statements could be interpreted as vague expressions of support for increased economic ties between Djakarta and Moscow, not a single word was said about Bloc military aid to Indonesia, which by this time was, after all, an acknowledged fact from which the communists could have derived much propagandistic advantage. Presumably, sweetness and light did not prevail in the relations between the Indonesian and Soviet parties; Aidit had only just returned from a trip to the Bloc, when the plenum was held, but was whisked back again almost immediately afterward, as Moscow was preparing for the CPSU's Twenty-first Congress. It was not until another year had passed (and the PKI had decided that a crisis atmosphere over West Irian might be useful for internal reasons) that the party's leadership consented to express any kind of support for Indonesia's military buildup. However, there was still no reference to the important part played by the Bloc in sending arms, nor was there as much as an indirect expression of gratitude.[102] Moreover, even this grudging gesture of support was withheld until September 1959, three years after the first military contacts with the Bloc, and well over a year after the arrival of the first Soviet jets. Perhaps still more time would have elapsed but for the fact that, on this particular occasion, the PKI's Sixth Congress, the army was persuaded only with difficulty to permit the communists to gather at all and insisted on having its military stenographers prominently ensconced throughout the proceedings. Thus the communists may have felt obliged to make some vague noises that might appease the officer corps, such as saying a few kind words about the need for new military equipment.

The Buildup at Sea

In the meantime, the center of gravity of Bloc military assistance had gradually shifted from the air force to the navy. The only

100 In other words, that preference be given to Moscow's aid, which was advertised as being free of "strings."
101 *World Marxist Review*, vol. 1 (1958), no. 1.
102 PKI, *Material for the Sixth National Congress of the Communist Party of Indonesia* (Djakarta, 1959), p. 100.

ships from communist countries to arrive in Indonesia prior to the winter of 1958/59 had been the twelve Soviet vessels whose military significance has already been noted[103] and a few East European freighters. The importance of these ships in defeating the rebels was later emphasized by Indonesia's minister of shipping, who pointed out that a decisive proportion of the merchant vessels had been "used for military purposes."[104] However, there was still no indication at this date that actual warships—as opposed to militarized freighters—were arriving from communist countries (except Yugoslavia, which, of course, did not belong to the Bloc). Yet the Indonesian military mission, whose publicized journey to Eastern Europe at the outset of 1958 had symbolized the start of overt military relations with the Bloc, was known to have visited Poland, an aspiring naval power, as well as Czechoslovakia, a supplier of aircraft.

At that time, an agreement was signed in Warsaw concerning an "exchange of experts," including, as later emerged, the dispatch of thirty Polish naval officers to Indonesia. Although Djakarta insisted that these were members of Poland's merchant marine,[105] needed in connection with the simultaneous Polish offer to let Indonesia charter 50,000 tons of coastal shipping,[106] there was some doubt on the matter in view of the avowedly military nature of the January 1958 Warsaw talks. The forthcoming arrival of the Polish officers was revealed in April 1958, and it became known some weeks later that a Polish trade delegation would also be coming to Djakarta to conclude a final agreement on the transfer of ships to Indonesia.[107] Then, however, it was announced that the Djakarta talks would deal only with general economic relations, and the question of the vessels would be settled at parallel discussions in Warsaw.[108] Later in June 1958, it was stated that agreement had been reached in Warsaw on the purchase of twenty-four new Polish merchant ships, amounting to 62,000 tons and costing more than $39 million, to be implemented within the framework of a general trade pact.[109] In spite of this development, the parallel discussions in Djakarta dragged on for another six weeks before a new trade agreement was finally negotiated, including the ship-

[103] See chap. 8, "Soviet Vessels for Indonesia."
[104] Medan, North Sumatra, regional broadcasting service, October 10, 1958.
[105] Antara, in English, April 1, 1958.
[106] AFP, in English, January 17, 1958.
[107] Antara, in English, June 17, 1958.
[108] Ibid., June 19, 1958.
[109] Djakarta Radio, domestic broadcast, June 28, 1958.

ping deal among its provisions but sidestepping the question of additional Polish credit commitments.[110] Not until the end of August 1958 were there some hints of the real reason for such apparent duplication and confusion. A Djakarta broadcast honoring the Polish chargé d'affaires, Wink, mentioned casually that an Indonesian delegation visiting Warsaw "in the spring" had "obtained military equipment on a credit basis."[111] In the light of this admission, the actual course of events may be reconstructed along the following lines: the Indonesian military mission to Warsaw in January 1958 probably concluded an agreement in principle on the acquisition of Polish naval vessels and the dispatch of Polish naval officers to Indonesia. After the training and maintenance questions had been settled, perhaps with these same officers, a second Indonesian delegation "in spring" (mid-June 1958) apparently negotiated two credit agreements in Warsaw, one, in secret, to cover the purchase of the Polish warships and connected expenses, and another, in public, to pay for the acquisition of the twenty-four Polish freighters. The simultaneous talks in Djakarta, on the other hand, were clearly concerned with the trade implications of these arrangements, including the choice of Indonesian goods to be exported in repayment for the Polish credits.

A prolonged training period was required to teach Indonesians to handle the more complex of the new naval purchases. An additional complication concerned Poland's capabilities with regard to naval equipment, which were by no means equivalent to those of Czechoslovakia in the aircraft industry. Most of the "Polish" naval craft were Soviet vessels built in the early 1950s and handed over in the 1955–1957 period. It was evident from the very beginning that any large Indonesian orders would have to be met, at least in part, from Soviet stocks, while even the items that could be sent directly from Poland were in short supply and would have to be replenished by the Russians. Thus one of the earliest large deliveries of Bloc naval craft to Indonesia, belonging to a fairly simple type that could be transferred after relatively brief training periods, apparently involved Soviet rather than Polish vessels. This occurred in December 1958, when eight submarine chasers of some 300 tons each were handed over to the naval authorities in Surabaja.[112] The more sophisticated of the new acquisitions, however,

[110] Antara, in English, August 7, 1958.
[111] Djakarta Radio, overseas broadcast, in English, August 31, 1958.
[112] Jane's Fighting Ships, 1964.

started arriving only during the following summer, after the first
Indonesian crews had learned to operate them; beginning in June
1959, Surabaja port was frequently placed under stringent security
measures to prevent leakage of early news about the country's
naval buildup. In August 1959, it was admitted that Indonesia
was receiving new submarines, although it was claimed that no
Bloc experts would be required to aid in running these vessels.[113]

On Armed Forces Day in October 1959, the Indonesian navy
already was able to display two submarines purchased from Poland (apparently early models of the W class with a wide range
but without missiles), two destroyers of the Skoryi class (with a dis-
placement of some 2,600 tons and a range of 4,000 miles), and seven
assorted submarine chasers of Yugoslav and Soviet origin, as well
as minesweepers, troop carriers, and a Yugoslav LCT. The destroyers were reported to have been improved by the Poles, who
had installed new guns and torpedo tubes.[114] It would appear,
however, that neither the speed of the training process nor the
number of crews produced were sufficient to enable Indonesia to
implement her naval buildup according to plan. For that matter,
standards of training do not seem to have been high enough to
ensure proper maintenance, as was indicated by the fact that,
within months, one of the Polish submarines had to be sent back
for overhaul.[115] The naval chief of staff of that period, Vice-
Admiral Subijakto, who had returned in June 1959 from a visit to
Yugoslavia and Poland, reported that both governments had offered to train additional Indonesian sailors, apparently in Eastern
Europe rather than in Surabaja.[116] Since many of the vessels that
were to be displayed on Armed Forces Day had by this time already arrived in Surabaja, it is to be presumed that the new offer
concerned the preparation of crews for additional ships to be purchased by Indonesia. At least two more Polish Skoryi class destroyers did, in fact, arrive in Surabaja in the months following
the 1959 Armed Forces Day.[117]

Poland, at this stage, had become deeply involved both with
Indonesia's navy and with her merchant marine, having extended
additional credits to aid Indonesia in the construction of ship-

[113] Reuters, August 29, 1959.
[114] Antara, in English, October 5, 1959.
[115] *Jane's Fighting Ships,* 1964.
[116] Antara, in English, June 25, 1959.
[117] *Jane's Fighting Ships,* 1964.

yards;[118] however, as has been noted, the Poles were quite unable to fulfill all of Indonesia's requests, and there were many instances of direct Soviet intervention in this sector.

Russian interest in Indonesia's maritime situation was in evidence continuously, starting with the dispatch of the twelve Soviet freighters and tankers in the spring of 1958. In the summer of 1958, the Soviet Union initiated the first move in its protracted operation to establish the Soviet presence in the oceans around Indonesia, a campaign that relied heavily upon scientific and, especially, oceanographic expeditions. It may be presumed that the USSR was concerned with the Pacific and Indian oceans as operational waters for submarines and as proving grounds in the missile, thermonuclear, and space age, where the Russians could shadow U.S. tests as well as the movements of the Seventh Fleet. In any event, the scientific ship Zarya visited Indonesia in the summer of 1958 and, in the fall, a Pravda correspondent went to spend a week on the strategic island of Ambon studying fisheries and other maritime activities.[119] Some months later, it was announced that the USSR was enlarging its $100 million credit to Indonesia to cover the building of a technical institute at Ambon, which would be devoted to fishing problems and to naval and oceanographic studies.[120] In the subsequent period, a Soviet scientific mission arranged to provide an Indonesian university with satellite tracking equipment and with Soviet technicians to train Indonesians in the use of this equipment.[121] The same delegation signed an agreement with Indonesia concerning the participation of Indonesian scientists in a Soviet maritime research cruise in the Indian Ocean.[122]

In the meantime, the USSR had dispatched the first submarine chasers to Indonesia, as well as two naval oilers,[123] and soon thereafter gave Djakarta twenty amphibious tanks, possibly of the PT-76 type, which were displayed on Armed Forces Day in 1959.[124] It was reported later that, in addition to the Poles, the Soviet Union itself was dispatching W class submarines to Indonesia sometime in 1959/60. During that particular period alone, the

118 Antara, in English, February 25, 1959.
119 Djakarta Radio, domestic broadcast, November 13, 1958.
120 Ibid., July 8, 1959.
121 Antara, in English, February 25, 1961.
122 Ibid., March 1, 1961.
123 Jane's Fighting Ships, 1964.
124 Antara, in English, October 5, 1959.

Russians may have sent as many as six of these vessels to Sura-baja.[125] The training program of Indonesian naval crews in Poland was consequently accelerated, including the dispatch of additional men for an eight-month course in underwater salvage operations, a step that could not be interpreted as a conspicuous vote of confidence in the safety of the new submarines.[126]

The tightening of relations between the Indonesian navy and the Bloc, however, by no means led to an abandonment of arms purchases from the West, and the same held true of the other services. In fact, Indonesia's military buildup in 1958–1960 proceeded in an atmosphere of all-round competition, both between the great powers and between the various armed services, organizational control over which was carefully subdivided by Sukarno in 1959. Domestically and externally, the Indonesian President performed a tricky tightrope act, during the 1950s, between Moscow and Peking, East and West, the army and the air force, the civilians and the military, as well as the PKI and its adversaries. His complex maneuvers in the international arms market merely reflected the tactics followed in the implementation of his over-all policy.

[125] *Jane's Fighting Ships*, 1964.
[126] Djakarta Radio, in English, February 7, 1960.

10   Aftermath

For some time it seemed as if the Indonesian President had drafted the ideal prescription for maintaining himself in power without a serious possibility of challenge. He managed to have his position affirmed for life, and honorific titles were showered upon him. However, during the early 1960s he himself began to disturb the equilibrium he had so dexterously created. Congenitally averse to dealing with the difficult and undramatic questions of everyday life (and probably incapable of grasping the true magnitude of this task), Sukarno ignored the staggering material and social problems facing his nation: the catastrophic rural overpopulation of Java, the dependence of the Indonesian economy on the export of a few raw materials whose price on the world market fluctuated wildly, the dizzying inflationary process menacing the country's stability,[1] and the cancer of corruption that undermined his administration.

Instead, Sukarno tried to externalize these problems and engender artificial national unity by embarking upon a program of territorial expansion and conflict that resulted in magnifying Indonesia's economic difficulties to the point of near bankruptcy. A three-year campaign to annex West Irian (rather than allow this

[1] During six years, in the 1950s, the price of rice almost tripled, the price of sugar doubled, meat and other proteins more than tripled, vegetable oils more than quintupled, and clothing increased more than ten times. Even so, this was but a modest inflation compared with the subsequent devastating rise in the cost of living during the 1960s, prior to Sukarno's removal from the scene.

territory to gain eventual self-government, as proposed by the Dutch), followed by a prolonged and unsuccessful "confrontation" with Malaysia, led to vast additional arms purchases from the Soviet bloc, estimated, in the end, at well over $1 billion. Many of the acquisitions, such as a hulking cruiser of the Kirov class, bore no conceivable relationship to Indonesia's real military needs; for that matter, several items received through the economic and technical assistance programs from the communist countries, including a huge sports stadium in Djakarta, belonged to the realm of psychological compensations rather than to the field of practical necessities. The more deeply Indonesia sank into the mire of belligerency, economic disruption, and frustration, the more numerous the imaginary enemies with which Sukarno surrounded his country. Increasing virulence and vituperation accompanied his every comment about the Western world and, as time proceeded, even about the USSR.

Sukarno's increasingly anti-Soviet and pro-Chinese slant mirrored a trend along similar lines in the policies pursued by the PKI. Since the early 1950s, D. N. Aidit, determined to revitalize the party after the 1948 Madiun catastrophe, had pursued a "rightist" policy of collaboration with the national bourgeoisie—in the person of Sukarno. Ideologically speaking, this approach should have brought the PKI into the camp of Khrushchev rather than of Mao. However, such a development was precluded for several objective reasons: (a) Soviet military assistance to Djakarta, whatever its ultimate motivations, in fact supplied weapons to the very power group that, from the PKI's point of view, had to be regarded as basically antagonistic and dangerous, namely, Indonesia's armed forces; (b) Aidit relied for financial support primarily upon the country's large and prosperous Chinese minority, which, while by no means "communist" in outlook, found in the PKI its only consistent ally against Indonesian racist elements, who repeatedly instigated anti-Chinese pogroms. Peking, for prestige reasons, was determined to act as protector of the Overseas Chinese and, in this role, found a useful partner in the PKI.

As the Sino-Soviet conflict became increasingly overt, both Sukarno and the PKI started to gravitate toward Peking.[2] As early

---

[2] The author has elsewhere presented a detailed exposition of developments during 1962–1966, which are summarized here: See Uri Ra'anan, "The Coup that Failed: A Background Analysis," in *Problems of Communism*, March–April 1966; also his chapter on Indonesia in William Andrews and Uri

as 1961, at the time of the CPSU's Twenty-second Congress, Aidit had refused to follow Moscow in its diatribes against China's satellite, Albania. By the fall of the following year, according to a PIA report in November 1962, Aidit acidly "congratulated" Khrushchev for belatedly (and temporarily) canceling the sale of Soviet MiGs to India, which was then embroiled in open conflict with Communist China. In the spring of 1963, at the preliminary Afro-Asian Journalists' Conference, held at the Djakarta sports palace (constructed, it will be recalled, with Soviet money and skill—as *Pravda* bitterly noted at the time), Sukarno's representatives initiated a campaign against participation by the "European" USSR;[3] the PKI showed its overt approval of the government's stand. Yet Indonesia had received some $1½ billion in military and economic credit commitments from Moscow and other East European revisionist capitals and, moreover, was defaulting on its repayments; in addition, the USSR had been very forthcoming in assisting Sukarno to blackmail the West into surrendering West Irian, as well as sending him hardware calculated to lend credibility to his "confrontation" with Malaysia.

By mid-1963, Aidit was condemning the "modern revisionists" for providing sophisticated weapons to the armed forces rather than to the people of Indonesia;[4] undoubtedly, this was a reflection of the PKI's dismay at seeing its military antagonists equipped by a supposedly "communist" state, the USSR. During the summer of 1963, Aidit bearded Khrushchev in the Kremlin with a demand for increased Soviet emphasis on aid to the "National Liberation Movement" at the expense of Russia's own "economic construction."[5] Khrushchev pointedly reminded the PKI leader that "the struggle for national independence cannot succeed without the help of the socialist countries." Aidit remarked that this sounded suspiciously like a threat that "communists who are struggling for national independence shall not dare to give expression to opinions that differ from those of certain socialist countries because the result would be that their own country would be deprived of as-

---

Ra'anan, eds., *The Politics of the Coup d'État* (Princeton, N.J.: D. Van Nostrand Company, 1969). The author is obliged to the publishers of these studies for their consent to utilize this material.

[3] Reuters, Singapore, February 16, 1963.

[4] Aidit's July 19, 1963 address at the Indonesian Naval Staff and Command School.

[5] Sudisman's address to Djakarta PKI gathering, October 27, 1963.

sistance."[6] According to PKI claims, following this quarrel, the "modern revisionists" retaliated by letting Sukarno know that it would be a mistake to include PKI members in the Indonesian cabinet, on the transparent grounds that this might be regarded in the West as a provocative act.[7] However, in spite of Moscow's repeated moratoria on the repayment of his debts, Sukarno refused to follow Soviet advice and proceeded to align himself ever more closely with the PKI and with China. While the Russians, increasingly disgusted with Afro-Asian gatherings that excluded them as "Europeans," swung their support behind nonaligned conferences (of the Belgrade type), Sukarno spoke and worked in the opposite direction. After he had raised two PKI leaders to ministerial rank, Sukarno was publicly praised by Aidit as a nationalist who was genuinely opposed to imperialism and, as such, was preferable to certain "revisionists" who embraced the West, namely, Khrushchev.[8]

The Russians reacted by encouraging the domestic opponents of the PKI. During the previous spring, the Indonesian army, in spite of PKI and Chinese opposition, had supported Indonesia's adherence to the Moscow test ban treaty. In the fall of 1963, a visiting Soviet delegation clashed with the PKI leaders and subsequently stressed its belief that the sound forces among the Indonesian people (that is, the army) would oppose those who had "minimized" the test ban treaty (namely, the PKI).[9] Defense Minister Nasution was invited to Moscow, where he received warm endorsement of his approach toward the Malaysian "confrontation."[10] Suddenly revising the previously bellicose PKI line, Aidit responded by warning against "adventurism," since "some people" (that is, the Defense Minister and his supporters) were allegedly planning to exploit the Malaysian conflict as an excuse for imposing a state of emergency and banning the PKI.[11]

In April 1964, at the preparatory Second Afro-Asian Conference, Sukarno's representative asserted that Indonesia was no longer "nonaligned"[12] and, together with the Chinese, foiled all attempts

[6] Aidit's December 23, 1963 report to the PKI Central Committee; see also *Harian Rakjat*, October 2, 1963.

[7] Sudisman's address, October 27, 1963.

[8] Aidit's report to Kwantung Party School, Canton, September 25, 1963.

[9] September 5, 1963 statement of Soviet trade union delegation to Indonesia.

[10] Reuters, November 26, 1963, quoting Antara.

[11] PKI press release, October 6, 1963; also *Harian Rakjat*, October 14, 1963.

[12] R. Abdulgani's address to the conference, March 25, 1964.

to have the USSR accepted as a full member of the conference.[13] To unmask the USSR as a colonialist state, Aidit actually went so far as to dig up an obscure quotation from Lenin, reproaching a certain Soviet leader for demanding self-determination in far-off places while keeping "silent about Uzbeks, Bashkirs, etc."[14]

Sukarno's increasing abandonment of neutrality in the Sino-Soviet dispute, and in the conflict between the PKI and its various domestic opponents, produced growing concern in certain Indonesian quarters. During the late spring of 1964, the "Trotskyite" (actually Tan Malakist) Murba, the army's political organization (IPKI), and several Moslem groups called for a "dissolution of parties," meaning the suppression of the PKI. Sukarno and his PNI (Indonesian Nationalist Party) followers opposed this demand. Aidit, saying "we will never forgive the revisionists," broadly hinted that it was the Russians who were trying to destroy the PKI because of its stand on Afro-Asian affairs.[15] The PKI's newspaper openly accused Moscow of using the "Trotskyites" (Murba) to split the PKI.[16] In addition, Aidit called for "self-reliance," that is, liberation from dependence upon Soviet military and economic aid. He stressed that he had learned in Peking that Moscow was capable of misusing aid for the purpose of applying political pressure.[17] Njoto, Aidit's colleague, warned the Indonesian government not to beg the Russians for further moratoria on debts, since "the modern revisionists . . . like very much to be repaid by others for their benefactions."[18]

At this point, in June 1964, Mikoyan arrived in Djakarta and indicated that, if irritated long enough, the USSR might yet do Indonesia the favor of letting her rely on her own resources. On a previous occasion, Mikoyan had shown skepticism about the efficacy of pouring aid into Indonesia; he had quoted an alleged oriental proverb, saying "if you take money, you will spend it; if

[13] AFP, Singapore, April 14 and 15, 1964.
[14] Aidit's address, April 21, 1964, to Indonesian-Soviet Friendship Association.
[15] NCNA, international service, in English, June 6, 1964, quoting Aidit's address of May 2, 1964.
[16] *Harian Rakjat,* June 11 and 12, 1964, quoting Aidit's Surabaja speech of May 23, 1964.
[17] NCNA, international service, in English, June 6, 1964, quoting Aidit's address of May 2, 1964.
[18] *Harian Rakjat,* June 9 and 10, 1964, quoting Njoto's address of June 3, 1964.

you take wisdom, it will stay with you."[19] During his 1964 visit,
Mikoyan went out of his way to stress that no one had helped
Russia when she had to construct her economy and, moreover, that
the Russian people were now weighed down with their own defense burdens.[20] Taking aim at Sukarno, he said that Moscow continued to support Indonesia's "confrontation" with Malaysia, but
"with a sense of responsibility."[21] He also reiterated that the USSR,
unlike Sukarno, considered "nonaligned" meetings as important
as "Afro-Asian" gatherings.[22] Referring to the PKI boycott of his
appearances, Mikoyan noted dryly that he was experiencing "both
hot and cold weather."[23] He did, however, woo the Indonesian
army, making constant references to Soviet military aid and
stressing that Indonesia was now better armed than any power in
Asia (including the Chinese).[24] In the end, Mikoyan consented
to yet another postponement of Indonesia's repayments and even
left the door open for possible further aid, provided Sukarno
ceased opposing Soviet participation in international gatherings.[25]

The army's newspapers immediately responded to Mikoyan's
approach and urged Sukarno to support Soviet participation in
Afro-Asian conferences so that Indonesia might receive further
Soviet assistance.[26] The PKI, on the other hand, publicly advised
Sukarno to resist Soviet pressure and went so far as to demand
"vigilance" against possible "sabotage" by the "revisionists."[27] The
army clearly did not accept Aidit's call for "self-reliance" and the
jettisoning of Soviet aid. However, Air Force Chief Omar Dhani,
supported by Sukarno, began to demand the application of "self-
reliance" to the armed forces.[28]

In order that the air force might gradually become independent
of Soviet supplies, Dhani restricted his shopping list in the Bloc
to repair and maintenance facilities, spare parts, and manufac-

[19] *Pravda*, July 23, 1962.
[20] Moscow Radio, overseas broadcast, in Russian, July 27, 1964; in English,
July 3, 1964.
[21] TASS, in English, June 22, 1964.
[22] *Pravda*, June 27, 1964.
[23] Djakarta Radio, domestic broadcast, July 2, 1964.
[24] Antara, in English, June 26, 1964.
[25] AFP, Singapore, July 2, 1964.
[26] Editorial, *Warta Berita*, July 11, 1964.
[27] Third Plenum of the PKI Central Committee, July 6 and 7, 1964; also
Harian Rakjat, July 15, 1964.
[28] Djakarta Radio, domestic broadcast, April 8, 1965.

turing licenses; eventually, he even ceased sending officers to the USSR for training.[29] Later in 1965, as the PKI intensified its pressure for the arming and training of the "masses," it was again to be Dhani, supported in the end by Sukarno, who consented—while Army Chief Achmad Yani and Defense Minister Nasution remained opposed—to arming "civilians" under PKI influence and to instituting a system of political commissars in the armed forces.

Following Mikoyan's departure, Army Chief Yani visited Moscow, and a slight détente appeared to develop in the relations between the two countries. However, Sukarno himself quickly recreated Soviet-Indonesian tension, personally quarreling with Khrushchev during a visit to the Russian capital in the fall of 1964.[30] Immediately afterward, in open disregard of Soviet pleas, he used a nonaligned summit conference in Cairo as a platform for violent assaults upon the concept of peaceful coexistence between Washington and Moscow.

During Sukarno's absence from Djakarta, Khrushchev fell from power, the Chinese exploded a nuclear device, and rumors reached the Indonesian capital that the President's health was finally giving way. The PKI leadership speedily became aware just how much the apparent communist successes of the recent past had really depended upon the personality of Sukarno. Even Foreign Minister Subandrio, who had seemed to be an unquestioning supporter of Sukarno's increasingly close alignment with the PKI, suddenly revealed unexpected deviations. While the PKI was rejoicing at the thought that, with Peking's nuclear test, "we" now possessed the bomb,[31] Subandrio condemned the explosion on the grounds that it might contaminate Indonesia's atmosphere and, in any case, was contrary to the test ban treaty; nor would he support Peking's call for a global nuclear summit.[32] When the PKI assailed the noncommunist Indonesian press for condemning the Chinese test, Aidit was told that these newspapers reflected the personal views of Subandrio.[33] Moreover, while the PKI was hailing the downfall of its archenemy Khrushchev, certain official circles in Djakarta were heard to express regret.[34] It seemed as if Subandrio was, in fact,

---

[29] Ibid., March 2, 1965.
[30] As revealed by Njoto in *Harian Rakjat*, April 23, 1965.
[31] *Harian Rakjat*, October 19, 1964.
[32] Djakarta Radio, domestic broadcast, October 20, 1964; Antara, October 22, 1964.
[33] *Duta Masjarakat*, October 24, 1964.
[34] *Suluh Indonesia*, October 17, 1964; *Harian Rakjat*, October 17, 1964.

AFTERMATH   241

preparing to align himself with such anticommunist elements as the Murba and the army for the purpose of taking over the succession to Sukarno. Graphic illustration for the new lineup appeared to be provided by the positions that the various politicians adopted during the sharp conflict then raging in the Indonesian capital over the symbolically important issue of a boycott of foreign films. What is more, army and Murba leaders soon joined hands to establish a new "Body for the Promotion of Sukarnoism" (BPS), intended to combat the PKI. In typically Javanese fashion, the opponents of the President and his procommunist line were using Sukarno's name and "ideology" as a weapon with which to beat the PKI.

The importance of Sukarno's personality to the PKI was illustrated vividly when the President, recovering from his illness, suddenly returned home; following a brief and mysterious trip to Peking, he immediately dropped Indonesia's objections to the Chinese nuclear test, and Djakarta officials even congratulated China on her achievement,[35] supporting her global initiative on the nuclear issue. Moreover, Sukarno supported the PKI on the issue of the foreign film boycott and proceeded to dissolve its most prominent rivals, first the "BPS," and then the Murba itself. In other words, Sukarno personally suppressed the "Body for the Promotion of Sukarnoism."

During this period, the Soviet leadership, highly irritated by the constant provocations from Djakarta, was beginning to retaliate by placing limitations on Russia's military support for Indonesia. The PKI even accused Moscow of imposing a temporary embargo on arms to Djakarta in order to enforce a change in Indonesia's policies;[36] it seems that Soviet military experts were gradually being withdrawn.[37] At this precise moment, however, Russian policy toward Indonesia was temporarily immobilized by Khrushchev's ouster; his successors even briefly toyed with the thought of conciliating the PKI.[38] Aidit brusquely declined to have any dealings with Moscow's projected conference of selected communist parties.[39]

[35] Martadinata, November 3, 1964; Mrs. Sukarno, November 27, 1964.
[36] Kuala Lumpur (Malaysia) Radio, in Indonesian, October 29, 1964.
[37] Djakarta Radio, domestic broadcast, November 20, 1964, stated that personnel at the Military Institute had once again become purely Indonesian.
[38] On November 11, 1964, Soviet Ambassador Mikhailov called on the PKI leaders with an "explanation" of recent events in Moscow.
[39] PKI announcement, December 14, 1964.

In the meantime, Indonesian relations with China were becoming ever more intimate; moreover, both Sukarno and Peking appeared increasingly to appreciate the importance of ensuring the long-term dependability of Subandrio as the only possible successor to the Indonesian President. In January 1965, the Indonesian Foreign Minister, together with one of the PKI leaders and the chief of police, was dispatched to Peking, where he huddled together with the Chinese leaders for prolonged sessions that, judging by the participants, seem to have been devoted to questions of Indonesia's internal security.[40] Some hints emerged that, in return for Subandrio's collaboration, China might even play a part in assisting Indonesia to become a nuclear power.[41] During his visit, Subandrio announced that Chou En-lai and he had exchanged thoughts on the bad experiences both countries had suffered at the hands of certain great powers, leading them to conclude that "self-reliance" was the best policy; he also attacked "manipulation" of the United Nations by the "U.S. and *other big powers.*"[42]

The new Djakarta-Peking axis caused Indonesian military relations with the USSR to wilt still further. Purchases of equipment from the Soviet Union were increasingly limited to workshops for repairs and maintenance.[43] Receiving the new Soviet ambassador in May 1965, Sukarno reviewed all spheres of relations—except the military.[44] At the same time, the Indonesian President, in a speech at the new Defense Institute, said Mao had told him that Chinese officers sent "abroad" (namely, to the USSR) had returned unable to apply their knowledge to Chinese conditions, and that Ho Chi Minh had regaled him with similar experiences;[45] Sukarno indicated that these conclusions applied to Indonesia as well. In June, Subandrio remarked publicly, "It was sufficient that the USSR was on our side for ten years and protected us from imperialism, but that is not enough [now]."[46] In July, the organ of the army reported that "certain socialist countries" were now unwilling to sell

[40] NCNA, international service, in English, January 27, 1965.
[41] Antara, February 2 and March 16, 1965; Djakarta Radio, domestic broadcast, March 16, 1965.
[42] NCNA, international service, in English, January 28, 1965 (author's emphasis).
[43] Djakarta Radio, domestic broadcast, May 24, 1965.
[44] Ibid., May 19, 1965.
[45] Antara, May 20, 1965.
[46] MENA, June 30, 1965.

arms to Indonesia, although it pointedly refrained from appor-
tioning blame for this development.[47]

Just as Sukarno, in mid-1965, was pushing Indonesia into an
evermore one-sided relationship with Peking against Moscow, so
was he also abandoning what remained of his precarious domestic
neutrality and openly taking sides with the PKI against the
army leadership. He came out on the side of Aidit and of air
force Chief Dhani in agreeing, at least in principle, to the "arming
of the masses"; on Indonesia's National Day in August 1965, he
publicly told the army that the people could live without the military but the military could not live without the people. He added
that the masses had a constitutional right to be armed. The position of the army leadership was thus becoming ever more precarious.

At this point, both major rivals in the Indonesian power struggle,
the army and the PKI, had good cause for alarm: the former
faced increasing threats (by the PKI, the air force, and the President) to its military power base; the latter, having learned in the
previous fall how much its future depended upon Sukarno's continued participation in political life, was consequently dismayed to
receive reports that the President's health had deteriorated once
again. Thus both sides had cogent reasons for taking immediate
preparatory steps, knowing that an open confrontation could not
be postponed for very long.

On September 30, 1965, the inevitable confrontation took place.
The PKI's "youth" organization, together with elements of the air
force, two mutinous battalions from radical East and Central Java,
and a unit of the presidential palace guard, apparently with Sukarno's connivance, kidnapped and murdered several of the army's
top leaders as part of an attempted coup. However, the plot failed,
since Defense Minister Nasution managed to escape, and the commander of the army's Strategic Reserve Corps, Suharto, was able
to rally his forces and defeat the putschists. Sukarno attempted to
extricate himself from the debacle, fighting a vigorous political
rearguard action against the victorious generals; gradually, however, Suharto succeeded in limiting the President's power and undermining his prestige so that, finally, Sukarno could be removed
altogether from the public arena. In the meantime, the army, aided
by Moslem and other anticommunist youth groups, began to

---

[47] *Berita Yudha*, July 20, 1965; AFP, Singapore, July 21, 1965.

avenge its slain leaders by initiating a nationwide massacre of PKI adherents and other opponents.

The new Suharto regime was eager to repair the economic ravages of the Sukarno era as well as the military damage that the "Great Leader" and his air force cronies had caused with their policy of "self-reliance." On both counts, Djakarta now needed the assistance of the USSR and other European communist governments, who constituted Indonesia's main source of hardware while also being her leading creditors. Overlooking the insults and injuries suffered during Sukarno's last years and closing more than one eye to the hundreds of thousands of communist bodies littering the Indonesian countryside, the Warsaw Pact powers granted Djakarta further moratoria on repayments for assistance received during the previous decade and resumed shipments of spare parts and ammunition to the Indonesian armed services.

It is, of course, perfectly true that Moscow saw no reason to shed tears over Sukarno's decline or over the debacle suffered by the anti-Soviet PKI; moreover, additional investments in Indonesia appeared to constitute the only way of salvaging old debts. However, such blatant disregard of "fraternal solidarity" for fellow communists in distress was bound to cause embarrassment for the Kremlin, especially at a time when last-ditch efforts were being made in the Soviet capital to resuscitate some form of international communist organization.[48] The fact remains that Soviet military assistance during the 1950s had failed to give Moscow leverage over Djakarta because of Sukarno's adroit manipulation of the international and domestic options open to him; in the early 1960s, the new Djakarta-Peking "axis" neutralized whatever influence the USSR might have been able to achieve as a result of increasingly massive shipments of Russian hardware and other goods. During the crucial moments of September–October 1965, when Indonesia's political future was being decided (perhaps for decades to come), Moscow's ability to affect events in Djakarta was practically nonexistent, in spite of the delivery of Russian military equipment valued at more than $1 billion, ostentatious Soviet economic and technical assistance, and Russian support during the West Irian and Malaysian crises. (At least in the latter instance, the Kremlin paid a fairly high diplomatic price for its stand, since nonaligned

48 In 1968/69, as a result of these conflicting considerations, Moscow began to publish repeated attacks on the Suharto regime, without, however, being able to regain the support of the majority faction of the underground PKI.

countries tended to sympathize with the Malaysians.) There can thus be relatively few illusions in the Soviet capital about the gains that may be scored by resuming shipments to the post-Sukarno regime, whose anticommunism, to be sure, is mainly directed against the Chinese but whose general posture is one of moderation and reconciliation with the West.

The question arises why, in view of the obvious disappointments suffered during recent years, the Kremlin has not decided on a policy of retrenchment and eventual disengagement in Afro-Asia. In the immediate aftermath of Khrushchev's overthrow, there were indications that such thoughts were beginning to be discussed among the Soviet leaders. However, ideological factors apparently constituted a primary obstacle to the adoption of a policy drawing the logical conclusions from the failure of Khrushchev's decade of overcommitment in the Third World. During an era in which the thermonuclear stalemate prevents major advances across the "frozen" lines of Europe and the North Pacific, meaningful gains can be scored with impunity only in the relatively "fluid" zones of Afro-Asia. Disengagement from that part of the world, therefore, is feasible only if the USSR is willing to settle for the maintenance of the present global balance, at least during the next few decades. However, the Kremlin, in spite of the "pragmatism" generally imputed to Kosygin and Brezhnev, has not yet divested itself of the belief in the dialectic, the assumption that to stand still means to be thrown upon "the rubbish heap of history." Consequently, setbacks and high costs notwithstanding, the USSR continues to commit itself, in the economic, military, and diplomatic sectors, as well as psychologically, to its clients in the Third World. Such a policy is not devoid of danger to peace, precisely because Moscow lacks meaningful leverage over its unpredictable Afro-Asian associates.

Index

Abakumov, V. S., 87
Abdel-Malek, Anouar, 83n
Abdulgani, Ruslan, 191, 237n
Adenauer, Konrad, 152n
Afro-Asian conferences, 222, 236, 237–238
  compared to "nonaligned" meetings, 239
  Soviet participation in, 222–223, 236, 237–238, 239
"Agricultural machinery," Soviet arms as, 69, 80
Aidit, D. N., 177, 184–185, 228, 243
  and Peking, 185, 235–236, 237, 240
  "self-reliance," 238, 239
  and USSR, 185, 228, 241
  on West Irian, 204
  see also PKI
Al-Ahram, 63, 66; see also Haykal, Muhammad Hasanayn
Ambon, USSR and, 232
Amer, Muhammad Abdul Hakim, 122
Anglo-Egyptian agreement (1954), 15, 40, 45, 48, 49
Ankara, Soviet-Egyptian contacts in, 71, 72–73, 74
"Anti-Party group," 100n
Arab-Israeli conflict, 23, 29, 33
  1948 (Arab-Israeli war), 23, 45, 49
  1956 (Suez-Sinai), 14, 29, 49, 51, 52, 53n, 153, 159, 169, 181, 209
  1967 (June war), 169, 169n, 170, 172

  see also Gaza incident
Arab League, 15, 15n, 45, 52, 53
Arbenz Guzmán, Jacobo, see Guatemala
"Arming of the masses," 10, 178, 239, 240, 243
Arms balance, Near East, 26, 27n, 50–56 passim, 56n, 57n; see also NEACC
Arms Deal, the Egyptian (1955)
  Chinese role in, 5, 7, 57–60, 141–143, 145
  chronology of, 5, 6, 7, 30, 30n, 31, 33–34, 36–37, 59–61, 76–77, 82–83
  as "Czech" transaction, 58, 75, 76, 81–82, 153, 154, 190, 199
  and factional struggles, Soviet, 5, 6–7, 40, 84–85; see also Kremlin factional struggle
  implementation of, 33, 33n, 61, 145–146, 148, 154
  precedents for, 28–29, 30
  purposes of, 29–30, 44, 53, 54, 55, 57, 58, 158–161; see also Leverage, Soviet
  source material on, 2, 3–4, 5, 6, 13–14, 38, 38n, 62–68, 76–78
  Soviet "benefits" from, 10, 126n, 157n, 158, 169–172
  supply routes for arms, 73–74, 75–76, 91
  traditional versions of, 57–63
  Western reaction to, 8, 24–25, 59,

Books Published Under the Auspices of the Research Institute on Communist Affairs, Columbia University

Diversity in International Communism, Alexander Dallin, ed., with Jonathan Harris and Grey Hodnett, Columbia University Press, 1963.

Political Succession in the USSR, Myron Rush, published jointly with the RAND Corporation, Columbia University Press, 1965.

Marxism in Modern France, George Lichtheim, Columbia University Press, 1966.

Power in the Kremlin: From Khrushchev to Kosygin, Michel Tatu, (trans. Helen Katel), published in French by Grasset, 1967, and in English by Viking Press, 1969.

Vietnam Triangle: Moscow, Peking, Hanoi, Donald Zagoria, Pegasus Press, 1967.

The Soviet Bloc: Unity and Conflict, Zbigniew Brzezinski, revised and enlarged edition, Harvard University Press, 1967.

Communism in Malaysia and Singapore: A Contemporary Survey, Justus van der Kroef, Martinus Nijhoff, The Hague, 1967.

Radicalismo Cattolico Brasiliano, Ulisse Alessio Floridi, Istituto Editoriale Del Mediterraneo, 1968.

Marxism and Ethics, Eugene Kamenka, Macmillan, 1969.

Stalin and His Generals, Seweryn Bialer, ed., Pegasus Press, 1969.

Communists and Their Law, John N. Hazard, University of Chicago Press, 1969.

Dilemmas of Change in Soviet Politics, Zbigniew Brzezinski, ed., Columbia University Press, 1969.

The USSR Arms the Third World: Case Studies in Soviet Foreign Policy, Uri Ra'anan, The M.I.T. Press, 1969.